Glorious Summer
Class struggle in Britain, 1972

Glorious Summer
Class struggle in Britain, 1972

*Ralph Darlington
and Dave Lyddon*

BOOKMARKS

London, Chicago and Sydney

Glorious Summer: Class Struggle in Britain, 1972 – Ralph Darlington and Dave Lyddon
First published 2001
Bookmarks Publications Ltd, c/o 1 Bloomsbury Street, London WC1B 3QE, England
Bookmarks, PO Box 16085, Chicago, Illinois 60616, USA
Bookmarks, PO Box A338, Sydney South, NSW 2000, Australia
Copyright © Bookmarks Publications Ltd

ISBN 1 898876 69 X (Hardback)
ISBN 1 898876 68 1 (Paperback)

Printed by Redwood Books
Cover by Roger Huddle
Cover photograph Syndication International Limited

Bookmarks Publications Ltd is linked to an international grouping of socialist organisations:
- **Australia:** International Socialist Organisation, PO Box A338, Sydney South
- **Austria:** Linkswende, Postfach 87, 1108 Wien
- **Britain:** Socialist Workers Party, PO Box 82, London E3 3LH
- **Canada:** International Socialists, PO Box 339, Station E, Toronto, Ontario M6H 4E3
- **Cyprus:** Ergatiki Demokratia, PO Box 7280, Nicosia
- **Czech Republic:** Socialisticka Solidarita, PO 1002, 11121, Praha 1
- **Denmark:** Internationale Socialister, PO Box 5113, 8100 Aarhus C
- **Germany:** Linksruck, Postfach 304 183, 20359 Hamburg
- **Greece:** Socialistiko Ergatiko Komma, c/o Workers Solidarity, PO Box 8161, Athens 100 10
- **Holland:** Internationale Socialisten, PO Box 92025, 1090AA Amsterdam
- **Ireland:** Socialist Workers Party, PO Box 1648, Dublin 8
- **New Zealand:** Socialist Workers Organisation, PO Box 13-685, Auckland
- **Norway:** Internasjonale Socialisterr, Postboks 9226 Grønland, 0134 Oslo
- **Poland:** Pracownicza Demokracja, PO Box 12, 01-900 Warszawa 118
- **Spain:** Izquierda Revolucionaria, Apartado 563, 08080 Barcelona
- **United States:** International Socialist Organization, PO Box 16085, Chicago, Illinois 60616
- **Zimbabwe:** International Socialist Organisation, PO Box 6758, Harare

Contents

Acknowledgments

The research for this book was financially assisted by grants provided by the Economic and Social Research Council (R000222876) and the British Academy (SS-1821/APN8398). Thanks are due to Alain Kahan at the Working Class Movement Library in Salford, to all those whom we interviewed, and to Fred Lindop for jointly writing Chapter 5 with us. Thanks also to Ian Birchall, Donny Gluckstein, John McIlroy, Angus McKendrick, Jack Robertson, Paul Smith and Alan Woodward, who read and commented on part or all of the draft of this book, to Dave Renton for helping to compile the index, and to Carol McFarlane and Mary Issitt for their support throughout.

About the authors

Ralph Darlington and Dave Lyddon teach industrial relations at the University of Salford and Keele University respectively. They are both longstanding members of the Socialist Workers Party.

Abbreviations

AEF	Amalgamated Union of Engineering and Foundry Workers (1968-71)
AEU	Amalgamated Engineering Union (until 1968)
ASLEF	Associated Society of Locomotive Engineers and Firemen
ASW	Amalgamated Society of Woodworkers (predecessor of UCATT)
AUBTW	Amalgamated Union of Building Trade Workers (predecessor of UCATT)
AUEW	Amalgamated Union of Engineering Workers (unless otherwise stated, this refers only to the Engineering Section of the union. Now Amalgamated Engineering and Electrical Union, AEEU)
AUEW(E)	AUEW Engineering Section
AUEW-TASS	Technical, Administrative and Supervisory Section of AUEW (now Manufacturing, Science and Finance Union, MSF)
BRB	British Railways Board
CAWU	Clerical and Administrative Workers' Union (later APEX, now part of GMB)
CBI	Confederation of British Industry
CEGB	Central Electricity Generating Board
CIR	Commission on Industrial Relations (1969-74)
COSA	Colliery Officials Staffs Association (white collar section of the NUM, now Colliery Officials and Staffs Area)
CP	Communist Party (of Great Britain)
CSEU	Confederation of Shipbuilding and Engineering Unions
DATA	Draughtsmen's and Allied Technicians' Association (became AUEW-TASS in 1971)

DC	district committee (of AUEW)
EC	executive committee (of CSEU)
EEF	Engineering Employers' Federation
EETPU	Electrical, Electronic Telecommunication and Plumbing Union (in 1972 still occasionally referred to as EETU-PTU. Now Amalgamated Engineering and Electrical Union, AEEU)
F&GPC	Finance and General Purposes Committee (leading subcommittee of TUC General Council)
FTAT	Furniture, Timber and Allied Trades Union (now in GMB)
GEC	General Electric Company (now Marconi)
GEC-AEI	General Electric Company-Associated Electrical Industries (name used by some GEC factories)
GKN	Guest, Keen and Nettlefold
IRA	Irish Republican Army
IS	International Socialists (now Socialist Workers Party)
LCDTU	Liaison Committee for the Defence of Trade Unions
LOSC	labour-only sub-contracting (in the building industry)
MFGB	Miners' Federation of Great Britain (forerunner of NUM)
NACODS	National Association of Colliery Overmen, Deputies and Shotfirers
NALGO	National and Local Government Officers' Association (now UNISON)
NASD	National Amalgamated Stevedores and Dockers Union (now in TGWU)
NATSOPA	National Society of Operative Printers and Assistants (now Graphical, Paper and Media Union, GPMU)
NBPI	National Board for Prices and Incomes (1965-70)
NC	national committee (of AUEW)
NCB	National Coal Board
NFBTE	National Federation of Building Trades Employers
NFBTO	National Federation of Building Trades Operatives (dissolved before 1972)
NGA	National Graphical Association (now Graphical, Paper and Media Union, GPMU)
NIRC	National Industrial Relations Court (1971-74)
NJC	National Joint Council for the Building Industry
NJNC	National Joint Negotiating Committee (of Ford Motor Company)

NPLA	National Power Loading Agreement (between NUM and NCB)
NUGMW	National Union of General and Municipal Workers (now GMB)
NUM	National Union of Mineworkers
NUPE	National Union of Public Employees (now UNISON)
NUR	National Union of Railwaymen (now National Union of Rail, Maritime and Transport Workers, RMT)
NUVB	National Union of Vehicle Builders (now in TGWU)
PROP	Preservation of the Rights of Prisoners
SOGAT	Society of Graphical and Allied Trades (now Graphical, Paper and Media Union, GPMU)
SWP	Socialist Workers Party
TASS	Technical and Supervisory Section of AUEW (otherwise AUEW-TASS)
TGWU	Transport and General Workers Union
TSSA	Transport Salaried Staffs' Association
TUC	Trades Union Congress
UCATT	Union of Construction, Allied Trades and Technicians
UCS	Upper Clyde Shipbuilders
UKAPE	United Kingdom Association of Professional Engineers
UPW	Union of Post Office Workers (now Communication Workers Union, CWU)
USDAW	Union of Shop, Distributive and Allied Workers

Introduction

The enduring political and industrial symbol of the 1970s is the so called 'winter of discontent' of 1978-79, popularly identified with the Labour Party losing the 1979 general election, and ushering in 18 years of reactionary and often vicious Conservative government. But to quote another phrase from the opening speech of William Shakespeare's *Richard III*, there was also a 'glorious summer'[1]—lasting most of 1972. It was the high point of the strike wave in Britain during the years 1969-74.

This is still remarked upon. For example, Seumas Milne, writing in the *Guardian* just before the 1997 annual Trades Union Congress (TUC), recalled some of the events:

> Five…dockers jailed for defying anti-union legislation were carried
> shoulder high from Pentonville prison after the Tory government was
> forced to release them in the face of a TUC-threatened general strike.
> And…Arthur Scargill was catapulted to national fame in the first of
> two devastating miners' strikes that drove the Heath administration
> from power.[2]

What distinguishes 1972 from many other peaks of working class struggle in Britain is not just the spirit of rebellion shown by the workers involved, or the militant tactics adopted and pursued by them, but their relative success: 'The miners made their…strike effective by large-scale picketing of power stations, sending mobile groups of pickets to areas remote from the coal fields. The dockers and building workers copied this tactic… Sit-ins and factory occupations occurred in the engineering disputes'.[3]

Yet, even before the 'winter of discontent', labour historian Royden Harrison had noted a paradox. The victories of the coal miners in 1972 and then 1974 had been 'taken almost for granted' despite the fact that they were 'unprecedented in British history':

> First, they compelled the Prime Minister [in 1972] to receive them in
> 10 Downing Street—which he had sworn he would never do—and

forced him to concede more in 24 hours than had been conceded in the last 24 years. Then two years later their strike led him to introduce the three day week—a novel system of Government by catastrophe— for which he was rewarded with defeat at the General Election. Nothing like this had ever been heard of before!

More generally, according to Harrison, 'the Labour Unrest of 1970-1974 was far more massive and incomparably more successful than its predecessor of 1910 to 1914'.[4] Whether or not we accept this judgement, the early 1970s undoubtedly witnessed the most intense period of class struggle in Britain since the 'Great Unrest' before the First World War and the turbulent years from 1919 to 1926.[5] After the boom of 1919-20, some of the largest disputes ended in defeat, particularly the long lockouts of the engineers in 1922 and of the miners in 1921 and 1926.

The British experience then was part of a wider convulsion in Europe symbolised by the Russian Revolution of 1917. Similarly the British strike wave of 1969-74, however dramatic in a purely national context, was only one fragment of the international revolt of the late 1960s and early 1970s. This embraced the capitalist heartland of the US, embroiled in an unwinnable war in Vietnam. It included the largest general strike in history in France in May 1968, followed by the 'hot autumn' in Italy in 1969. It saw the end of the fascist states of Portugal and (eventually) Spain, and of the military dictatorship in Greece. The state capitalist regimes of Czechoslovakia and Poland were challenged in quick succession. And, of course, there was the Catholic uprising against the Unionist state in Northern Ireland.[6]

While the events covered in this book were primarily industrial, there was a political edge to the five main disputes. Four of them have already been mentioned. The most important were the miners' national official pay strike of January and February, which shattered the Conservative government's public sector incomes policy, and the dockers' unofficial dispute over the impact of containerisation, which brought them into serious and successful conflict from March to July with the new and highly restrictive 1971 Industrial Relations Act.

The building workers' official strike over pay began in June with action at selected sites and then escalated dramatically in August, when local action committees wrested control of the dispute from national officials and organised all-out stoppages. The employers conceded a high pay rise in September. Another national pay dispute in engineering saw sporadic action around the country with the re-markable spectacle of some 30 factory sit-ins in the Greater Man-chester area, spread over a period from March to August. A fifth dispute was the on-off official industrial action on the railways from April to June. The railway workers faced a government desperate to reassert control over public sector pay after the miners' victory and farcically trying to use the Industrial Relations Act to assist it.

This book is the first systematic attempt to bring together and analyse the major industrial movements of 1972. An introductory chapter, identifying some of the key background issues leading up to that year, is followed by five that cover the major disputes in turn before some common themes are drawn together in the conclusion. The account is drawn mainly from newspapers and political weeklies, supplemented by those union and employers' records that are open to public access. The 30-year rule operated by government, and some unions and employers' associations, on their internal documents means that many of them have not yet become available. Interviews were also conducted with several key participants both at national and local level—government ministers, union leaders and rank-and-file activists.

Strike levels have been at record lows in recent years in Britain. We are constantly told, particularly by Labour prime minister Tony Blair, that 'the class war is over'.[7] Socialists currently look to France for examples of workers taking direct action. This book demonstrates that the British working class has a tradition of struggle too.

Chapter 1

The industrial and political background to 1972

In the spring and summer of 1972, British miners, railwaymen and dockers each in turn successfully defied the Heath Government. On no previous occasion in British history has the administration of the day suffered such a sequence of reverses from groups of workers.[1]

The immediate background to these events, and to the engineering sit-ins and the successful building workers' strike, is explored in this chapter, which concentrates on the period from the mid-1960s. But first we need to appreciate the impact on workers of the long post-war boom.

The long boom

British trade union membership had slumped from a brief high of 8.25 million (45 percent of the workforce) at the end of 1920 to 5.5 million two years later, with a low point of 4.35 million (22.9 percent) at the end of the depression in 1933. As a result of economic recovery, the effects of rearmament (from the mid-1930s) and the full employment generated by the Second World War trade union membership had doubled to 9.1 million by the end of 1948.[2] Instead of a repeat of the slump at the end of the First World War there followed more than two decades of 'full' employment. Until the mid-1960s unemployment levels were typically 2 percent or less. Workers becoming unemployed could often find work within two or three weeks—and that was only for those who bothered to sign on at the labour exchange because they could not immediately walk into another job.

A major study of the car industry, for example, argued that the 'lifting of manual workers' expectations which followed several years of post-war high employment and rising wages' was one important factor in the car workers' confidence in challenging their employers.[3] Such attitudes were reinforced by the post-war consensus whereby both Labour and Conservative governments accepted the need for 'full' employment, a 'mixed' economy (though with some disagreement about the exact proportions) and a welfare state.

But an overall rising standard of living could not mask the general insecurity of earnings that manual workers in particular experienced. Thus government figures for the early 1970s showed, 'The higher the earnings the higher the proportion of manual workers who were liable to experience drastic reductions in the following year'.[4] This was particularly the case for male workers, due to sometimes wildly fluctuating piecework or overtime earnings.

While conditions were generally favourable to union growth, there was only a modest rise to just under 10 million union members by the end of 1969. And the proportion of the workforce in membership—44 percent—was still lower than it had been in 1948 (and in 1920).[5] But it was a changed, and changing, labour force and trade union movement. 'King Cotton', 'King Coal' and the railways were in rapid decline, and in their former place of prominence were the engineering industry in particular and the manufacturing sector in general. Unions were at the beginning of the great expansion that would add 3 million members between 1968 and 1979—including over 1.5 million more in the public services (health, education, and central and local government) and an extra 600,000 among white-collar workers in manufacturing—which was to further reshape the movement.[6]

Inside many unions there was a slow but growing shift of authority away from full-time officers to shop stewards, reflecting the increasing importance of workplace bargaining in a number of sectors. This was bitterly contested by many employers and managers, particularly in the strategically important car industry where there was a strong tradition of victimisation of stewards until the early 1960s.[7] By 1966 there were an estimated 175,000 shop stewards in Britain compared to perhaps 3,000 full-time union officials.[8] Yet despite the large numbers of stewards their organisation was very uneven. Shop stewards' bodies were also, in the words of Tony Cliff and Colin

Barker, 'largely speaking, politically apathetic'. There was not a 'shop stewards' *movement*' as in the First World War, but the 'new tradition of "do-it-yourself" reforms' expressed workers' 'growing self-reliance and self-assertiveness' (original emphasis).[9]

It was a confident working class, having experienced no serious defeats in more than a generation, that was confronted with the increasing politicisation of industrial relations from the mid-1960s as governments tried to find solutions to companies' squeezed profit margins, low economic growth, balance of payments crises and rising inflation rates. The Conservative government of 1970-74 polarised opinion more on class lines than had its Labour predecessor. Geoffrey Goodman, a long-serving industrial correspondent, has argued, 'The Heath Government in 1970 and 1971 was viewed with just as much hostility by the trade unions as was Mrs Thatcher's 10 years later.' People who have experienced Margaret Thatcher but not Edward Heath might find this hard to believe, but the latter was the first to try to 'break with *postwar consensus politics*' (added emphasis).[10] Cooperation rather than confrontation with the unions had been part of this bipartisan approach. Increasingly governments' concern, if not obsession, with the international competitiveness of British capitalism put such consensus under strain.

There were three main issues that generated massive anatagonism to the 1970 Conservative government and helped to fuel the solidarity action that was so essential a part of the workers' victories in 1972: incomes policy, anti-union legislation and unemployment. These are analysed in turn. The first two of these issues were not unique to the Conservatives and were central in the Labour government's defeat in 1970. We start, therefore, with the standard analysis of industrial relations in the mid-1960s.

The Donovan Report

In the wake of the notorious *Rookes* v *Barnard* judgment (1964), which had opened up unions to damages claims in the courts for the first time since the passing of the 1906 Trade Disputes Act, the then Conservative government had suggested an inquiry into trade unions. When Labour was elected to office in October 1964 it quickly closed the legal loophole with a very short act, but prime minister Harold

Wilson was initially against an inquiry, as royal commissions 'take minutes and spend years'. Yet as the journalist Peter Jenkins observed, a 'Commission served the useful purpose of doing something about an awkward problem without actually doing it now'.[11]

When the Royal Commission on Trade Unions and Employers' Associations, chaired by the judge Lord Donovan, reported in 1968, three years after its establishment, it highlighted three main features of British industrial relations that had been raised in the voluminous evidence to it. First, recorded strikes in industries other than mining had trebled from the mid-1950s to the mid-1960s. Almost all such strikes were 'unofficial'—lacking union approval—and 'almost invariably' were 'unconstitutional'—in breach of the appropriate procedure agreement.[12] While days lost due to unofficial strikes were relatively low compared to time off through sickness or accidents, the impact of such strikes, and even the threat of them, was much greater:

> If an employer forestalls a strike by making concessions in the face of threats…or by refraining from introducing changes which he believes to be necessary in the interests of efficiency, then the economic consequences of his doing so may be more serious than those to which a strike would have given rise…
>
> A manager…may be under severe pressure from customers to produce goods or materials by a particular deadline, and in a competitive market such pressure is not easy to resist. No doubt it should be resisted if the alternative is to surrender to blackmail exerted by unofficial strikers. But it is not surprising if managers sometimes make unwise concessions…
>
> The economic implications are obvious and serious; the country can ill afford the crippling effect which such managerial attitudes are liable to have on the pace of innovation and technological advance in industry. We have no hesitation therefore in saying that the prevalence of unofficial strikes, and their tendency…to increase, have such serious economic implications that measures to deal with them are urgently necessary.[13]

Second, the 'gap' between industry-wide agreed pay rates and actual earnings—made up of piecework, overtime and factory additions to basic rates—was growing (it was known as 'wage drift'). Of particular concern to government was that earnings were believed to be rising faster than productivity and thus pushing up unit costs. The third feature was that the 'formal system of industrial relations offers no means for negotiating the relaxation of restrictive practices enforced by work groups'.[14]

In the memorable phrase of Allan Flanders, an influential industrial relations academic, workplace bargaining was 'largely informal, largely fragmented and largely autonomous'.[15] It was informal 'because of the predominance of unwritten understandings and of custom and practice'. It was fragmented because it was 'conducted in such a way that different groups in the works get different concessions at different times'. It was largely autonomous of trade unions and employers' associations.[16] Full employment had 'increased the influence of the work group', which would often determine its own rules on issues such as overtime, ceilings on piecework earnings and whether to work with non-unionists. This in turn provided the basis of 'the shop steward's power'.[17] The shop steward, however, was not generally believed to be a 'troublemaker'—most were seen as 'more of a lubricant than an irritant'.[18] The *Economist*, the employers' weekly, also argued that 'even shop stewards are helpless in the face of small groups of men with the power to stop production'.[19] Such views contrasted strongly with popular caricatures of shop steward behaviour propagated in the very different films *I'm All Right, Jack* (1959) and *The Angry Silence* (1960).

The suggested solution to the above 'problems' was to introduce comprehensive productivity agreements (with clear procedures for grievances, redundancy and discipline) negotiated mainly at individual factory level.[20] This fitted neatly with the agenda of the National Board for Prices and Incomes (NBPI), which was constantly advocating means for increasing productivity. But while the Donovan Report argued that there was a need for some legal reform of industrial relations, in general it rejected laws against strikes. The Labour government, finding it difficult to sustain its policy of wage restraint and under pressure from the Conservatives to get tough with the unions, became attracted to legal intervention. The combination of its wages policies, which affected all workers, and its proposed strike laws, particularly aimed at the more militant groups and occupations, further fed the massive disaffection among Labour supporters and resulted in election defeat in 1970.

Incomes policy

In the full employment post-war economy, both Labour and Conservative governments had periodically attempted to restrain the growth of wages to provide a more favourable environment for British capitalism to flourish. Throughout the 1960s and 1970s there were few years without some form of incomes policy. The most formalised was that operated by Labour from 1965 to 1970. It included a statutory wage freeze in 1966 and then a series of 'norms'. These were policed by the NBPI, which issued a huge number of reports, particularly emphasising the scope for productivity bargaining, in which it was hoped that workers would give up restrictions in return for higher wages.

Vic Allen long ago noticed that incomes policies in Britain tended to follow a cycle. They start with exhortation and consent, move to compulsion, and then to exceptions, ending with collapse.[21] In Labour's case the collapse took the form of a pay explosion in 1969-70, most obviously manifested by the record number of separate strikes in those two years.

'Traditionally militant groups…[were] prominent…but what has been remarkable has been the spread of industrial conflict to virgin territory.' Three particular groups were distinguished by Richard Hyman: public service workers, who had rarely taken action before this point; 'sections of workers among whom trade unionism is new'; and 'the "organized-unorganized"—traditionally unionized workers among whom rank-and-file activism has never previously developed or has been suppressed by a union leadership committed to industrial pacificism'.[22]

'Perhaps the most astonishing thing about the "dustmen's strike"'— an example of public service action—'was that the leaders on neither side had any idea they were sitting on a volcano until it erupted.' In late September 1969 Hackney dustmen stopped work unofficially for a £20 basic wage. The strike spread: 'Within a fortnight dustcarts had vanished from practically the whole of London and in many other areas.' Other groups of council workers came out in support: 'Thousands of tons of garbage were piled in the streets, parks and lavatories closed, and funerals postponed'.[23] In 1969-70 there was an explosion of action among schoolteachers (the majority of them women), starting with half-day and one-day strikes in limited areas, followed by three waves of selective two-week strikes, culminating in indefinite strikes in three carefully selected areas.[24]

An example of Hyman's second category of trade unionists was the strike of 800 workers at the heavy engineering works of Centrax in Newton Abbot in Devon, one of the lowest paid areas in Britain, from November 1969 to March 1970.[25] The third group (the 'organized-unorganized') included, 'The strike of Leeds clothing workers...in February 1970...[which] was remarkable in the way it snowballed. Day after day, factory by factory, workers joined the strike.' Official estimates suggest 14,570 mainly female workers at 45 factories eventually stopped work.[26] A women's strike of much greater significance had taken place in June 1968 when sewing machinists at Ford's Dagenham factory, followed by those at Halewood, came out for equal pay. Lasting three weeks and stopping all Ford car production, the strike had started unofficially but was quickly backed by the main unions involved. Before it had finished Barbara Castle, secretary of state at the new Department of Employment and Productivity, had announced that the government would introduce an Equal Pay Bill (which became an act in 1970).[27]

When the Conservatives were elected in June 1970 with a pledge not to have a statutory incomes policy this did not mean that they were uninterested in the pay explosion. Brendon Sewill, the special assistant to the Chancellor of the Exchequer, Tony Barber, admitted that in the autumn of 1970 'we in the Treasury had to cobble together a makeshift policy' on pay.[28] The chair of the NBPI under Labour, Aubrey Jones, a former Conservative government minister, described it as follows:

> In so far as the new government had a philosophy about prices and incomes it was that, if the Government set an example in the public sphere, the private sphere would automatically follow. This indeed had been the philosophy of another Conservative Administration some ten years earlier; and the private sphere had not automatically followed...
>
> The Government's policy for the public sector may be summarized in the formula 'N minus 1'—that is, each settlement in the public sector was required to be one percentage point less than the previous settlement of N per cent.[29]

The first public sector group to come into conflict with the government over pay was the local authority manual workers in what was known as the 'dirty jobs strike'. Following their successful unofficial action in the previous year, there was official strike activity from 29 September until 13 November 1970 involving over 120,000 workers.[30] It was 'a rolling programme of selective industrial action, [which] not only made less demands upon the union [the National Union of Public Employees] for strike pay, but also proved unpredictable and disruptive for employers'.[31]

During the dispute the employers and the unions approached the Department of Employment, but the senior civil servant there, Denis Barnes, wrote, 'It would not be right for the conciliation service of the Department to be used to seek a settlement at a higher level'.[32] The two sides then agreed to bring in an independent committee, but they could not appoint a judge as chair because of government interference. The report, which recommended increases of £2.50 per week as against the employers' final offer of £1.75, included the comment:

> Given the pace of inflation in the country as a whole, there is no chance that it can be arrested by a somewhat smaller pay increase for local authority employees. All that would achieve would be a deterioration in their position without a significant benefit to the country as a whole.[33]

Heath was 'infuriated' and appeared on *Panorama* on BBC television to complain about this 'nonsensical' argument. It 'sent the wrong signals to other workers' rather than reinforcing the government's and employers' message that wage increases caused inflation. Hugh Clegg, an industrial relations professor and the main author of the Donovan Report, had been the union nominee on the committee but was not reappointed as chair of the Civil Service Arbitration Tribunal the following year. Labour leader Wilson complained of 'government by vendetta'.[34]

While this dispute was on, a widespread unofficial strike of miners also started over pay. It eventually involved about one third of the workforce, some 100,000 (see Chapter 2). A few weeks after the miners had settled, 125,000 power workers then began a national work to rule and overtime ban.[35] At last the government was able to make a stand. Barber, the chancellor, declared that 'if the supply is interrupted or cut off, the unions are deceiving themselves if they think that the consequences will drive the Government to connive at an unjustifiable settlement'.[36] Heath later recalled, 'A general view, which I broadly shared, was…that at some point we would have to face down at least one strike in the public sector… A dispute in the electricity industry provided an opportunity for making the stand that we all sought'.[37]

On the second day of the action, 8 December 1970, peak period power cuts totalled 31 percent. The 'effects of the work to rule were magnified by the employers'. It was not until the end of the first week that schedules were drawn up to deal with power shortages. Not all generating resources were brought into operation. It was also not until the end of the week that network 'splitting' was carried out so that hospitals could be spared power cuts.[38] Meanwhile there was a vicious campaign in the media against the power workers:

> ...on television the Industry Secretary, John Davies, urged the community to demonstrate its disapproval in a virtual incitement to violence... These remarks had a distinct effect: electricity workers and their wives were abused, assaulted, denied medical treatment, had their car tyres slashed and their windows broken; David Frost's provocation on a television show led to one of our shop stewards getting punched in the face.[39]

The government declared a state of emergency on Saturday 12 December. The four manual unions joined with management to ask for a court of inquiry on Sunday and, when this was agreed, called off their work to rule the next day. The action continued unofficially at some power stations for several days.[40] While the subsequent award was thought to be more generous than portrayed, the government had successfully intimidated this strategically powerful group of workers.

Douglas Hurd, Heath's political secretary at the time, wrote an important memo to him on 14 December when the official industrial action was called off:

> There is a chance that the Government's success in handling the electricity dispute can be used to transform the general situation. For the first time public opinion has clearly and unmistakably made the connection between a particular wage dispute and the general struggle against inflation. A great prize awaits the Government if it can turn this dramatic happening to long-term account.
>
> This will not happen automatically. It will surely depend on
> a) a successful outcome to the court of inquiry...
> b) a fresh look at plans for future public sector disputes, designed where possible
>   i) to bring the negotiating body concerned to offer a good deal less at the outset than has hitherto seemed practicable.

ii) to ensure that in future effective and practical pressure can be exerted against industrial action before it begins, e.g. by making offers conditional on there being no such action...

iii) to examine again the practical side of contingency planning for mitigating the effects of future disputes. This did not look impressive this time...

c) to look again at private sector claims...

It would be a great pity if the impetus of these last days were lost... The Government need not worry so much about being seen to take a hand.[41]

The opportunity to take a tough line arose very quickly with the postal workers' dispute. A final offer of 8 percent was made on 14 January 1971, after which 'industrial action of some sort was inevitable'. The Union of Post Office Workers general secretary Tom Jackson was reported as saying that 'if we go on negotiating for a few weeks we might lose control of our members'. It was later claimed that, following the vilification of the power workers, Jackson had argued 'for a "short sharp shock", in which a national strike of all the Union's members would cause a complete closure of the postal system and a major disruption of telecommunications'.[42]

The national strike of 180,000 workers lasted from 20 January to 6 March. In terms of days lost (6,299,100) it was the biggest single action since 1926. Labour shadow minister Castle argued that the government had 'deliberately chosen this union and this strike to make an example of, because they thought the union was weak'.[43] The *Times* asserted that 'it is more important to the Government not to "lose" this strike than to preserve the postal service from contraction'.[44]

The union had no strike fund and had to set up a hardship fund. There was a flow of money into this from both official union sources, and workplace and other collections. But even if the union had paid dispute benefit, a national strike of its membership would have exhausted its resources very quickly. In 1972 the miners were to show that strike pay was not necessary to sustain a dispute, but also that active support from other trade unionists considerably enhanced workers' chance of success. The postal workers were beaten because of this latter factor. Their historian recognised, 'For most purposes the telephone system was now able...to do more or less automatically what had until very recent times been done by letters and telegrams'.[45] Yet there were still significant numbers of telephone operators, especially for international calls, and even the automatic equipment needed to be maintained or repaired.

The postal workers returned to work on the basis of an independent committee of inquiry which met one month later and, taking account of 'the national interest', awarded a mere 9 percent.[46] 'One effect of the [postal] strike was to teach other unions the danger of isolation. It also stirred up mass resentment. The Conservatives, full of their apparent success, misread this resentment for resignation'.[47] More generally 'many workers regarded the n-1 policy with an outraged sense of injustice, since it implied that their position in the wages queue was likely to be more important than the "justice" of their claim'. This same commentator argued:

> How can the Government avoid the damning political consequences of isolating and picking off groups of public sector employees? They all have votes and a much greater sense of injustice than would be the case if they believed that they were not being isolated and discriminated against.[48]

British Rail train drivers then operated a national work to rule and overtime ban for ten days in April 1971 before settling (see Chapter 3). But during the rest of the year the Conservatives were seen to be winning on the wages front.

Anti-union legislation

As with incomes policy, there was a common thread running from Labour to Conservative on industrial relations legislation. The Conservatives published their proposals early in 1968, even before the Donovan commission had reported. In the process they set an agenda which the Labour government felt that it could not ignore. *Fair Deal at Work* was a classic statement of Conservative thinking on trade unions and their activity. It was the result of three years work,[49] and was based around encouraging 'responsible trade unionism' and strengthening 'constitutional union authority'.

It proposed narrowing the definition of a lawful 'trade dispute' by excluding sympathy strikes, blacking,[50] inter-union disputes and strikes to enforce the closed shop. Collective agreements were presumed to be legally binding unless the parties agreed otherwise. This was aimed mainly at breach of procedure by workers and the accompanying phenomenon of 'unconstitutional' action. The Minister of Labour would have powers to apply to a special court to 'delay or stop' a strike for up to 60 days if the strike would 'seriously endanger the national interest'. During this period a secret ballot on the employer's 'last offer' could be forced on the workers.[51]

Given the interference of the later 1970-74 Conservative government in disputes of public sector workers, it is interesting to note the following comment in *Fair Deal at Work*:

> Some people consider that the present conciliation functions of the Ministry of Labour should be transferred to an outside body... [W]e reject this proposal. The Ministry's record is excellent and the impartiality of their industrial relations officers is rarely questioned.[52]

Of even more concern, and something that was to form the basis of the opposition to the Conservatives' 1971 legislation, was that a new Registrar with sweeping powers was proposed. Registration would give unions immunity from civil proceedings only where the union was acting 'in furtherance of a lawful trade dispute which was not in breach of agreement'. In return, the Registrar would supervise unions' own rules. Union members would not be liable to discipline if they refused to take industrial action in breach of agreement. Any expulsion or fine from a union could be appealed to a special industrial court. 'The status and responsibilities of all officials, including shop stewards' was to be 'clearly defined'. Postal ballots were to be used for certain union positions. There was a plethora of new rules concerning internal union finances. Finally, various restrictions on the operation of closed shops were recommended.[53] Not all of these proposals found their way into the Industrial Relations Act, which was repealed by Labour in 1974, but many were enacted in a different form by the Thatcher governments in the 1980s and have been maintained by the 1997 'New' Labour government.

When the Donovan Report was published 'it did not, on the whole, receive a good press', mainly because it did not propose major legal reforms. Labour would have preferred 'to do rather less than a "hawkish" Commission had recommended... [But] in order to hold the centre ground of British politics he [Wilson] now had to aim higher than Donovan while lower than the Tories.' Wilson was particularly attracted to the proposal on compulsory ballots after the engineering union had called a national strike without one in October 1968 (in the event it was cancelled—see Chapter 4).[54]

A White Paper, *In Place of Strife*, was published in January 1969 under the authority of Castle at the Department of Employment and Productivity. While it mainly followed the reforming agenda of Donovan, it added a number of highly contentious proposals. A 'conciliation pause' of up to 28 days could be imposed by the secretary of state where there were unconstitutional strikes. If industrial action were not stopped, then 'financial penalties' could be imposed by an 'Industrial Board' on unions 'or [the] individual striker' (presumably in the case of unofficial strikes), which could be collected by 'attachment of earnings' orders. Secret ballots could also be ordered by the secretary of state where 'a major official strike' was threatened. There were further proposals potentially involving unions in fines or damages.[55]

While there was significant Labour backbench opposition in parliament, the White Paper led to 'the post-1926 *omerta* [conspiracy of silence] on political strikes' being broken.[56] The Liaison Committee for the Defence of Trade Unions (LCDTU), a Communist Party (CP) controlled body formed in 1966 to campaign against government wage restraint, called for a one-day unofficial stoppage to take place on 27 February 1969. This was to coincide with a conference of executive committees of unions affiliated to the Trades Union Congress. Estimates of the numbers who came out range from 65,000 to 150,000, but there was little action outside Merseyside or Scotland. A second strike took place on 1 May, this time with more support. Between 90,000 and 250,000 took action, including many dockers, printers in London and Glasgow (with official support for stopping the national newspapers), and engineering union districts in Liverpool, Manchester and the West of Scotland.[57]

The TUC—whose main function is to lobby government on behalf of the trade union movement—was recalled for a special congress on 5 June. The government promised not to produce a bill on industrial relations before this. A huge majority at the TUC voted to express 'unalterable opposition to statutory financial penalties on work people or on trade unions'.[58] In the next couple of weeks Wilson and the TUC leaders met several times. Eventually Wilson backed down when he realised the strength of the revolt—first in the Parliamentary Labour Party and then in his own cabinet—against the proposed sanctions on unions and workers. *In Place of Strife* was dropped on 18 June 1969 when the TUC entered into a 'Solemn and Binding Undertaking' to try to control strikes.[59] Exactly one year later Labour lost the general election.

The incoming Conservative government issued a consultative document on industrial relations legislation on 5 October 1970, with only a few weeks available for comments. The main proposals were similar to those first enunciated in *Fair Deal at Work*.[60] A few days later the Secretary of State for Employment, Robert Carr, met TUC leaders to tell them that the government's proposals rested on 'eight pillars'.[61] He said that the government 'could not compromise' on these. Later he admitted that 'that was, with the wisdom of hindsight, an unwise thing to say'.[62]

Hugh Scanlon, president of the Amalgamated Union of Engineering Workers (AUEW), recalled that this intransigence 'left us with no option, either accept it or fight it'.[63] On 15 October a special meeting of the TUC General Council (its sovereign body between annual congresses) agreed to break off discussion and to mount a mass publicity campaign on behalf of its affiliated membership, over 90 percent of all union members in 1970. Michael Moran claimed that the General Council 'had now all but accepted the inevitability of an Act'.[64] This was shown by the decision to 'prepare for a Special Congress at a time when, if the proposals appeared likely to become an Act, the Movement would need to determine its attitude to such an Act'.[65]

The LCDTU was 'highly critical of the General Council's leisurely approach' and organised a large conference on 14 November, which agreed to a call for a one-day strike on 8 December 1970. This was denounced by the General Council, which 'strongly' advised unions 'not to support in any way the activities of unofficial bodies who may be arranging conferences or demonstrations or recommending stoppages of work'.[66] In the event somewhere between 350,000 and 600,000 stopped work in 'the biggest political strike since 1926'.[67] National newspaper production was stopped as print union SOGAT officially supported the stoppage, despite a court injunction.[68] TUC general secretary Feather remarked that 9.5 million trade unionists had worked 'in the face of attempts by a front organisation to mislead them'.[69]

The General Council then called for demonstrations to be held outside working hours on 12 January 1971. The Transport and General Workers Union (TGWU) supported these inside working hours and the

AUEW left it to district committees. With the LCDTU urging strikes, some 180,000 working days were lost in industrial action that day (and perhaps 50,000 more on 1 January, then a working day, when some AUEW districts had struck).[70] A TUC demonstration on Sunday 21 February brought at least 140,000 trade unionists on to the streets in what was claimed to be 'the biggest demonstration of the century—the biggest since the Chartists...130 years earlier'.[71] By now, the TUC's total opposition to strikes against the bill was being ignored.

A special national conference of all four sections of the AUEW on 4 February agreed to instruct the union's executive council 'to call a series of one-day national strikes prior to the introduction of the Act and to press the TUC to organise similar action'. The AUEW raised this at the executive of the important Confederation of Shipbuilding and Engineering Unions on 11 February, and it was agreed to circulate the proposal to affiliated unions.[72] Strikes were arranged for 1 March and 18 March, when another special congress was held. As well as the AUEW membership, the Boilermakers' Society came out on both days and SOGAT on the second.[73] But this was to be the last action, official or unofficial, against the legislation until 1972.

Meanwhile the Industrial Relations Bill was proceeding through parliament. It was 'the longest piece of legislation' in the post-war era, other than finance bills. It also 'occupied more parliamentary time' than any other non-financial legislation, as its committee stage was conducted on the floor of the House of Commons 'in the belief that it would expose divisions within the Labour Party'. While the left within the parliamentary party dominated the debates, reinforced by Eric Heffer's promotion to the front bench, even Castle wished to 'mend her fences with the trade union leadership and with her own back benches'.[74]

> Labour's essential problem was to demonstrate...to the unions its goodwill after the differences over *In Place of Strife*. As one backbencher remarked: 'We will not convince hon Members opposite by our arguments, but I hope that we can convince...the trade union movement'.[75]

According to Moran, the debates were a 'shambles' with backbench contributions being 'largely a rambling farrago of political abuse, anecdote and misused statistics'.[76] They also allowed Tory MPs to pontificate. One, William Clark, managed this contribution: 'The British working man is a decent chap... But he is lethargic and...his lethargy permits others to take control.' This view was in tune with Labour leader Wilson who spoke of 'unscrupulous unofficial leaders' and of the bill as a 'Trots' charter' (significantly Trotskyists, rather than Communists, were seen as the enemy). Castle complained that the ballot procedures were a 'charter for militants', but she was heavily compromised by her advocacy of ballots in *In Place of Strife*.[77] As the government possessed a comfortable parliamentary majority, few changes were made to the bill. On 5 August 1971 it received royal assent, and its provisions were implemented in stages until it was fully operative on 28 February 1972.

Effective opposition could only come from the trade union movement. There were three main shades of opinion within the TUC General Council. Using Moran's terms, the 'extreme constitutionalists', such as the electricians' leader Chapple and Jack Peel of the dyers and bleachers, believed that 'government must govern' and that unions should cooperate with the act. The 'moderate constitutionalists', who formed the overwhelming majority, believed with the first group that repeal would come through the ballot box but advocated passive resistance, particularly through the 'perfectly legal' policy of non-registration. If unions registered, not only was 'complete entanglement' with the institutions of the act unavoidable (with all the consequences that brought in its train) but, very importantly, 'the problem of repeal would be enormously complicated'. The third group, the small number of 'qualified constitutionalists', led by Scanlon, was prepared to defy this particular law.[78]

'Registration was the coping stone of the Tory proposals... Mass non-registration could lead to the collapse of the whole structure'.[79] Thus the TUC's policy hinged on non-registration of unions or, when unions were placed on a provisional register, on de-registration. The General Council majority position at the special congress in March 1971 was to 'strongly advise' unions not to register. An alternative motion to 'instruct' unions was lost. But this permissive policy was unlikely to stick. Jack Jones, general secretary of the TGWU, the largest union in Britain, had voted for the tougher line. A few days after the congress he told the *Guardian* that 'if other major unions like NALGO do...[register] then our executive will have to reconsider the position'.[80]

Over the summer of 1971 a number of unions 'had become alarmed at the behaviour of some TUC members' and switched their support to a policy of instructing unions not to register. This was then narrowly passed at the annual TUC in September.[81] Employment secretary Carr was forced to admit that the act 'might not work effectively' because of this policy.[82] Yet no commentator at the time believed that the TUC would hold the line on de-registration. Even when the general and municipal workers' NUGMW and the local government officers' NALGO accepted the TUC line in the early summer of 1972 there were still several large unions that had not yet agreed.[83] The imprisonment of the dockers, who had consistently defied both the National Industrial Relations Court and the TGWU, transformed the situation (see Chapter 5). 'The Iron and Steel Trades Confederation, EETPU [electricians] and USDAW [shop workers] finally decided against registration during the industrial action against the incarceration of the "Pentonville Five".' A number of unions were suspended from the TUC during the summer, and at the September 1972 congress 32 (mainly small) unions with a membership of about 500,000 were formally suspended for a year.[84]

'Lame ducks' and unemployment

A third area of conflict with the trade union movement was the Conservative government's philosophy of denationalisation and its refusal to rescue 'lame ducks'. Under the self-proclaimed 'quiet revolution' the frontiers of the state were to be rolled back from private industry, which would be left to look after itself in the competitive atmosphere of a free market economy. At the Tory party conference in the autumn of 1970, industry secretary Davies announced that he would 'not bolster or bail out companies where I can see no end to the process of propping them up'.[85] But in November 1970 the government pumped money into an otherwise bankrupt Rolls-Royce and then, in February 1971, 'the Cabinet decided unanimously to take responsibility for the company's aero-engine, marine engine and industrial divisions'.[86]

This was intensely embarrassing for a government committed to reducing the size of the public sector. But a more traumatic reversal of the 'lame duck' policy occurred in the summer when Upper Clyde Shipbuilders (UCS) went bust. In February 1971 Davies had announced the separation of the Yarrow naval shipbuilding yard from UCS, and that no new public funds would be made available to the rest. On 14 June a request for a £6 million loan was turned down. A week later a meeting of representative organisations in the West of Scotland, including 800 shop stewards but also 'clergymen of several denominations', agreed on a mass demonstration. On the afternoon of 24 June 1971 more than 100,000 workers in Glasgow stopped work and half of them demonstrated through the city.[87]

Davies confirmed the liquidation of the company on 29 July, with the closure of two of the four yards and the loss of 6,000 out of 8,500 workers' jobs. The following day the workers of UCS took control of the yards, led by a joint shop stewards' committee with a number of prominent CP shop stewards including Jimmy Airlie, Jimmy Reid and Sam Barr. Concerned to win 'public opinion', the stewards adopted the strategy of a 'work-in', rather than an occupation strike, and this meant cooperating with the government appointees to finish ships. Nevertheless their battle for the 'right to work' won considerable sympathy and financial support from trade unionists across the country.

On 10 August a meeting of 'over 1,200 shop stewards from all over Scotland and the north of England' endorsed a proposal for a strike and demonstration on 18 August. The stewards also appealed to the whole British working class for financial support for the work-in. Six days later the first ever special congress of the Scottish TUC was held. On 18 August some 200,000 Scottish workers took solidarity strike action and about 80,000 of them went on a demonstration.[88] The government was thrown on the defensive. Strathclyde's chief constable, David McNee, warned that mass disorder, on the scale of the events in Northern Ireland, was a real possibility in Glasgow. Government minister Peter Walker later admitted, 'There was a genuine feeling that unless some action was taken social disorder of a type not seen in this country could have taken place in the city'.[89]

The work-in continued unmolested. On 28 February 1972, the day that the victorious miners returned to work, Davies announced £35 million aid for the three Glasgow yards and 'unspecified financial assistance' for any prospective buyer for the Clydebank yard.[90] The three yards became independent on 1 July as Govan Shipbuilders, while an American company, Marathon, a builder of oil rigs, took over the fourth on 10 October. The work-in then ended, having raised the huge sum of £485,000 from the trade union movement and general public to help to pay the wages of workers technically redundant. Various concessions over working rules, however, were made to Marathon.[91]

Although the occupation tactic had been used in a wave of student occupations from 1967 onwards in Britain, and more effectively in the French general strike of 1968, the UCS action massively popularised it among British workers. It helped to spark a spate of factory occupations across Britain, which included the Plessey plant in Alexandria, Scotland, and the River Don Steelworks in Sheffield. But perhaps the most significant was at the Fisher-Bendix factory in Kirkby on Merseyside in early 1972. In the summer of 1971 a nine-week strike had succeeded in staving off threatened redundancies. But when the company, owned by the Thorn group, made it clear that it intended to close down the whole factory a number of stewards visited the UCS yards, established a combine committee with other Thorn factories and laid plans for a fightback. When the management deadline for the first redundancies drew near in January 1972, a group of militants met to organise a demonstration inside the plant. About 14 workers marched towards the administration block, joined by others on the way. One related what happened:

> We...marched...to...the boardroom. There was this big oak-panelled door...and behind it all the decisions are made... Outside there was an incredible noise with about 100 or 200 people yelling and shouting... Then someone threw a chair and the door burst open and the chair slid across the room. Silence, complete silence, in there, and then...somebody stood up and closed the door. It was immediately kicked open again and there were more shouts... All of a sudden it went very quiet. We...didn't know exactly what to do... A fellow in the Communist Party and me...were both nodding to each other, but no-one really wanted to be the first to go in... Other people were starting to say that we had made our demonstration now and we shouldn't do anything more... Just then I pushed the CP member...and once he was in, we were all in...
>
> The convenor said 'I think at this stage I had better give you a period of time to reconsider your closure plans. I will give you no more than ten minutes.' They left the room... [The convenor] said that he didn't think there was much chance of them reversing their decision but that we were in a position of strength now that we were in the boardroom. They

came back...and said that they were very sorry but they could not reverse the decision... Then someone dropped the... master keys to the factory...on the table and said 'Well, this factory is under occupation. Out!' We gave them five minutes to get out. You should have seen their faces.[92]

A mass meeting of 800 workers voted unanimously to occupy the factory. Jack Spriggs, AUEW convener, told them, 'It's far better to occupy, to control from within rather than to stand out in the rain and cold, the fog and wind, trying to stop scab vehicles'.[93] Committees were elected to run the occupation on a 24-hour, six-shift basis. They included press, propaganda, security, hygiene, attendance, refuse collection, canteen and entertainment. Every worker was provided with an attendance card and expected to report to a committee for duty. Financial support flooded in and, following an appeal from the joint shop stewards' committee, dockers 'blacked' all Thorn products coming in and going out. In Liverpool on 26 January there was a one-day solidarity stoppage. Initially called in support of the Fisher-Bendix workers, it was linked with the miners' strike, then in its third week (see Chapter 2), and an unofficial one-day national dock strike.

The issue looked like snowballing into a general fight against redundancies. Following intervention by Labour leader Wilson (the local MP) a new company, IPD, agreed to keep the plant open at least until the end of 1973.[94] It was a wonderful victory that showed the advantage of a militant occupation, and it helped to inspire the developing sit-in movement in Greater Manchester engineering from mid-March 1972 (see Chapter 4). But also in early 1972 the unemployment total touched 1 million for the first time since the 1947 fuel crisis. This generated further antagonism towards the Conservatives, who still bore the stigma of presiding over the mass unemployment of the inter-war years.

Official strikes, union leaders and politics

The background to 1972 shows that official national industrial action was becoming more common, and presented governments with another and very different problem from the Donovan Report's concern over localised short unofficial strikes. The tables below indicate the growth in importance of official strikes during the 1969-74 strike wave.[95]

Official and unofficial strike activity, 1963-74

Days lost in strikes (000s)

	Official	Unofficial	Total
1963-67*	678	1,750	2,428
1969	1,613	5,233	6,846
1970	3,320	7,660	10,980
1971	10,050	3,501	13,551
1972	18,228	5,681	23,909
1973	2,009	5,188	7,197
1974	7,040	7,700	14,740

Workers involved in strikes (000s)

	Official	Unofficial	Total
1963-67*	84	634	718
1969	283	2,371	2,654
1970	296	1,497	1,793
1971	376	1,395	1,771
1972	635	1,087	1,722
1973	396	1,117	1,513
1974	467	1,134	1,601

*1963-67 are annual averages. Figures for 1962 and 1968 are not comparable with other years because of the distorting effects of three one-day official national engineering strikes.

These tables underestimate the true extent of official industrial action as they exclude work to rules and overtime bans (for example, those of the power workers in 1970 and the railway workers in 1972) and all 'political' strikes (many of which were officially called). While the absolute number of official strikes was still very low (between 3.1 percent and 7.2 percent of all recorded stoppages during the years 1969-74), the size and length of the biggest ones (particularly those directed at government as employer or legislator) significantly altered the industrial and political atmosphere. They also brought national union leaders into much greater prominence, which requires us to assess their role.

The Socialist Workers Party (SWP) has often been accused of holding an oversimplified view of the distinction between full-time union officers (the 'bureaucracy') and rank-and-file union members. Yet the notion that trade union officials hold an intermediate position between employers and workers is not peculiar to the SWP. It originates with the Fabian socialists Sidney and Beatrice Webb over 100 years ago. In fact, Lenin learned a great deal from them as he translated their masterpiece, *Industrial Democracy*, into Russian when he was in exile in Siberia.[96] The Webbs' studies led them to the conclusion, 'The salaried official of a great Trade Union...belongs neither to the middle nor to the working class.' They quote at length from 'a graphic description of Trade Union life...by a skilled craftsman', a passage that can hardly be bettered:[97]

> To the ordinary Trade Unionist the claim of the workman is that of justice. He believes, almost as a matter of principle, that in any dispute the capitalist is in the wrong and the workman is in the right. But when, as a District Delegate [full-time officer], it becomes his business to be perpetually investigating the exact circumstances of the men's quarrels, negotiating with employers and arranging compromises, he begins more and more to recognise that there is something to be urged on the other side.
>
> There is also an unconscious bias at work. Whilst the points at issue no longer affect his own earnings or conditions of employment, any disputes between his members and their employers increase his work and add to his worry. The former vivid sense of the privations and subjection of the artisan's life gradually fades from his mind; and he begins more and more to regard all complaints as perverse and unreasonable.[98]

The Webbs make other points concerning changed lifestyle but these are secondary to the above. What applies to the general run of local union officialdom is even more apposite for the national leaderships. But this would be a one sided and misleading view if we were to leave it at that. There are periods when union leaders take a much more aggressive stance in support of their members. In a study of American union leaders in their heyday from the mid-1930s to the late 1940s, the sociologist C Wright Mills described them as 'manager[s] of discontent'. The union leader 'organizes discontent and then he sits on it, exploiting it in order to maintain a continuous organization... He makes regular what might otherwise be disruptive, both within the industrial routine and within the union'.[99]

In Britain in the mid-1960s, after several decades of almost no national disputes,[100] and with most local strikes being over very quickly, it was relatively easy to overlook the role of union leaders—especially in those sectors then identified with strong workplace organisation, which included engineering, mining and the docks. But, with the growing confidence of workers, there was from the late 1960s 'a gradual recognition by union officialdom that attempts to suppress rank-and-file militancy may prove unsuccessful... To keep some form of control over the situation, a degree of endorsement of militant action may well appear the most prudent course'.[101] This is particularly well illustrated by two big strikes at the Ford Motor Company.

In 1969 a pay agreement signed by most unions represented on the Ford National Joint Negotiating Committee (NJNC) was repudiated by a significant section of members, who at that time were still not consulted by their unions over pay offers. An unofficial strike of the three Halewood factories led the opposition to 'penalty clauses' in the pay agreement. The unions with the majority of the membership at Ford, the AEF engineering union,[102] and the TGWU, made the strikes official and called out their other members. In the process a senior TGWU official, who had signed this appalling agreement, resigned from his post 'under pressure'. It was not surprising that Ford challenged in the courts the unions' revocation of a signed agreement (unsuccessfully, as it happened). After three weeks Ford was forced to shut down all production and the following week it withdrew the contentious clauses.[103]

Two years later 15,000 copies of a detailed pay claim were distributed to union members at Ford, demonstrating the company's ability to afford wage parity with car workers in the Midlands. When British Leyland offered £40 (soon raised to £42) per week to production operatives at Cowley, near Oxford, compared to the £25 paid to equivalent workers at the much more profitable Ford, the situation was explosive. Ford's derisory £2 offer caused spontaneous walkouts at Halewood and Swansea before strike action spread. Despite the unions being signatories to an agreement which still had one month to run they had no alternative but to make this strike of 42,000 workers official. After nine weeks, with the strike still solid, Jones and Scanlon dramatically intervened. Going over the heads of the NJNC members they negotiated a settlement and recommended it in a company-organised ballot.[104]

Their behaviour provoked much condemnation at the time as most Ford workers rightly believed that much more could have been squeezed from the company. Clearly Jones and Scanlon had one eye on such a big strike's effect on their respective unions' funds. But, probably more importantly, their behaviour was consistent with a typical feature of negotiating practice—that too high a pay settlement can cause several long term problems for union negotiators. It raises expectations for the future among the immediate group as well as in other sections of membership where it may be harder to deliver. It can also damage the bargaining relationship with the company in question.[105]

The end of the 1971 Ford dispute also demonstrates that the act of making strikes official in the first place gives union leaders the opportunity to withdraw support when they deem it appropriate. Jones and especially Scanlon (referred to in the media as 'the terrible twins') were on the left of the national trade union leadership.[106] This almost definitely affected their intervention in the 1969 strike—as right-wing leaders would not have torn up a signed agreement—and their support for the unofficial walkout in 1971. But Jones and Scanlon behaved no differently from the right wing when they forced through a return to work in 1971.

Only the various small Trotskyist groups (such as the International Socialists, forerunners of the SWP) were prepared to criticise their behaviour. The CP, whose members and supporters formed a significant network of militants across industry, was silent or apologetic. The roots of this behaviour went back to the foundation of the party in 1920, following the 1917 Russian Revolution. The CP drew on several traditions in the British labour movement. One was the First World War shop stewards' movement, epitomised by the slogan of the Clyde Workers' Committee: 'We will support the officials just as long as they rightly represent the workers, but we will act independently immediately they misrepresent them.' Another tradition was that of the South Wales miners' 'Unofficial Reform Committee', whose policies encouraged militants to take official positions within the union.[107] Both strands manifested themselves in the turbulent early 1920s, but 'the decisive shift to the right…was spurred on by the establishment of the Anglo-Russian Trade Union Committee' in 1924. This body, a grouping of senior union officials from both countries, gave 'a false radical credibility' to the 'lefts' on the TUC General Council and this was used 'to discourage independent rank-and-file initiatives during the 1926 General Strike'.[108]

From this point, loyalty to Moscow—which now meant the needs of Soviet foreign policy as decided by Stalin, who was to become the gravedigger of the revolution—particularly dictated the twists and turns of the CP's trade union work. For decades, however, the CP continued to attract many of the best working class militants who genuinely believed that they were building for a revolutionary change in society. The year 1956 was a watershed in the fortunes of the British party. With Khrushchev's 'secret speech' on Stalin's crimes, and the Red Army's brutal suppression of the Hungarian Revolution, members left in droves, and the party's once-famed internal discipline (particularly over members who were full-time union officials) was never to be the same again.

The emphasis in the CP's post-war programme, *The British Road to Socialism*, had already marked its formal abandonment of a revolutionary path. Its 1968 version proclaimed that 'the labour movement will find the way to throw off its right wing leadership; that new political alignments will come about and create the conditions for the election of a Parliamentary majority and government pledged to a socialist programme'.[109] At the same time the CP's own small vote in general elections was declining. The 'broad church' of the Labour Party with its huge affiliated trade union membership did not leave sufficient space for a second significant reformist party.

Within the unions, the CP's general support for militant policies within the workplace was subordinated to an electoral strategy. But the ballot-rigging scandal in the CP-dominated Electrical Trades Union, which was exposed in a High Court case in 1961, seriously damaged its authority. While 'ballot-rigging was never central to the CP strategy…[and] was a temporary and foolish lapse…[it] was symptomatic of an electoral orientation'.[110] Following this debacle there was greater emphasis on promoting Broad Left factions rather than organising separate CP groups within unions. John McIlroy has suggested that there was a common core to 'Broad Leftism' in its various guises—'a drive to "get inside" and operate the official machinery of the unions, viewed uncritically as neutral engines of class advance with the correct hands on the wheel'.[111]

By 1967, Colin Barker could write:

> For Party members and non-Party lefts alike, the Party has provided a career structure within certain unions, in line with its essentially reformist emphasis on getting 'left' candidates into office. Once in office,

> many of these 'left' officials have succumbed to the pressures of their positions and have lost the militancy that gave them their support while they were on the shop floor... But the Party...will defend its officials against criticism from dissatisfied rank-and-file militants.[112]

Despite this:

> In 1970-71 the Communist Party was still the major activist force in the engineering industry in Sheffield and Manchester, in shipbuilding on the Clyde and in the Scottish and Welsh coalfields, and was influential in...the engineering industry throughout London, the building industry in London and Birmingham.[113]

Several of these sectors would be involved in the big disputes of 1972, and necessarily CP members would play an important role. But the CP as a national organisation was no longer capable of serious and sustained intervention. Organisationally it was in serious crisis. Before its conference in November 1971, it was publicly admitted that it was suffering from 'a slowly falling membership and a rapidly ageing cadre force, burdened with the Herculean task of holding branches together, collecting money...and selling the *Morning Star*'.[114] Politically the CP promoted illusions in left-wing union leaders, thus disarming workers at critical moments, while some of its members in practice often formed an effective and militant opposition to right-wing leaders. This contradictory mix helps us to explain the shape of events in 1972.

Chapter 2

The miners' greatest victory

The national miners' strike of 1972 rudely thrust the coal industry back into the centre of British politics. The strike, along with the subsequent ones in 1974 and 1984-85, joined the earlier generation of epic miners' battles stretching from 1893 to 1926. But this was their greatest victory.

Under public ownership from 1947, the industry had been systematically run down since the mid-1950s. Coal was giving way to other fuels, and pits were closed to cut capacity. Increased mechanisation in the remaining pits meant a massive and continuing contraction of employment in the industry under both Conservative and Labour governments. While employment had held up at around 700,000 until 1957, it had fallen to about 300,000 by 1970.[1]

The miners had not taken national action since their shattering defeat in the massive lockout of 1926 (the largest single industry dispute ever).[2] But that did not mean that they were quiescent. Coal had traditionally been cut under the piecework payment system that, because of constantly changing geological conditions, necessitated regular and very localised bargaining. This spilled over into a rising trend of strikes from the late 1930s (under private ownership) until the late 1950s when the (nationalised) industry started to contract. In 1957 three quarters of all strikes recorded by the Ministry of Labour were in coal mining.[3] But these strikes were generally very short and very small. Rarely was strike solidarity displayed across a colliery, let alone beyond it. Given the extensive use of arbitration in the nationalised industry, all strikes until 1961 were in breach of procedure and hence also unofficial.[4]

As the proportion of mechanically-cut coal increased, there was pressure to reduce the numbers employed on piecework (some 42 percent of the manual labour force in 1955—mainly but not exclusively faceworkers).[5] District power loading agreements started to be made and eventually the National Power Loading Agreement (NPLA) was introduced in 1966. The intention was to pay all miners moving onto new coal faces a flat rate, with a phasing-in period finishing in 1971. The changeover involved many miners having their wages cut. First of all, cuts in money wages for those whose piecework earnings had been higher than the new flat rates and second, cuts in real wages for miners in the higher rated areas with easier coal seams (such as Nottinghamshire and Yorkshire) as they received smaller annual pay rises (below the rate of inflation) while miners in lower rated areas caught them up.

A further 70,000 underground workers were then brought under the Third National Daywage Structure in June 1971 (the first national daywage agreement was in 1955). Again, a significant percentage of these stood to have their pay reduced when moving to a new job. Against the background of rapidly increasing prices in the late 1960s, miners had not only slipped down the 'league table' of earnings relative to other workers, but large numbers of them had also experienced actual wage cuts. For example, Jack Collins, a National Union of Mineworkers (NUM) executive member for Kent but still a working miner, was earning £5 per shift at the beginning of 1972 compared to £5.50 in 1963.[6] Whatever the intentions of the National Coal Board (NCB) and the NUM leadership (which had historically opposed piecework), the unforeseen effect of the NPLA was to 'nationalise' dissatisfaction over wages across the coalfields.[7] The official historian of the post-war mining industry was in no doubt: 'It was the complicating changes in the wage structure that united the interests of mineworkers in aggressive national action'.[8]

In the early 1960s left-wingers in the NUM had difficulty in making common cause between coalfields, but electoral considerations eventually facilitated the establishment of a national miners' forum in 1967, consisting of representatives who were both working miners and full-time officers. Paramount in their minds was the need to avoid splitting the national left-wing vote in the election to replace Communist Party (CP) member Will Paynter as union general secretary (a four-way split in the left's vote in 1960 had let in a right-winger as NUM president). They succeeded in getting Lawrence Daly from Scotland, who had left the CP in 1956 but remained a left-wing socialist, elected in December 1968. CP member Mick McGahey, also from Scotland, was later unsuccessful in his challenge for the presidency in 1971 against the right-wing Joe Gormley from Lancashire, who had been the NUM representative on the Labour Party National Executive Committee since 1963 and had only narrowly lost to Daly in 1968.[9]

The left in the union, mainly concentrated in Scotland, South Wales, Kent and Derbyshire, was particularly concerned with changing the union's collaborationist policies on wages and closures. Among other things, this required getting control of one of the big right-wing areas to counter the right-wing control at national level. With the disproportionate rundown of some of the older coalfields, Yorkshire had become the largest area in the union. Its election system, along with the pending retirement of officers, also made change potentially much easier there than in Nottinghamshire or Durham.[10]

Around this time reorganisation of the NCB in Yorkshire into four areas had raised the status of the four NUM 'panels' (pit groupings in North Yorkshire, Barnsley, Doncaster and South Yorkshire) in relation to the area union. These more closely reflected the changing mood in the Yorkshire coalfield. Despite its dominant right-wing leadership, Yorkshire had been one of the three most strike-prone regions in the industry. With the NPLA's changes to the payment system, the normal expressions of discontent (especially over falling wages) were temporarily suppressed and waiting for an outlet.[11]

According to Vic Allen, Arthur Scargill, a Labour Party and former Young Communist League member and branch official from the Woolley pit near Barnsley, was active in helping to form the Barnsley Miners' Forum in 1967.[12] Scargill was one of a number of Communist, Labour and other non-aligned left-wing activists, who met monthly in this forum which was open to militant miners throughout the coalfield:

> The Forum…was attended by hundreds of miners who listened to speeches by Lawrence Daly, Michael McGahey, Emlyn Williams [South Wales], Jack Dunn [Kent] and others. For the first time many young miners heard arguments against pit closures, in favour of higher wages and a shorter working week. Through this medium Scargill acted as a catalyst…and worked closely with a small group of Barnsley miners including Peter Tait, George Wilkinson, Ron Rigby and Don Baines…
>
> [T]hese miners…were competent branch officials who…had struggled in the isolation of their branches. They had never controlled the Barnsley panel but collectively they began to discover that they could influence its proceedings. Within a relatively short period of time they controlled it in much the same way as the Doncaster one was controlled by Ian Ferguson, Jim Oldham, Owen Briscoe, Mick Welsh and Tommy Mullany. These representatives of the Barnsley miners began to meet with the Doncaster ones to discuss policy and strategy.[13]

Rising national frustration over the failure to reduce the long working hours of surfaceworkers boiled over during the 1969 pay claim, when the NCB used the Labour government's incomes policy as an excuse for further delay on this issue. While action had been threatened in some coalfields, nothing happened until a dramatic meeting in Yorkshire on Saturday 11 October. When the area council chair ruled a strike motion out of order as it would constitute an unofficial strike he was voted out of the chair. The motion was overwhelmingly carried. Here was a classic example of the blurring of the boundaries between official and unofficial action. The strike was unofficial in terms of the union's rule book and in being outside the industry's agreed procedures. But the area council was the ruling body of the Yorkshire miners, and all collieries but one were shut on Monday 13 October.

The left-wing activists organised a strike committee that excluded those area officials hostile to the strike. They systematically adopted the tactic of the 'flying picket'—which had played a limited role in unofficial Yorkshire strikes in 1955 and 1961—to bring out pits in other areas across the country. Scargill recalled:

> ...the first thing...was every pit in Yorkshire out? ...the answer was 'yes'...the next step was to get out every other pit in Britain... So we sent emissaries to Scotland and to Wales... And then we launched pickets into Nottinghamshire and Derbyshire. We decided that the best way that we could produce an effective stoppage was to have a rapid mobile picket... We launched from the coalfield here squads of cars, minibuses and buses, all directed onto pre-determined targets, with five, six, seven-hundred miners at a time...[T]his strike was totally unofficial.[14]

Frank Cave, branch delegate at Brodsworth pit, similarly remembered:

> The 1969 strike brought home to me the importance of picketing, the flying picket, that type of organisation. In Doncaster we had a strike headquarters and we had branch officials...who had been in the army, held positions in the Coldstream Guards, who drew up a map of what we had to picket in Notts and Derbyshire. It was like a military strategy.[15]

An area delegate conference in South Wales called for an official national strike as an alternative, but vigorous picketing within this coalfield brought out some 16,000. In Scotland a delegate conference belatedly supported the strike but did not attempt to extend the piecemeal action that saw about two thirds of Scottish miners on strike at some point. At its height the strike involved 130,000 miners from 140 pits across Britain. For the first time since 1926 a strike had spread across the boundaries of a coalfield. This was despite the fact that the recently elected general secretary, Daly, called on the strikers to return to work even though in Yorkshire the strike was being led by the very people who had campaigned for his election. Allen notes that 'the striking miners did not expect Daly to advocate an extension of the strike [as it was outside the rule book] but they did expect him either to argue their case or to keep quiet'.[16]

While the strike was on, negotiations were proceeding on the national pay claim that had been submitted in September 1968 but had been delayed for 12 months under incomes policy. The NCB took the unprecedented but probably wise step of conceding the pay claim in full but did not compromise on the hours issue. The strike ended on 27 October when the Yorkshire strike committee got a promise from the TUC general secretary that he would try to get an independent inquiry on surface workers' hours.[17]

Despite the mixed result of the 1969 action and 'some recrimination among the strike leaders, particularly in South Wales and Scotland',[18] the militant action had affected official attitudes within the union. Hence when the NCB rebuffed the union's 1970 pay claim as this time it was in conflict with the recently elected Conservative government's public sector pay policy, the NUM national executive committee agreed to ballot on a national strike. For the majority on the executive it was merely a negotiating tactic, but it allowed extensive campaigning for a strike vote. In Yorkshire this was conducted by the unofficial group based around the Barnsley and Doncaster panels, while in Scotland the officials and area executive members addressed pithead meetings. The national vote of just over 55 percent in favour was not enough to meet the two-thirds majority then required by the NUM rule book.

When negotiations restarted with only a very small concession from the NCB, unofficial action again took place. In Yorkshire the Brodsworth miners came out, and persuaded the Doncaster panel to support them and organise pickets, but only half the Yorkshire miners struck this time. Scotland and South Wales were once more the main other areas taking action. Some 103,000 miners from 116 pits were on strike at some point before the unofficial movement collapsed after nearly four weeks and a majority, including 60 percent of Yorkshire miners, supported the revised offer in a national ballot. While this strike was not as widespread or well-organised as the 1969 dispute, it was a further indicator of the changing mood of miners. The main outcome was general agreement to change the voting rules for a national strike. The executive compromised between a simple majority and the existing two thirds rule by supporting a change to 55 percent at the 1971 annual conference.[19]

Thus by the end of 1971 the miners now had some of the ingredients for a successful national strike: the motive—a significant percentage of members aggrieved by below-inflation wage rises or even actual wage cuts; the opportunity—a national wage structure which united the mining workforce for the first time in decades, along with a reduced hurdle to overcome to win a strike ballot; the weapon—flying pickets (though these were still in their relative infancy); and the agent—sufficient numbers of left-wing activists who believed in taking industrial action and making it work.

The national strike

The 1971 pay claim, originating from conference motions from Yorkshire, Scotland and South Wales, was unanimously approved by the NUM annual conference in July 1971. It demanded pay increases ranging from 17 percent to 47 percent (£5 to £9) depending on the grade, with consultation 'on various forms of industrial action'. The claim was answered by a derisory offer of £1.60.[20] Derek Ezra, appointed NCB chairman in July 1971, felt his ability to negotiate a compromise was constrained by the government's insistence on keeping to their pay limit:

> In fact, they were pulling the strings… It was made very clear to us that we had to stick to the government guidelines… We didn't have much direct dealing with the Prime Minister, but we were in touch with Carr and, of course, the Department of Energy throughout… Our main concern was to see how…we could negotiate something that could solve the dispute…but…whichever way we tried we couldn't get anything that was remotely within the government's guidelines… We kept in close contact with Gormley throughout, we were both keen to resolve the thing. He always said another 2 or 3 percent and we could resolve it, although I'm not so sure… But the government wouldn't wear it.[21]

NUM executive members were aware of this interference. One commented, 'You'd have a meeting with him and you'd know he'd just come from a meeting with Carr or Heath or someone like that'.[22] They concluded that the government, having clearly defeated the postal workers earlier in the year, was not afraid of taking on the miners in its pursuit of reducing pay settlements. A special NUM conference on 21 October 1971 unanimously voted in favour of an overtime ban from 1 November and a ballot on strike action. The pithead ballot, with a recommendation for strike action, took place later in November and secured a 58.8 percent majority on an 85 percent turnout.[23]

Allen suggests that initially the dominant view on the executive and among the officials was that the overtime ban 'was an act in its own right, an alternative to strike action'. A second view—the 'official one'—was that it would make inroads into coal stocks, thus giving a strike more chance of success. A third was that the ban was a 'delaying tactic', but one that allowed time to campaign. The operation of the ban itself inevitably led to a number of disputes. More importantly, it concentrated miners' minds on how low their basic wages were: 'It had an enormous politicizing influence which no one really foresaw… The attitudes of many of the 41.2 per cent who had voted against the strike were transformed… If the strike vote had been taken at the end of the ban the percentage against would have been derisory'.[24]

Not without some trepidation (especially among the left), the NUM executive gave one month's notice of a national strike to start on Sunday 9 January 1972. Gormley and Daly continued to meet the NCB negotiators, and the full NEC also met them twice, but the concessions were paltry and were rejected, along with the NCB's offer of arbitration.[25] On the eve of the strike Gormley and Daly were invited to meet conciliation officers at the Department of Employment. They refused to go.[26] The pay offer was then withdrawn, which was later considered by the previous NCB chief, Lord Robens, to have been 'a serious tactical error'.[27]

The government did not particularly want a strike but felt confident that it would be defeated. The press consistently played down the threat posed by the strike. Woodrow Wyatt in the *Daily Mirror* wrote that the miners did not stand a chance:

> The coming coal strike billed for Sunday is the saddest industrial cock-up since the war. Rarely have strikers advanced to the barricades with less enthusiasm or hope of success… Even if the strike lasts two and a

half months, it would have little effect on electricity supplies... Alas it is as if some mystery siren is luring [the miners] zombie-like to destruction. They have more stacked against them than the Light Brigade in their famous charge.

The *Economist* urged the government into battle, insisting the miners 'cannot stop the country in its tracks as they once could have done'. The *Times* predicted that 'coal stocks away from the pits are large enough to withstand a strike for weeks, if it does not spread, with only marginal disruption to industry and commerce as a whole'.[28] The *Guardian* urged the miners 'to think again, and settle' because 'they are likely to be defeated after a long stoppage, damaging to them and their industry'.[29] But just before the strike Daly challenged the high level of stocks, arguing that the coal was not necessarily where it was needed. And the *Times* was prepared to admit that stocks in power stations near the Midlands and Yorkshire coalfields had been hit particularly hard by the miners' overtime ban.[30]

From the first day of the strike all 289 pits were closed. But also from the beginning of the strike those miners active in it clashed with the wishes of the national and area NUM leaderships for 'orderly' behaviour. This can be seen particularly over the issues of safety cover and the role of office staff. The situation on secondary picketing is more confused, but periodically the pickets went further than the area and national leaders wanted.

Safety cover

The withholding by miners of safety cover during strikes had always constituted a serious threat to the physical integrity of underground workings due to the risk of fire, flooding or roof falls. It had therefore rarely been used in practice (see Chapter 7 for earlier examples). In the 1972 strike the NUM instructed its members to carry out safety work and to permit deputies, members of the union NACODS, also to do this.[31] But it was clear just before the strike that the official national line on safety would not hold. For example, 3,000 South Derbyshire miners voted at a mass meeting to withdraw all safety men. North Derbyshire area council and Cumberland did likewise.[32]

On the very first day of the strike more than half the pits were deprived of NUM safety cover. On the second day only 46 had full cover.[33] Gormley appeared on *Panorama* on BBC television on the second night, appealing for miners to provide safety cover. He then complained on the third day that 'the men are being a damn sight more militant than we would want them to be', following this up the next day with the comment that 'some men have been over ambitious in applying the strike'.[34] By 16 January only 38 of the 289 pits had full cover, a figure which gradually fell to 30 by the end of the strike. The 133 pits with absolutely no NUM cover on 16 January also slowly increased to 152 by 31 January. And half of those pits with partial NUM cover only had the winders present (55 pits on 23 January, 52 on 27 January).[35]

As the strike progressed the NCB became infuriated at the escalation of unofficial action over safety cover, particularly when pickets began stopping NACODS officials attending the pits to do safety work.[36] On 24 January the NCB deputy chairman claimed that 'at an increasing number of pits, mainly in the Midlands, miners' pickets are hell-bent to stop even our limited management resources getting underground'.[37] But it was much more widespread than that, and the following examples mainly refer to the larger incidents.

As early as the beginning of the second week, on Monday 17 January, officials were turned away at Cadeby in South Yorkshire. There were clashes at Calverton in Notts on 19 January, then at Gedling, also in Notts, over the following two days. Lynemouth and Ellington collieries in Northumberland were affected on 25 and 26 January respectively.[38] On 27 January pickets succeeded in keeping NACODS members away from seven Yorkshire pits. The next day NACODS members stopped work at several Derbyshire pits following alleged threats of violence, which also affected deputies in Notts, and 60 NACODS members were prevented from getting to Murton colliery in county Durham.[39] On 31 January 250 pickets clashed with 300 police escorting 68 deputies for work at Clipstone colliery in Notts. Twenty miners were arrested including the NUM branch secretary and president, and several committee members.

The picketing was often in defiance of area as well as national union policies. For example, because the Leicestershire area union was obeying national instructions and providing safety cover there was an attempt by nearby South Derbyshire miners to reverse this by direct action. This started on Monday 24 January, when 60 pickets stopped NACODS deputies entering Measham colliery. They then moved to Donisthorpe, and on Wednesday to Elliston. A fist fight between the Leicester area strike committee and a delegation of South

Derbyshire miners was 'only narrowly averted', and the latter were told 'in no uncertain terms' to keep out of the area.[40]

Not all pickets were so easily put off. The South Wales area executive twice reaffirmed (on 17 and 26 January) its initial decision of 7 January that safety men should work. But there was widespread flouting of this instruction—clashes over a number of days at Penrhiwceiber colliery culminated in a mass picket of 300 on 4 February, after which NACODS members there declared that they would not work under any conditions.[41] And despite an instruction from the Durham NUM executive, 250 pickets delayed deputies for four hours on 1 February at Usworth colliery at Washington, while others had to be sent home at the nearby Glebe colliery. On the same day, 500 pickets prevented deputies' buses entering Ellington colliery in Northumberland. There were also clashes at Renishaw and Ireland collieries in Derbyshire and, two days later, on 3 February, 18 miners were arrested when 400 pickets tried to stop deputies at Markham colliery.[42]

On 7 February, six miners were arrested at Kilnhurst colliery, near Rotherham, while deputies got through at Cadeby colliery, near Mexborough, for the first time in three weeks (apparently railway sleepers had been put across the road to block entry). The NCB estimated that there were at that time some 1,600 pickets trying to stop safety cover at Yorkshire pits alone. On the same day the Yorkshire area council voted 58 to 22, against the advice of full-time officers, to ask the national executive to ban all safety work—in the belief that it would end the dispute earlier.[43] This attitude probably accounted for Yorkshire having the least safety cover of any area apart from the tiny Kent coalfield.[44] On 9 February pickets kept deputies away from ten of the 21 pits in North Yorkshire.[45] The next day saw yet another (very long) internal NUM circular: 'We feel no helpful purpose can be served by picketing either colliery officials or management,' but clashes continued.[46] The *Economist* argued early in February that pickets 'still hope to close the power stations, but more than anything else they are relying now on the thought of all that beautiful machinery causing Mr Ezra's nerve to break'.[47]

Office workers

Another source of conflict between rank-and-file mineworkers and the national union leadership was the question of NCB office workers. The NUM national executive had instructed the union's white-collar section (COSA) members to stay at work initially to handle wages for the week in hand and then to process weekly tax rebates. The Inland Revenue had also told the union that it would be unable to staff special centres to pay out tax rebates if COSA members went on strike. The COSA leadership then worked out that this would require 35 percent of its members 'and that the selection of that 35 per cent was bound to cause aggravation'.[48]

There was picketing of NCB centres in Notts on the first Monday of the strike. Later in the first week 500 workers at the coal industry's research centre came out after a call for support.[49] On 13 January 1,200 COSA members in South Wales decided to join the strike two days later.[50] Given the general wave of militancy at the beginning of the strike, many white-collar NUM members were anxious to join it. The COSA general secretary, Leslie Story, argued that 'we only remained at work because of the executive instruction. But we found it impossible to obey the directive and decided unanimously that we should join the strike.' As a result 12,500 COSA members came out on strike on Monday 17 January.[51] One consequence of this was that a week later COSA leaders in Lancashire, Staffordshire, North Wales and Cumberland voted to call out 200 of their members who had been helping with pit safety.[52]

The problem for NUM members was that the 5,500 NCB employees in the Clerical and Administrative Workers' Union (CAWU) did not join the COSA strike. The CAWU general secretary, right winger Roy Grantham, announced that his members would not work any overtime, do COSA work, 'or try to go through picket lines if this is likely to cause trouble'—which it soon did.[53] Strong picketing at Coal House in Doncaster led COSA to estimate that the number working there fell from 500 on Monday 17 January to 250 by the Friday of that week. The 500 COSA strikers from Coal House and the 1,000 others from local pits were not prepared to stand idly by, especially as some white collar workers had allegedly left COSA to carry on working. Two hundred and fifty had picketed on the Thursday, and this grew to 600 on the Friday when night workers were trapped and day workers prevented from replacing them. Office workers were eventually forced to walk through a corridor of pickets for about 200 yards to get to the building, and some jostling took place. The press had a field day, ignoring any provocations to the pickets.[54]

Despite the press furore, the assistant chief constable of Doncaster, who was in charge of the police at the time, said on Yorkshire television, 'The behaviour of the strike pickets today has been splendid. I have nothing but praise for them'.[55] But the national union was clearly on the defensive and employment secretary Robert Carr took advantage of this, referring to it in parliament (and was interrupted by the former miner and left-wing Labour MP Dennis Skinner):

> Mr Carr: I am glad…to see that the union has taken action about that—
> Mr Skinner: Some miners have.
> Mr Carr:—which, I hope, is being put into operation today, because I am sure that what went on at Doncaster on Friday did not accord with the wishes of the leadership of the union.[56]

Even the militant local NUM panel also appealed for miners to picket the power stations instead. Picketing of the Doncaster offices effectively stopped but was restarted a fortnight later when it was discovered that priority coal had been diverted there.[57]

Elsewhere there were some successes. In South Wales picketing of NCB area offices at Ystrad Fawr (in the Valleys), Tondu (near Bridgend) and Llanishen (Cardiff) also started on Monday 17 January. At Ystrad 400 CAWU members were turned back on the Tuesday and the Friday. On the Tuesday another 90 clerks were prevented from entering the West Wales area wages office at Pontardulais (near Swansea). The following Monday and Tuesday, 24 and 25 January, some 900 clerks were unable to get into Pontardulais, Tondu and Ystrad. The next day the South Wales NUM area executive instructed its members not to picket the NCB offices, but there were reports of clerks still being stopped the next week.[58] Throughout the third week of the strike, 24 to 28 January, there were some 200 pickets every day at the north Durham NCB headquarters at Whitburn (north of Sunderland).[59] Other sites of significant office picketing included Alloa (near Stirling), where there was a report of 300 pickets in one incident,[60] and Edinstowe in north Nottinghamshire.[61]

Secondary picketing

The control of the dispute from below became most evident around a third issue, namely the use of pickets away from the collieries. An NUM circular went out a few days before the strike listing ports handling coal. But apparently one providing the locations of power stations, both oil-fired and coal-fired, was held back in case of a last-minute settlement.[62]

However, 'Even before 9 January the [Yorkshire] Panels had laid their plans and were able to seal off coal supplies from the start.' Thus the huge Ferrybridge power station complex was reported to be under siege, with almost all coal movements stopped by the end of the third day of the strike.[63] Very early in the strike a picket was mounted at the Coalite Smokeless Fuel plant in Grimethorpe, near Barnsley, to prevent road tankers delivering oil. A series of clashes over several days, which included pelting the tankers with coke, saw the picket numbers grow to 300, and the police were forced to close the plant. But this was only after its management had agreed that no smokeless fuel would be moved unless a driver could produce an NUM docket that it was going to an approved destination (such as schools, hospitals or pensioners).[64] 'After this success the tactic of the mass picket became the standard weapon of the Yorkshire miners'.[65] Allen elaborated on this: 'A picketing strategy began to emerge in Yorkshire through a series of *ad hoc* decisions arising out of practical problems as they cropped up'.[66] Similarly, on the third day of the strike, groups of up to 300 miners disrupted coal supplies to power stations at Kincardine-on-Forth, Longannet and Cockenzie in Scotland. The next day pickets were switched from Longannet to Kincardine after lorries had gone into the latter.[67]

Effective picketing required support from other trade unionists, particularly transport workers. This was forthcoming from the railway unions even before the strike. On 6 January the National Union of Railwaymen (NUR) instructed that members 'should not go into collieries' and 'should not work oil into power stations where, due to the strike, a switch is made from coal to oil'. A Manchester NUR spokesperson backed this up immediately: 'If anyone has ideas of changing to oil to beat this we will ban the handling of that as well.' The *Guardian* complained that the order by the train drivers' union ASLEF that 'extra freight trains carrying coal and other fuel which could have a bearing on the dispute should not be worked' was 'an astonishingly vague instruction, leaving it open to militants to refuse to handle almost any fuel'.[68]

On the second day of the strike, Monday 10 January, an emergency meeting of the TUC's 'inner cabinet', the Finance and General Purposes Committee (made up of the most senior union leaders), considered a request from the NUM for support from TUC unions 'whose members were involved in handling and transporting coal'. The committee decided that a special meeting 'of unions whose members transport coal or oil' was not necessary as the NUM had already approached most of the unions concerned. Jack Jones, Transport and General Workers Union (TGWU) general secretary, stressed that his 'members would not pass picket lines', and it was generally agreed that 'it would be helpful if pickets were mounted by the NUM on those places from which they did not want coal to be moved'.[69] Jones, whose road haulage members would be critical to the strike's outcome, declared after the meeting, 'Clearly no picket lines will be crossed and there will be opposition to any abnormal movement of coal or other fuels to try to break the strike'.[70] The Morning Star was able to print the headline 'Don't Cross Picket Lines—TUC Call'.[71]

The Times commented that the TUC order 'will not prevent shipment, road transport, or internal movement of coal stocks unless the miners' union can post pickets at points far from coalfields'. But Gormley immediately publicly announced, 'We shall put pickets wherever necessary—within the law—to make sure that this strike is a success, even if it means picketing power stations'.[72] The journalist Paul Routledge later argued, 'Thus was born, quite accidentally, the aggressive picketing campaign which brought the Central Electricity Generating Board to its knees'.[73] While this is hard to prove, the TUC's support for respecting picket lines was to be given a much wider meaning than had originally been intended.

TUC general secretary Vic Feather met the miners' leaders the next morning at NUM headquarters and at midday an NUM press statement was released: 'Mr Gormley and Mr Daly said that official pickets were being posted and welcomed the TUC assurance that the Trade Unions would firmly instruct their members not to cross such picket lines in any circumstances'.[74] This was an important shift from what had actually been agreed at the TUC but it was not contradicted. On the same day an NUM circular was sent to area secretaries which repeated that 'a further assurance has been received from the TUC that the Unions whose Members are engaged in the distribution of coal will issue firm instructions' not to cross picket lines. It also called for 'immediate steps to place pickets at such places as coal stock yards, open cast sites, Docks and Power Stations'.[75]

On the Wednesday, official NUM 'instructions to pickets' stated that their aim was 'to prevent the movement of coal *or alternative fuels*', and that 'pickets should…be placed at strategic road and rail access points'. Another circular to area secretaries attached a list of power stations in their coalfield with the request that 'major' power stations be picketed, but others only when 'manpower is available'. There was also advice that 'at oil fired power stations fuel *in excess* of normal deliveries should be halted where possible' (added emphasis).[76] At this stage the national office was responding to the momentum developing in the more militant coalfields while simultaneously trying to set minimum standards for the others.

In the small Leicestershire coalfield, for example, which had returned only a 37 percent vote for the strike 'there was some difficulty recruiting sufficient pickets at first because the men had not been involved in an official strike before and were uncertain as to their role'. Even here unofficial action played a significant role: 'At the end of the second week…about fifty men…invaded the Swannington pumping station, which kept Whitwick and Snibston mines free of water, with the intention of stopping the NUM pumpmen from working.' After 'a heated meeting' with the area secretary, also called Jack Jones, 'the men called off their action' but 'agreed to act as official power station pickets'. During this first fortnight members of Desford NUM lodge had been picketing Leicester power station but, 'through inexperience', only between 9am and 5pm and 'so had not prevented oil tankers from going through' at night. Twenty-four-hour pickets were then instituted at the local power stations and open cast sites.[77]

The national circulars of 11 and 12 January had both stressed 'peaceful' picketing. The mass pickets in evidence already in Yorkshire and Scotland were not necessarily what the national office intended. That they were usually effective meant that they provided a model for others to follow. Thus once the 24-hour picketing was operating at Leicester power station 'we got a tip-off from one of the power workers…that oil tankers…were going to join together in a convoy and force their way through at midnight. By 10 o'clock we had organised a mass picket to combat it, about 100 men from as far afield as Coalville. They did not get through that lot'.[78]

Even in traditionally militant areas pickets still found it hard going to establish their supremacy. In the small Kent coalfield the miners from the three collieries had problems stopping the movement of coal from

Dover docks in the first week and had received little assistance from the local TGWU full-time officer: 'It was felt that if they could not close the docks within a few miles of their own pitheads...there were considerable doubts about whether they could close anywhere else.' A concerted effort on Monday 17 January led to unionised drivers recognising the picket, but the non-union drivers continued through. On the Tuesday a mass picket of 150 tried to block the road. More miners and women from the mining communities arrived and intensive picketing continued. Eventually, on the Thursday night, an agreement was reached between the NUM and TGWU on the one hand and the coal distributor on the other, with the police acting as witness and guarantor. The 'Dover Agreement' allowed union drivers in to collect priority loads only—coal for domestic purposes and for schools, hospitals and old people's homes—and pickets would be limited to six per entrance. The police admitted privately that 'the widespread nature of the miners' offensive and the numbers of men involved had stretched police resources to their limit'.[79]

Yet before most area unions had even sorted out the picketing of coal users in their own coalfields the dispute was dramatically escalated. The *Morning Star* had intimated this on the first Wednesday of the strike when it reported that 'from next week miners will move into non-coal producing areas to man picket lines at strategic points'.[80] The NUM executive meeting on Thursday 13 January took literally the TUC's apparent licence to target power stations and ports in non-mining regions. Responsibility for different parts of the country was allocated to the various area unions.[81] Away from any close supervision by the official national and area union leadership, the activists showed a remarkable organisational ability.

Kent and the Midlands area were allocated London and the south east of England to picket. Thanks to the work of Malcolm Pitt we have a record of the Kent miners' campaign. Seven 'flying squads' were quickly sent out to investigate—four to London and three along the coast. Within 24 hours, after finding power stations in London and trying to get picket lines established, 'the ad hoc organisation...began to show signs of breaking down under the magnitude of the tasks which their expedition was beginning to reveal'.[82] On Sunday 16 January Terry Harrison, a Betteshanger committee member, and Joe Holmes, Kent area president, arrived in London to set up a London picket office, which they established by taking over the NUM research officer's room in the union's head office in Euston Road. The next day over 200 Kent miners set off by coach and car for London.[83]

Many of the 21 power stations that Kent miners were responsible for picketing were along or close to the River Thames: 'The pickets felt very strange standing outside the massive brick pile of a power station, over a hundred miles from home, with nowhere to sleep, blasted by a bitterly cold wind and waiting to see what would happen when the first lorry came up.' As the power workers had their own wage claim, many of them saw the sense in helping the miners. Their stewards 'would usually show the miners where to put the picket line and tell them when to expect deliveries of fuel and chemicals'. Despite the TGWU's instruction to its members not to cross NUM picket lines, 'there were continual reports...that drivers were claiming that they had not received any such instructions'. Yet the pickets managed to turn back from the power stations all deliveries of fuel, including oil.[84]

At the same time, Monday 17 January, the NUM Scottish area general secretary, Bill McLean, announced that Scottish miners would be trying to stop oil entering oil-fired power stations. On Friday 21 January, a new NUM circular 'ratified what was already current practice on the picket line', that 'oil fired power stations are now taking extra loads...and supplies should...be stopped'. Further, 'a 24 hour picket line must be maintained unless the other local unions give firm assurances that they will contact the NUM should fuel be moved'. It was also reported that 'oil tanker drivers in the TGWU have been told not to cross our picket lines'.[85] For example, at the beginning of the second week, Alan Law, the West Midlands TGWU trade group secretary, declared that although oil tanker drivers could not black oil deliveries to power stations, they would not cross picket lines outside power stations.[86]

As many London power stations had been designed to receive supplies from the riverside, Kent miners arranged a water-borne picket, and on Monday 24 January 'the Miners' Navy was launched from Westminster Pier'. It provided 'an important cover for dockers and power-workers when they refused to handle fuel which they could justifiably claim had passed through the NUM picket line'.[87] Meanwhile in Kent itself the pickets were still having a hard time. In the Gravesend area, for example, pickets were spread between two cement works and a coal depot. Non-union drivers were the problem, as they had been at Dover. Eventually it was decided on

Wednesday afternoon, 19 January, that 'instead of attempting to picket the three sites, the picket should be concentrated' on one. The next day an agreement similar to the one at Dover was reached.[88] Each area of the union devised its own solutions to picketing. In north Notts, for example, picketing was organised on rotas of six hours, day and night, seven days a week. There was a 'Flying Squad' of 'people in cars, on standby 24 hours a day'.[89]

The biggest travelling army of pickets was from the Barnsley area. East Anglia had been allocated to the whole Yorkshire area but was given to the Barnsley panel because it had far fewer coal-using installations in its vicinity than the other panels.[90] After exploratory visits, the first 200 pickets left for East Anglia on Tuesday 18 January. They faced a daunting task—15 ports and seven power stations in their allotted area. The Barnsley panel secretary, Don Baines, established an office at the agricultural workers' union premises in Norwich. Scargill claims that he pushed for mass picketing at each site in turn, but that the Barnsley strike committee only agreed to this after several days of the pickets being spread around ineffectively.[91] On 22 January the Norwich strike office informed Barnsley that coal movements had generally stopped, but that Ipswich was causing problems. By Monday 24 January there were some 1,000 Yorkshire miners in East Anglia, and mass picketing did eventually stop coal going into the Cliff Quay power station that day. Two days later, after several days of picketing at Ipswich docks, the TGWU agreed to black all future oil deliveries to the nearby power station.[92]

Once agreements had been established that certain goods should not cross picket lines the pickets were mainly a token presence. In many places it suited local police to keep a low profile. Thus:

> At one colliery the village policeman even gave the strikers lifts in his police car to and from the picket line. On another picket...the strikers had set up a tent complete with heater, cooker and portable television; the lone representative of law and order frequently took advantage of these facilities.[93]

But there were other experiences: 'A telephone request for pickets to go to a certain location was made to the Barnsley offices of the NUM. Within a few minutes police had arrived at the scene of the alleged picket—a turnip field'.[94] The pickets themselves were sometimes not averse to taking the law into their own hands:

We were at Thorpe Marsh [power station near Doncaster]…and an oil lorry went through… [T]here were a kid there and he said, 'Can I get a car, I want to go back to pit.' He were [a] blacksmith… He came back about four hours later. He'd been in pit yard in forge and he'd made some things which you throw on floor and chance which way you throw them there's a spike stuck up to throw under wheels. He'd made about a dozen at pit yard.[95]

Surveying the experience of Notts and Derbyshire miners, a *Financial Times* reporter noted, 'Picketing may be an uncomfortable way of filling in time, but it is a way. It givers strikers a sense of purpose and even greater direct involvement than the simple fact of being on strike.' These miners were also well aware of its importance, and told the reporter that the postal workers in 1971 'made the mistake of not closing the telephone service down, and they paid for it dearly'.[96]

Allen has argued that 'the scale and intensity of the miners' participation in the strike *distinguished it from all other strikes in recent trade union history*' (added emphasis).[97] His estimate of 500 establishments being picketed on a 24-hour basis by an average of 40,000 miners each day came from *Labour Research*, and may well have originated from Joe Ashton MP.[98] Allen also cites Daly's evidence to the Wilberforce court of inquiry, which gives a total of 60,000 pickets, as does the *Times* newspaper.[99] Exact figures are difficult to verify but there is no doubt that the picketing involved a significant proportion of striking miners. Thus Frank Cave, member of the Yorkshire area NUM executive, recalled that it was possible to 'pull 4-500 people anytime we wanted' from the 2,800 miners employed in his [Brodsworth] pit.[100] At the end of the strike a government statement declared that 263 people (mainly but not all miners) were arrested for picketing offences.[101] Compared with the 1984-85 miners' strike this number is tiny,[102] but it did not seem like that at the time.

The picketing was devastatingly effective. For example, by early February the Central Electricity Generating Board (CEGB) reported that it was 'in a state of siege', complained of the 'unrelenting blockade' of power stations, and later considered itself to be 'conducting a guerrilla war'.[103] The crisis was intensified by the pickets' decision to stop not just coal and then oil, but other essential materials. A bare two weeks into the strike it was reported that stocks of special oil to help coal burn and to ignite furnaces—vital to 40 percent of the 142 coal-burning power stations in England and Wales—were running low. The NUM was also considering how to cut deliveries of caustic soda, essential to clean furnaces of clinker.[104] Only a week later the CEGB's concern over possible power cuts was 'not…[due to] any immediate shortage of coal' but because of 'pickets preventing normal deliveries of other essential materials'.

At the same time a CEGB spokesman in the north east blamed 'extremists, apparently in defiance of official instructions from the National Union of Mineworkers' for preventing delivery of 'hydrogen, chemicals and other commodities essential for safe operation'.[105] Battersea power station in London was reported in late January to be close to shutting as supplies of sulphuric acid had not been delivered.[106] In early February there were even shortages of 'lubricating oil for the bulldozers that shift the coal about' in the power stations.[107] The *Economist* later explained the significance of hydrogen: 'The really big turbines in modern power stations are usually kept spinning continuously; if they are not called on to generate power, they windmill until a load is applied again. When they are windmilling they get hot and are cooled down by spraying with liquid hydrogen'.[108] The pickets had identified and exploited these dependencies and thus accelerated the impact of the strike.

Solidarity action

The pickets could never have been so effective without the assistance, both official and unofficial, of other workers. Such solidarity was expressed in numerous ways, most notably in the observance of TUC guidelines asking trade unionists to respect NUM picket lines. But rank-and-file activists in the transport unions were instrumental in implementing, and going much further than, such official guidelines. For example, the south-eastern and south-western areas of ASLEF blacked all movement of coal by rail.[109] The TGWU provided information about movements of coal, and its drivers generally complied with official instructions not to cross picket lines, though this took some time to sort out. Generally, the only lorries that tried to ignore the miners' action were driven by non-union drivers, often with police escorts. Early in the strike, 50 lorry drivers in Staffordshire were threatened with the sack for refusing to cross picket lines.[110] Dockers and seamen also provided information and support to help stop coal imports. Two weeks into the strike dockers at the Tilbury oil terminal were reported to be blocking the transit of oil in or out of the port.[111]

The national decisions of the railway unions and the TGWU to respect the miners' picket lines did not mean that all movement of coal magically halted. Drivers particularly had to be persuaded not to cross pickets. But the miners gained confidence from early examples of transport workers taking the initiative themselves. Thus, for example, on the first Monday of the strike ASLEF train drivers refused to move coal from depots at Port Talbot and Stoke-on-Trent, and from ships in Southampton docks. On the Tuesday a ship with foreign coal had to be diverted from Cardiff to Rotterdam. On the same day Middlesbrough dockers blacked a ship carrying 20,000 tons of power station coal. Their action was followed up by railway union members refusing to move empty coal wagons into the docks.[112]

On Friday 21 January a Kent miner reported that an ASLEF meeting at Hither Green in south-east London had agreed to black 'all movement of coal and allied fuels'. Three days later the NUR north London district council also voted to stop all coal and oil for power stations but was warned by the union head office that it did not have the authority. However, it was reported on 27 January that the more strategically important ASLEF had called on members not to take oil into power stations where there were picket lines.[113] This was a logical development of ASLEF's position at the beginning of the strike and a response to its members' local initiatives.

On 11 February the weeks-long blockade at Thameshaven on power station oil from two major refineries (Mobil in Coryton, and Shell-Mex/BP in Shellhaven) was extended to all oil when a train that was allowed through was later suspected of carrying CEGB supplies. When Kirkstall power station in Leeds was shut down on 14 February, a week after NUR and ASLEF members had blacked oil deliveries from Immingham, Ray Buckton, ASLEF general secretary, said,'When our members hear that there are pickets on they do not start the journey, so as not to block main junctions'.[114] In fact, some ASLEF members went even further than this. Long after the strike the *Times* gave a graphic example of their solidarity:

> The driver and second man of a goods train of oil tankers...refused to take their train out of the yards. They said there were pickets on the line. Management could see no pickets... The driver rang...[ASLEF] headquarters and asked for a picket. A frantic telephone call to the NUM...led to the immediate dispatch of two 'flying

pickets'. They unfurled a banner bearing the slogan 'official NUM picket' from an overhead bridge and the train did not run.[115]

Similarly, according to one source, 'Transport men in the Midlands…phoned up the local NUM centre to ask for one or two pickets to go to depots so that they would have reason to turn back'.[116]

Apart from the events at Saltley (see below) where strikes took place to reinforce the picket line, there were few examples of sympathetic strikes. But more than 100 TGWU members at a British Leyland car component factory, SU Carburettors in Birmingham, staged one-day strikes in support of the miners in late January and early February, leading to a further 1,000 workers being laid off.[117]

While strike action such as this was relatively isolated, there were more organised protests. Delegates at the joint Merseyside trades council meeting on 19 January—held to consider solidarity action with the Fisher-Bendix occupation—used the opportunity to support the miners. As local dockers had already agreed to support an unofficial national dock strike on Wednesday 26 January in protest against redundancies, the trades council called for a 24-hour stoppage on that day in support of Fisher-Bendix, the miners and the dockers. A 7,000-strong march in pouring rain to the Pierhead in Liverpool included car workers, engineers, shipbuilders and building workers. Among the construction workers on strike were 2,000 from the Shell Stanlow site, 800 from the Fiddlers Ferry power station and 500 from the Burmah oil site.[118] The next day some 12,000 trade unionists marched through Cardiff in support of the miners 'in one of the largest demonstrations ever seen in Wales'. There were solidarity demonstrations in London on Sunday 6 February and at the miners' lobby of parliament on Tuesday 15 February, with an estimated 6,000 and 10,000 respectively.[119]

As well as these public shows of support, there were innumerable small ones, such as the hundreds of shop stewards' committees and trade union branches which sent donations, with many workplaces organising a weekly levy. The London joint branches of the print union NATSOPA 'adopted' the miners' pickets at Bankside power station, providing them with food and accommodation.[120] Across the country miners were invited to speak to student meetings. Up to 1,000 Yorkshire miners were provided with free accommodation at the University of Essex until the university authorities threatened a High Court injunction. Students at the London School of Economics and Goldsmiths' College in south-east London housed Kent miners.[121]

The CP produced 250,000 'Black the Coal, Back the Miners' leaflets,[122] and held numerous solidarity meetings at which miners put their case, as did other left groups such as the International Socialists (later to become the Socialist Workers Party).

The NUM did not pay strike pay, though area unions paid some expenses to pickets. Gormley later acknowledged that:

> ...we originally had a deliberate policy of not asking for financial as-
> sistance, realising that physical assistance would be of more value.
> This was one of the lessons we learnt from the postmen's strike last year.
> But we were forced as a union, because of pressure by those of the
> trade union and labour movement who could not involve themselves
> physically, but who wanted to be involved in some way, to open up...a
> 'Campaign Fund'... This money helped to keep our picket lines going
> 24 hours a day, seven days a week.[123]

The power workers' dispute

Power station workers helped the strike greatly by providing miners' pickets with information about stocks, deliveries and where to place pickets. Such action was undoubtedly stimulated by the power workers' own long, drawn-out campaign for a wage increase.

The aftermath of the power workers' dispute in December 1970 had been a court of inquiry followed eventually by a negotiated settlement in late March 1971, backdated to September 1970. Unsurprisingly the Electricity Council was not in a hurry to start negotiations for the September 1971 claim. Ironically, in an attempt by both sides of the National Joint Industrial Council, the collective bargaining forum, to isolate 'unofficial groups in the industry', a conference of representatives from works committees and district joint industrial councils had been established to have some say in the negotiating process. The Electricity Council waited for this to meet before making an offer for the 1971-72 settlement. At the conference in late November there were some calls for industrial action, but the negotiators were put under a lot of pressure not to accept less than 11 percent. Hence when just under 7 percent was then offered, followed by a miniscule improvement, the electricity negotiations inevitably spilled over into the new year, with an agreement to resume talks on 20 January.[124] By then, however, the miners' strike was on and was beginning to bite. The electricity negotiations now became inextricably linked with the government's handling of the miners' strike.

On Friday 14 January the four unions (the EETPU electricians, the AUEW engineers, the TGWU and the NUGMW general and municipal union), after dismissing an informal approach from the Electricity Council, gave notice of an official overtime ban from 1 February if their demands were not satisfied the following week. In the first week of the miners' strike 'their sudden militancy could not have come at a more embarrassing time for the Government'.[125] The cause of it was undoubtedly the call for action already put out by the Power Workers' Combine, an unofficial national organisation of shop stewards (whose secretary was George Wake, a leading CP member). Its paper, *Power Worker*, had called for an overtime ban, no temporary upgrading of staff, no driving of workers' own vehicles, and workers to start and finish shifts from officially designated centres. Solidarity action with the miners was to be encouraged. A London-wide meeting of power workers was arranged for the evening of Wednesday 19 January and plans laid for a demonstration outside the Electricity Council's Millbank offices the following day when pay negotiations formally resumed.[126]

The unofficial meeting agreed to organise local liaison with miners and call mass meetings in the power stations over their own claim. On Thursday 20 January a delegation of Kent miners joined the power workers' picket of the Electricity Council, with banners declaring 'Power and Mineworkers Unite'. Under pressure from their members, the union officials threatened further industrial action beyond their already announced overtime ban.[127] Then, on 24 January, workers at West Ham, West Thurrock and Woolwich, among other power stations, imposed an unofficial overtime ban. Under this pressure the national union negotiators rejected an improved pay offer on 27 January, but delayed the start of the official ban for one week—until midnight on 7 February, to allow further negotiations on that day.[128]

Shortages of essential materials in power stations and a cold spell led to some voltage reductions for four successive days, from Sunday 30 January to Tuesday 2 February, in the fourth week of the miners' strike.[129] As the *Economist* noted, 'If the [overtime] ban had been in effect' in the power industry and not postponed, 'there would have been instant and probably widespread power cuts, and the militants in electricity are kicking themselves that they missed the chance. It will probably not come round again'.[130] Voltage reductions throughout Britain on Sunday 6 February were followed by strong warnings of power cuts the following day.[131]

'Just how close the country came to chaos may be judged from the fact that there was an argument on the trade union side about the possibility of joint action with the miners.' The electricity union negotiators split six to six over the increased pay offer on 7 February, with four NUGMW and two EETPU for it, and three TGWU, two AUEW and one electrician (Eric Hammond) against. Frank Chapple, the electricians' leader, used his casting vote as chair for acceptance, arguing that 'to bring down the Government by industrial action would only lead to a general election in which the Conservatives would be returned with a landslide majority'.[132] Chapple later elaborated on this, saying that 'such dual action would be seen as a challenge to the state, tantamount to a general strike… Industrial action for political ends is not for me and, so far, it is also alien to the TUC'.[133]

State of emergency

The very next day, Tuesday 8 February, the Conservative cabinet agreed to introduce a state of emergency in order to ration electricity supplies. There were three main reasons—'the general coal situation, the success of picketing in preventing essential materials in getting to power stations, and the tanker drivers' decision not to deliver oil to them'.[134]

This decision had probably already been made at the cabinet emergency committee the previous Thursday.[135] According to *Labour Research*, 'The CEGB and the government had gambled on a settlement with the power workers, and this involved putting off power cuts for as long as possible'.[136] While the government had been criticised for proclaiming states of emergency too quickly in other disputes, its main concern early in the miners' strike was fear that such action 'might stiffen union attitudes' in the negotiations in gas, water and particularly electricity supply, 'where a strike could not be faced'. But the electricity negotiations 'took longer than hoped',[137] thus dramatically reducing its room for manoeuvre.

The journalist John Torode argued that the government had already decided that the miners were 'a "special case", deserving more than the 8-per-cent offer dictated by a rigid application of the government's covert wage norm'. But 'first they had to get the power dispute out of the way. Otherwise the floodgates would have been opened. Once the miners were safely isolated, talks about a special case could begin'.[138] The *Times* similarly argued that the power workers' settlement 'makes it easier to admit the miners as a special case', especially 'now that the winter bargaining season is over' for the public sector.[139]

According to Sir Denis Barnes, then permanent secretary (the senior civil servant) at the Department of Employment, 'the government had…intended to "conciliate" in the miners' strike immediately after the electricity claim had been settled, but now decided that this would mean too open a retreat'.[140] However, secretary of state Carr did announce on the afternoon of Tuesday 8 February that 'we are going to start talks with both sides tomorrow'. The next morning he suggested to NUM and NCB negotiators 'that they might consider resuming talks on the basis that if a settlement ran for a period longer than 12 months, this might provide a possibility for some improvement in the cash offer'. Following those talks, the NUM executive rejected the offer the next morning, with Alex Eadie MP of the NUM telling parliament that 'it is a 22-month agreement, because the award starts on the commencement of work, whereas the previous offer was retrospective to November'.[141] According to the former newspaper proprietor Cecil King, 'The information at the CBI [Confederation of British Industry, the main employers' organisation] was that the Government was confident the offer made…[on 9 February] would be accepted. When it wasn't, they were utterly unprepared'.[142]

Gormley has claimed that, as the offer was clearly unacceptable to the majority of the NUM executive, he managed to avoid taking a vote on it—'if there *had* been a vote, it would soon have become public' (original emphasis) and any split would have weakened the union's bargaining position.[143] Further negotiations were held on the Thursday afternoon but the only NCB concession was to backdate the proposed 18-month deal to November. At this point talks collapsed and Carr then told them that he 'would immediately appoint a court of inquiry'. He asked the union negotiators to consider a return to work on the current offer without prejudice to the findings of the inquiry. On the Friday morning the executive not only threw this out as a sign that the inquiry 'would be subjected to government pressure', but also refused to be bound by the inquiry's recommendations.[144]

The battle of Saltley gates

Thursday 3 February was significant for two reasons. That day Fred Matthews, a 37-year-old miner from Hatfield Main colliery in Yorkshire, was killed whilst picketing outside Keadby power station near Scun-thorpe. He was run over by the rear wheel of an articulated lorry driven by a non-union driver.[145] Ten thousand people came to his funeral, with miners from all over the country and a representative from every pit in Yorkshire. Print workers in London and the provinces held one-hour token strikes as a mark of respect.[146]

The other event was the start of the picket at the West Midlands Gas Board coke depot in Nechells Place, Saltley, about a mile from the centre of Birmingham. It was the last major coke distribution point still operating, and contained an estimated 138,000 tons. On 3 February the *Birmingham Evening Mail* ran a story about a mile-long traffic jam as 'lor-ries from all over the country waited at Saltley'. It reported some 650-700 lorries arriving daily. A lorry driver from Bolton was quoted as saying of the miners, 'I'm amazed they haven't started picketing it already'.[147]

By that evening seven pickets from the NUM in Warwickshire and Leicestershire were stationed outside the Saltley gates,[148] and were re-inforced the next day by 200 miners from Stoke-on-Trent. There was some success in stemming the movement of coke. Officers of the TGWU 5/35 road haulage branch, which organised the great major-ity of lorry drivers in the Birmingham conurbation, warned drivers that their firms would be 'blacklisted' and their union cards withdrawn if they crossed the picket line. They organised a round-the-clock picket rota of union branch members, alongside the miners, to turn back TGWU drivers.[149] Such solidarity action resulted in a dramatic reduction in the number of lorries crossing, but employers responded by using non-union firms who were paid as much as £50 to £60 per day, plus a £50 bonus for every load (significantly more than a week's wages). This led the right-wing Midlands area NUM secretary, Jack Lally, who was nearly knocked over by a 20-ton lorry, to agree to CP suggestions to con-tact the union's national office to appeal for extra pickets. Local CP dis-trict secretary Frank Watters described Lally sitting down with him as 'like getting Ian Paisley to have a friendly chat with the Pope'.[150]

By Sunday morning, 6 February, miners had arrived from South Wales, the Midlands and Yorkshire. Scargill recalled the response from Barnsley: 'The telephone rang at four o'clock on the Saturday...within three hours we had 200 on their way. Within five hours we had 400 men on their way down to Birmingham in coaches'.[151] Scargill him-self arrived at 3am and went to the local CP headquarters where ac-commodation for the Yorkshire pickets had been provided.[152]

Hundreds of miners picketed the gates from the early morning on Sunday. Pickets had already agreed with the police and the Gas Board that only one gate would be used. During the morning some lorries were turned away, and the Gas Board then closed the gates for the rest of the day.[153] On the Monday morning over 1,000 were outside the gates, the numbers increasing through the day. Hundreds of police reinforcements were drafted in and there were frequent scuffles as dozens of non-union drivers attempted to drive through. A steady stream of pickets were arrested or injured. The entire Birmingham police force was put on special alert.[154] By the Monday evening the *Birmingham Evening Mail* had dubbed it the 'Battle of Saltley'.[155]

On Tuesday more miners arrived, particularly from Staffordshire, South Wales, Scotland and Kent. Two pickets were injured and a police chief inspector had his thigh fractured when a lorry pushed its way through. Every lorry provoked skirmishes between the police and pickets, and arrests and injuries continued to rise. One amusing incident was recounted in the *Times*: '...pickets let down the tailboard of a loaded lorry and about three tons of coke poured on to the road. Policemen had to shovel it onto the lorry to clear the way'.[156]

Officially the picketing of the coke depot fell under the authority of Lally. But while he was working behind the scenes Scargill, still only a branch delegate, was left in charge of the picket, aided by a team of stewards. Outside support started to build up. The lorry drivers' TGWU branch supplied mobile canteens. Dozens of shop stewards and union activists took time out to visit the picket line. On Monday workers from Bryant's and McAlpine's building sites, and from SU Carburettors, who had already struck in support of the miners, went on strike to join the picket. On Tuesday they were joined by nearly 2,000 car delivery workers, and by 200 workers from H F Ward and delegations from the (British Leyland) Tractors and Transmissions, Thorn Electrical and Thorn Radiation plants.[157]

But mass picketing had still not stopped the flow of lorries, so Scargill and Watters realised that they needed more extensive solidarity action. They decided to win the support of leading shop stewards for a one-day strike and mass picket. Of vital importance was the network of industrial contacts around the CP, which had about 800 members in Birmingham, including leading stewards and conveners in factories across the city, particularly in engineering.[158]

CP member Arthur Harper, convener at the British Leyland Tractors and Transmissions plant, played a pivotal role. Watters asked him if Scargill could address Tuesday evening's meeting of the AUEW East Birmingham district committee.[159] Harper, as chair, ruled in favour and Scargill made a 40-minute speech to this specially extended meeting of the committee, many of whose members were also conveners at large engineering plants. 'We don't want your pound notes,' Scargill told them. 'Will you go down in history as the working class in Birmingham who stood by while the miners were battered, or will you become immortal? I do not ask you—I demand that you come out on strike'.[160] He got a unanimous response, and an emergency district shop stewards' quarterly meeting was called for the following afternoon, with a recommendation that the district's AUEW membership join a mass picket on the Thursday morning.

The following day 200 stewards endorsed an appeal from Harper to call mass meetings and lead demonstrations from each factory to Saltley. Although the word 'strike' was not explicity used, it was understood that stoppages had to take place. Watters used his contacts so that Scargill obtained similar decisions from the district committees of the TGWU and the National Union of Vehicle Builders (NUVB).[161] In the NUGMW and the EETPU, rank-and-file activists agreed to try to get their members out unofficially, given the refusal of their local union leadership to call official action.

Birmingham was buzzing with stories about the picket. Accounts by union activists who had visited the picket line were told and retold in numerous workplaces. Local and national television and press carried graphic accounts and pictures. Now news of the call for a mass picket swept through the city. With the CP industrial network at its core, a momentum built up on the Wednesday. Delegations of miners toured factories and Birmingham Trades Council placed an advert in the *Birmingham Evening Mail* calling for support. What had begun as an unofficial initiative had now won significant official union backing and legitimacy, which further extended its pool of support. As Mick Rice, an AUEW district committee member, explained:

> I don't remember the CP putting out any leaflets…but…[b]ecause the CP put the main players together they were important… [A]lso because Harper was a natural militant and happened to be the [AUEW] district president he could give a lead. Without Arthur

Harper it couldn't have happened, no one else would have had the status to push something as strong with the district committee. And once he got it through…the ball was rolling.[162]

On Thursday morning there was an air of anticipation on the picket line. The chief constable, Sir Derek Capper, was quoted in the *Times* as saying, 'If these people come they will be there illegally and we shall take the necessary steps'.[163] Scargill takes up the story:

> …about ten o'clock…there was a hush over the Saltley area. 3,000 miners altogether, Welsh miners singing, Yorkshire miners, Nottinghamshire miners, Midlands miners. And yet nothing happened… And then over this hill came a banner and I've never seen in my life as many people following a banner. As far as the eye could see it was just a mass of people… There was a huge roar and from the other side of the hill they were coming the other way. They were coming from…every direction… And our lads were just jumping up in the air with emotion.[164]

From early in the morning shop stewards in numerous engineering and car factories across east Birmingham had organised meetings and appealed to their members to support the miners. Thousands responded by walking out on strike, with large contingents marching to Saltley from plants such as Rover Solihull, Tractors and Transmissions, Dunlop, GEC, Lucas, Wilmot Breedon, Salisbury Transmissions (GKN) and Pressed Steel Fisher. While local employers tried to play down the scale of the walkout and claimed that many returned to work after lunch, there is no doubting the impact it had on the situation at the coke depot. The *Morning Star* cited estimates of 6,000 to 10,000 pickets. Major-General Richard Clutterbuck, the counter-insurgency expert, cited police records that claimed 15,000 pickets at the peak.[165] This magnificent display of solidarity reflected the self-confidence and generally successful nature of the Birmingham engineering workers' own struggles in recent years.[166] They were joined by trade unionists from other workplaces, including building sites. A young engineering shop steward recalled, 'For the first time in my life I had a practical demonstration of what workers' solidarity meant. We all felt so powerful. We felt we could rule the world'.[167]

Nearly 1,000 police were banked against the massive throng that gathered. Scargill described what happened:

> …everybody was chanting…some were chanting 'Heath Out', 'Tories Out', 'Support the Miners', 'General Strike'… I got hold of the mega-

phone and I started to chant… 'Close the Gates!' …and it was taken up, just like a football crowd. It was booming through Saltley: 'Close the Gates!' …each time they shouted this slogan they moved and the police, who were four deep, couldn't help it, they were getting moved in. And Capper, the Chief Constable of Birmingham…said 'Close the Gates' and they swung them to. Hats were in the air, you've never seen anything like it in your life. Absolute delirium on the part of the people who were there.[168]

The chief constable had acted 'in the interests of public safety'. At 10.43am a Gas Board official walked across the yard and locked the padlock on the gates. At 11am it was announced that the gates would be closed for the rest of the day. The police asked Scargill to disperse the crowd and he agreed, on condition that they would allow him to use a police loudspeaker as his was 'knackered':

I…told them it was the greatest victory of the working class, certainly in my lifetime… Here had been displayed all that's good in the working class movement…what for years had been on a banner but had never been transferred…into reality. You know the words: 'Unity is Strength', 'Workers of the World Unite'… Here was the living proof that the working class had only to flex its muscles and it could bring governments, employers, and society to a total standstill. I know the fear of Birmingham on the part of the ruling class. The fear was what happened in Birmingham could happen in every city.[169]

Reginald Maudling, the Home Secretary, wrote in more measured tones in his memoirs:

The then Chief Constable of Birmingham [had] assured me that only over his dead body would they [the pickets]…succeed. I felt constrained to ring him…to enquire after his health! I am sure the decision he took was a wise one…[as] any attempt by the relatively small body of police who could be assembled to keep the depot open by force could have led to very grave consequences. Some of my colleagues asked me afterwards, why I had not sent in troops…and I remember asking them one simple question: 'If they had been sent in, should they have gone in with their rifles loaded or unloaded?' Either course could have been disastrous.[170]

Yet it was not clear even then that Saltley would remain shut. George Evans, the NUVB Birmingham district organiser, pointed out, 'We may have communications problems tomorrow but if they are foolish enough to open we shall have to mobilize a force greater than today'.[171] In the House of Commons John Davies, trade and industry secretary, equivocated when pressed about whether a priority scheme would be operated at Saltley. Birmingham Labour MP Denis Howell then declared that notice had been given 'that a much more widespread stoppage will be pursued on Monday, which will mean that not fewer than 20,000 workers will be disrupting the industry of Birmingham'.[172] For example, Alan Law had requested all 8,000 TGWU lorry drivers in the Birmingham area strike on Monday and picket Saltley.[173] Eventually the Gas Board capitulated on the Thursday evening, an agreement on essential loads was reached with the NUM and a token picket of 12 was established.[174]

Former chief superintendent Arthur Brannigan was one police officer who later claimed, from a policing point of view, 'there was no reason why the gates couldn't have opened again the following day.' The West Midlands Gas Board chairman Derek Beavis also tried to play down the effectiveness of picketing by arguing that 'we were already considering closing the plant before the Thursday, and limiting the supply to priority customers'.[175] But a decision had been made first to keep Saltley open, despite the growing effectiveness of the picketing, and second, to keep it shut after 10 February—and most people would draw the obvious conclusion why.

Roger Geary assembled a table from a number of sources to produce the following approximate picture of events:[176]

Picket and police activity at Saltley			
Date	Pickets	Police	Arrests	Lorries entering
Fri 4 Feb	200	48(est)	0	596
Sat 5 Feb	130	48	2	320
Sun 6 Feb	200	48	2	-
Mon 7 Feb	2,000	400	21	47
Tue 8 Feb	2,000	400	18	39
Wed 9 Feb	2,000	400	25	43
Thu 10 Feb	15,000	800	8	10

Power cuts start and picketing continues

During the week of picketing at Saltley voltage reductions, which had started on 30 January, had occurred intermittently. The day that the gates were closed coincided with the first actual power cuts. Under the emergency regulations 'complete power cuts were introduced throughout most of the country on a rota basis' on Friday 11 February. Areas were allocated 'a series of four-hour periods each week in which there was a high likelihood of disconnexion'.[177]

On the same Friday Carr's announcement of the court of inquiry to the House of Commons was followed by further details of the government's emergency powers. Industry secretary Davies explained that there would now be a ban from Saturday on the use of electricity for the heating of 'offices, shops, public halls, catering establishments and premises used for recreation, entertainment and sport'. More significantly 'from Monday on, most industrial consumers with an estimated maximum demand of 100 kilowatts or more will be required not to use any electricity on Sunday and on three other days in the week'.[178] It was estimated that 800,000 workers were laid off work on Monday 14 February and 1.6 million on Friday.[179]

An NUM circular on 14 February stated that 'it is now time for each Area to review the position so as to ensure only the minimum number of men should be involved essential for effective picketing'.[180] According to Mick Costello of the *Morning Star*, 'While this was first interpreted as a relaxation of picketing, I understand it is nothing of the kind, but is a measure to cut down on the union's enormous expenditure'.[181] It probably was an effort to make the miners' pickets less visible. After all, as Gormley had noted, with large-scale layoffs now starting in industry, 'This, we thought, was the moment that we would start to lose public sympathy.' To his surprise 'it didn't happen. The letters of support, and the contributions, came in unabated'.[182]

The weakness of the government's position was further underlined on Monday evening, 14 February, when Davies told parliament that of 4.8 million tons held by the CEGB 'about 2.2 million tons were denied to use…by picketing and other factors'. With the restrictions introduced three days earlier 'the anticipated endurance of the CEGB is approximately two weeks'. After this 'capacity will be down to approximately 20 to 25 per cent of normal load'. There was 'no experience in handling electricity supply at these low levels'.[183]

But not only did the miners keep public support, they ignored the request to reduce picket numbers. An NUM spokesperson explained the immediate lack of reaction to the union's request: 'This is not an army—we can't give an order which is effective overnight'.[184] But, as Allen notes, the miners 'would have been negligent of their own interests if they had dropped their most effective weapon at a time when they could sense victory'.[185] One result was another large confrontation—this time at Longannet power station in Scotland.

On Monday 14 February a mass picket slowly assembled at the power station, on the shores of the Forth in Scotland. Allegations of oil being delivered in foreign ships determined the miners to try to shut the station. At 4.30am five busloads arrived after a three-hour journey from Ayrshire to be greeted by large numbers of police. Eventually some 2,000 pickets faced 400 police. Thirteen were arrested—11 miners (including one full time official and one senior lay officer), one draughtsman and one research student. They were charged with the Scottish common law offence of 'mobbing and rioting' and detained overnight. When they appeared in Dunfermline Sheriff Court the next morning a crowd of some 200 outside convinced the sheriff 'to declare the whole of the court building to be his chambers, thus keeping out the public'. The accused were committed 'for further examination—in custody—and in the normal course of events [under Scottish law] would have remained in prison until the following week'. Widespread protests took place and McGahey 'declared that the miners would not resume work until the pickets had been released'.[186]

Picketing continued at Longannet with 1,500 present on the Tuesday, while on Wednesday 700 pickets faced 600 police.[187] The whole situation threatened to get out of control. The Lord Advocate, the senior government law officer for Scotland, flew to Scotland on the Wednesday and the whole legal process was speeded up, with the pickets appearing in court on Thursday and being released on bail. Before the court hearing, some 1,500 pickets, faced by 600 police, tried to block access to Longannet. Another six pickets were arrested during the day. Significantly it could be argued that the intervention of the Lord Advocate, as a government minister, was a more obviously political interference with the courts than was the involvement of the Official Solicitor in the dockers' cases later in the year (see Chapter 5). All 13 were acquitted at the subsequent trial.[188]

The settlement

The then Conservative prime minister Edward Heath has since argued:

> Confronted with the prospect of the country becoming ungovernable, or having to use the armed forces to restore order, which public opinion would never have tolerated, we decided to set up a powerful and independent inquiry into miners' wages.[189]

The composition of the court of inquiry was unusual. Often such ad hoc bodies would have a 'neutral' chair, such as a judge, lawyer or academic, and two other members—one a trade unionist and the other an employer. In this case the government, perhaps concerned with the sensitivity of the issue, appointed three apparent neutrals: Lord Wilberforce, a judge who had chaired the power workers' court of inquiry the previous year and who would give the all-important House of Lords judgment on the dockers' case in July, John Garnett, director of the Industrial Society (a body preaching harmony between employers and workers), and Laurence Hunter, an economics professor at Glasgow University. The court reported 'with more than normal urgency'.[190] 'Its three authors first met on a Sunday, candles ready for working into the night. Having studied the situation on Monday, they heard evidence on Tuesday and Wednesday, wrote their conclusions on Thursday and published them on Friday!'[191]

On Thursday 17 February, the day before the report was published, Davies read out the following dramatic statement to the House of Commons:

> Stocks of coal, lighting-up fuel and necessary chemicals…have diminished…with denial of available and necessary supplies still continuing as a result of unwillingness of other union members to cross picket lines… The combined effect [of the measures so far]…has been to reduce the consumption of coal at power stations by about 35 per cent…
>
> [D]irections for further restrictions to take effect on Wednesday… will allow supply to be maintained throughout next week at the still further reduced level, before reaching the point where we will be down to non-coal generated capacity—equal to 20-25 per cent of normal load— and sufficient to meet only the essential services…with very little left available for other users…
>
> If essential materials currently denied to the CEGB were made available, then the time by which this basic, essential services-only level would be reached would be extended by some seven to 10 days.[192]

At this point, government ministers were treading on eggshells and in the House of Lords the Minister without Portfolio, Lord Drumalbyn, answered a question about the distribution of priority supplies of coal by stating, 'We are extremely grateful for the way it has been carried out by co-operation between the coal merchants and the National Union of Mineworkers' branches'.[193] The Tory weekly the *Spectator* recognised that Wilberforce's task was 'to judge what is the least the miners will now settle for, and to dress up the award as cleverly as may be'.[194] The report makes interesting reading:

> In our view there are *two quite separate elements in any possible wage increase in this industry*. First, there is what we may call the *periodic increase*, which is designed to take account of the cost of living... But, secondly, there is what we may call the *adjustment* factor. This means that a time may come in any industry when a distortion or trend has to be recognized as due for correction. We are convinced...that the present is a time when a definite and substantial adjustment in wage levels is called for in the coal industry.[195] (original emphasis)

The report then made the extraordinary claim that 'the existence of these two quite separate factors seems to us to have been overlooked until the present inquiry brought it to light'.[196] John Torode was lost for words: 'If you believe that you will believe anything'.[197] After all, only two days after the report, Carr was telling the House of Commons, 'The miners always made it very clear to me...that [it]...was not a dispute of the winter of 1971-72 but a dispute arising from at least a decade of events'.[198]

Wilberforce then examined:

> ...the Coal Board's final offer. By amazing chance it stood at the government's ceiling for public-sector deals. By equally amazing chance the court found that figure 'perfectly fair' to settle the annual claim, which is what Wilberforce insists the Coal Board honestly thought it was trying to do. But instead the Board must meet the 'adjustment factor' too.[199]

In the report's own words, 'We are conscious of the difficulties of establishing any general principle, but we think that the need for reassessment is clear and that it can be reasonably quantified in money terms'.[200] Torode riposted, 'So saying, Wilberforce gave 'em the money. No attempt to explain why and no attempt to justify in detail the award'.[201]

But the court of inquiry's views on what was acceptable were not shared by Conservative politicians. Carr recalled, 'Heath [had] agreed to…[an] Inquiry under what we thought was the safe chairmanship of Lord Wilberforce… [W]hen they came up with over 20 per cent we were sunk.' Douglas Hurd, Heath's political secretary, similarly argued that the award was 'far too high for the national interest'.[202] The faceworkers' wage rise was £4.50, other underground workers £6 and surface workers £5. This meant individual increases of between 15 percent and 31.6 percent.

Copies of the report were made available at 10am on the Friday to the NCB, the NUM, Feather of the TUC and the CBI director general, who all met at the Department of Employment.[203] Earlier in the week Heath had called Feather to Downing Street and expressed his concern that 'the process of decision making in the NUM should be carried out…as soon as the Court of Inquiry's recommendations were known'.[204] As a result, he understood that Feather was 'willing to influence the NUM to react as quickly as possible to the report'.[205] In practice, Feather had little role to play on this day.

The NUM executive quickly decided that the amounts on offer, especially over a 16-month period, were not sufficient. Gormley suggests that it split 15 to 10 against acceptance at this point. According to the permanent secretary at the Department of Employment, the union was now in '*the strongest conceivable bargaining position*' (added emphasis). The government, despite its earlier reluctance, was now 'not able to avoid "conciliating"—and in the most unfavourable circumstances'.[206]

The NCB negotiators refused to budge on the size of the wage increases or the length of the settlement. They gave significant but not full concessions on holidays and the adult rate, items on which Wilberforce had made no recommendations. From 1 May 1972 there were to be five extra rest days, 'the timing of which should be agreed with the Colliery Manager in such a way as to enable the pit to continue in effective operation'. The full rise was given to 18 year olds and the adult rate at 18 was to be phased in over two years. At this point, the NUM executive voted by the narrowest majority, 13 to 12, to reject 'the Board's offer arising from the Court of Inquiry' and to authorise the three national officials to negotiate further on the basis that the union would settle on, and recommend, rises of £4.50, £7 and £6.[207] It was the Communist Jock Kane who argued that the executive should insist on the extra £1 for non-faceworkers, stating that 'we have the government on the run so let us keep it running'.[208]

Further negotiations with the NCB led to more concessions: corresponding increases were to be given to coke and by-product workers; the full appropriate increases to any remaining pieceworkers; clerical workers were to get the same increase as surface workers; winding enginemen were to get an extra 80p (to give a £5.80 rise); a new wage structure was agreed for lorry drivers; and 'consequential increases' for canteen workers and weekly paid industrial staff were to be negotiated later but to be effective from 1 November 1971. All these matters flowed, in one way or another, from the report, but the NUM also secured the extra concession of a national subsidised transport agreement which had to be agreed by 1 May 1972.[209]

Daly apparently even asked the members of the executive for further suggestions. Several other points, which were not part of the original claim but flowed out of the industrial action, were squeezed from the NCB: rent arrears for members in NCB-owned housing to be cleared up over a period 'up to twelve months'; and claims for wages lost during the earlier overtime ban were 'to be dealt with expeditiously'. Pitt argues, however, that 'many of the issues of considerable importance to the working miner were missed, like safety clothing, bathing time, etc'.[210]

As there was still no movement by either side on the pay question, Carr arranged for the NUM negotiators to see Heath: 'So the whole caravan moved off to Downing Street'.[211] Meanwhile a full cabinet meeting took place at 8.30pm—'by candlelight, appropriately'.[212] As Thatcher later recalled of that meeting, 'The dispute simply had to be ended quickly'.[213]

After the cabinet meeting Heath and Carr talked to Campbell Adamson of the CBI and Feather of the TUC at 9.15pm for about an hour, followed by a meeting with NUM leaders for another hour. Heath, who believed that 'Gormley was visibly under pressure from his colleagues', impressed on the three NUM national officials that he could not agree to the extra £1 claimed for non-faceworkers. During this meeting some members of the NUM executive became restless, as all but the negotiators had been relegated to watching television. But when Gormley returned to meet them he insisted that he wanted a settlement that night and that anyone deciding to leave would lose his vote. Meanwhile NCB officials met Heath and Carr briefly before resuming their negotiations with the NUM at 11.45pm. This final round led to the major concession of the bonus shift payment (a sixth shift's pay given to workers who were present for all five shifts in any one week) being consolidated into the normal five-shift basic week from 1 June, 'thereby [also] consolidating it in the calculation of overtime [pay]'. Gormley suggests that he thought that the union negotiators could only get this if they were to recommend acceptance of the whole package. He won a vote on this and put it to Ezra and his deputy, who then left the room to consult 'I suppose…the Government and everybody else in sight'. It was agreed.[214]

It was after midnight when the NUM executive voted by 16 to 9 to 'recommend the members to return to work on the terms negotiated and to consult the members through an individual ballot'. Pitt commented, 'The waverers of the centre of the miners' executive had left the hard-core of the left-wing isolated.' There had been an argument over the form of consultation, the left wanting area votes. Again Gormley insisted. Heath was not happy, given the potential delay involved, but Gormley later pointed out to him that 'you need a ballot vote to make sure you get the right type of majority'.[215]

The right wing on the executive then proposed that 'all the pickets be withdrawn forthwith', which was carried 14 to 11. According to the Communist Jack Collins, the executive member from Kent, 'it killed the strike stone dead'. Pitt argued that 'once the pickets were withdrawn, it would be impossible to reestablish the blockade on the power stations, and many men would make a virtue of necessity and vote for acceptance'.[216]

Heath was 'very depressed'.[217] By contrast, as Gormley left Downing Street he famously declared, 'We've won more concessions in the last 24 hours than in the last 20 years'.[218] The *Financial Times* charted how the NUM had progressively pushed the cost of settlement up: 12 October 1971, £25 million; 13 December, £28 million; 5 January 1972, £32 million; 10 February, £52 million; Wilberforce Report, £85 million. The final settlement added at least another £10 million.[219] The *Economist* thought the total cost 'will hardly be less than £117 million'.[220] Among the miners' supporters there was a feeling of elation, epitomised by this extraordinary letter in the *Times* from the historian Alan Taylor:

> Sir, Fifty years ago the miners were driven back to the pits by the lash of hunger. Successive governments combined indifference and brutality, and *The Times* applauded their attitude. Now the miners have

avenged the defeats of 1921 and 1926. I rejoice at the miners' victory and I record that February 19 will be long remembered as a glorious day in the history of the British working class.

Yours, etc, A J P Taylor, Magdalen College, Oxford.[221]

Another historian, Edward Thompson, wrote amidst the power cuts that 'for the future historian it will seem that his week of darkness, in February 1972, was an incandescence'.[222]

While the final act of the drama was being played out in London, picket activities had continued as normal around the country on the Friday. For example, 500 miners' pickets faced 200 police at Longannet power station,[223] 50 deputies were stopped by pickets from entering Wearmouth colliery in Sunderland, and 70 pickets at NCB area headquarters in Gateshead managed to stop some clerical workers getting to work. Nearly 1,000 tons of coal were shipped into three small ports (but not the main port, Douglas) on the Isle of Man 'under cover of a news blackout imposed by the Manx government in order not to alert striking miners into sending pickets'. Power cuts meant that electric train services remained severely hit—1,361 services were cancelled on the Southern Region, 480 on London-Midland and 132 on Eastern Region.[224] In London there was chaos on the roads as power cuts led to 'erratic traffic lights' resulting in huge jams.[225]

The sudden calling off of pickets following the settlement meant 'an undignified, unorganized and, in some cases, acrimonious ending' to the strike.[226] The leadership of the Kent miners, for example, initially refused to call off its pickets in protest at the national executive's pre-emptive move. On the Saturday morning:

> ...there was...chaos throughout the London picket line, and power-workers and tanker drivers were confronted by a serious problem. The national announcement that the...NUM had called off the pickets immediately left them wide open to attacks from management, and divisions in the solidarity of the men began to appear. There was talk of unofficial picketing, and the confusion began to breed ill-feeling.

Eventually 'by Saturday afternoon London was cleared of the "invading army" of Kent miners'.[227] During the next week the miners, still on strike but no longer picketing, voted in their ballot by 96.5 percent to accept the offer. The exact figures, declared on Friday 25 February, were 210,039 in favour and 7,581 against. But there was still unfinished business. For example, the Derbyshire NUM area council voted to continue the overtime ban on the return to work unless miners were compensated for being sent home because of the ban before the strike. After a couple of days back, the NCB agreed to pay.[228] In Notts, NUM leaders refused to allow miners to return over the weekend to undertake preparatory work before the full return on Monday 28 February.[229]

The miners and the Industrial Relations Act

As early as 1973 an official of the National Industrial Relations Court (NIRC) could write that 'the myth has since grown that the miners' strike took place before the [Industrial Relations] Act came into force'.[230] This confusion may partly have arisen because it was, by chance, not until the day that the miners returned to work, 28 February 1972, that the final sections of the act became operative, outlawing, among other things, secondary boycotts, blacking of supplies and picketing people's houses. Yet the emergency provisions of the act had been available since 1 December 1971. In all likelihood the scale of the government's defeat was not fully comprehended until after the events, and the notion that the relevant provisions of the act were not yet in force could give the government a retrospective excuse. But this was not the perception at the time and the evidence for this is readily available.

Even before the strike, the *Guardian* had argued that the new powers under the act could be used but the cabinet would not want to be seen using them 'at the first possible opportunity'.[231] Early in the strike the cabinet discussed whether to use the cooling-off provisions; and it was realised that 'a ballot forced on the NUM would lead to…a continuation of the strike, and perhaps also a hardening of attitudes'.[232] In debates in the House of Commons on the commencement orders for the parts of the act not yet operative, the issue was publicly aired. On 31 January 1972 Dudley Smith, the Under-Secretary of State for Employment, declared that any use of the emergency procedure 'would not be conducive to a settlement' in the strike. Two days later a Conservative MP even claimed, 'If the Secretary of State applied to the court now over the coal strike it is not certain that a ballot or cooling-off period would be allowed'.[233] When talks were set to resume, another Conservative MP suggested that a compulsory ballot be called on any improved offer.[234]

The *Economist* pointed out the government's dilemma regarding a 'cooling-off' period. There had already in effect been one as the strike had been called with a month's notice. If one was ordered 'would the miners obey? Mr Carr may not want to put idly to the test his long-held belief that the British actually are a law-abiding people'.[235] However, during the railway dispute in the spring of that year, it emerged that the Commission on Industrial Relations 'had an arrangement' to draw on the resources of the Department of Employment 'whenever a ballot might be ordered. *It carried out a similar operation during the miners' strike*' (added emphasis).[236] This may have been precautionary, but the government did seriously consider using the emergency powers of the act following the miners' rejection of Wilberforce, and 'as a matter of contingency planning' the NIRC 'put itself on full standby on the night of the 18/19 February'.[237]

Conclusion

The miners had won a historic victory. The settlement completely shook the confidence of the government. As Hurd remarked, 'It was hard to imagine an outcome that was worse than the one that happened'.[238] There was a hunt for scapegoats. The Tory weekly the *Spectator* argued 'that Mr Carr and his Department misunderstood the mineworkers, that Mr Davies and his Department miscalculated the consequence, and that Mr Maudling's Emergency Committee left matters too late'.[239] By contrast, the strike had given back to the miners their self-confidence, ending more than two decades of compliance with governments and their employer.

The miners had won so convincingly for four main reasons. First, several years of campaigning by the left within all levels of the union had built the necessary strike majority in the first place. Second, because of 'the spirit of aggression and zeal displayed by rank-and-file miners' exemplified by the use of flying and mass pickets during the strike.[240] This in turn had encouraged the third reason—the massive practical solidarity received from other trade unionists. Finally, following the Wilberforce Report's recommendations, the left minority on the executive had refused to compromise, which led quickly to further major concessions by the NCB.

It is fitting to end this chapter with a short extract from NUM general secretary Daly's introduction to the union's evidence to the court of inquiry:

> The Government has said that it has had to act now because of the effectiveness of our pickets. What it means is that it would have let this affair drag on even longer if we had not, through our picketing, brought forward the economic impact of the miners' strike...
>
> Our pickets have...[also] acted as ambassadors of the mining community in every city and port in this country. We have enjoyed in practical form, and with steadily growing effectiveness, the solidarity and support of the organized workers of this country. Instead of remaining isolated and alone beside our pits, we have built the unity of action and understanding that has been the immense positive feature of this strike...
>
> When the industrial workers of Birmingham marched in their thousands to join our picket line they showed that we do not stand alone, and that the purpose of our picket lines is understood by the working people of this country.[241]

Chapter 3

The railway work to rule

'The outstanding success of the miners simultaneously raised the expectations of the railwaymen and lessened the ability of the Railways Board to meet them'.[1] So wrote the railway historian Philip Bagwell.

The scale of the miners' victory made a railway dispute almost inevitable in the spring of 1972. When it came, it was a very muted affair compared to the miners, but it demonstrated once again the links between unofficial and official action. Its significance was twofold. First, it represented another very public defeat for the government's wages policy. Second, the government used the opportunity to invoke the Industrial Relations Act, precipitating a crisis for the Trades Union Congress (TUC) boycott of it.

The miners' legacy

Early in the railway wage negotiations the National Union of Railwaymen's (NUR) leader Sir Sidney Greene told the chair of the British Railways Board (BRB), Richard Marsh (a former Labour cabinet minister), 'All you've been saying for the last couple of hours is that you haven't any money.' Marsh noted, 'This seemed to me a fairly clear description of what I had been saying, and reasonably convincing as an argument.' Greene went on, 'British Rail has never had any money. If I'd listened to that argument I would never have put in a claim at any time in the past. *With the miners' claim settled, we have no alternative but to put in [such] a claim*' (added emphasis).[2] This was from a union leader described by his own union's historian as '[politically] well to the right of the Labour Party...[with] an intense dislike, at times approaching the pathological, of all members of the Communist Party', and by the *Economist* as a 'director of the Bank of England, pillar of the establishment and regarded as the sort of moderate trade union leader whom the Government needs to keep on its side'.[3]

Once the lowest-paid mineworkers had secured a £5 increase in their basic wage to £23 per week, the NUR's demand for a £2.80 rise to bring the lowest-paid rail workers onto £20 per week seemed eminently reasonable to the membership—especially as some 75,000 railway workers received basic pay less than this figure.[4] As the nationalised rail industry had seen a similar savage rundown in employment to the coal industry, and as most coal was moved by rail, there were natural affinities between the two groups of workers. The miners' settlement had also awarded clerical grades a £5 per week increase. The mines had been one of the comparator industries used by the Guillebaud committee on railway pay (1958-60), and the railway white collar union, the Transport Salaried Staffs' Association (TSSA), also wanted to restore relativities, requiring an increase of 16 percent.[5] The NUR and the much smaller craftist Associated Society of Locomotive Engineers and Firemen (ASLEF) had an acrimonious and long-standing rivalry which rarely allowed joint action. But in 1972 both ASLEF (concerned to maintain drivers' differentials which had been seriously eroded by a freeze on mileage and bonus payments since 1968) and the TSSA recognised that their own claims would be more easily furthered if the NUR won its minimum wage demand.[6]

When the union negotiators met the BRB in the wake of the miners' strike, they carried copies of the Wilberforce Report with them.[7] Not just the scale but the manner of the miners' victory opened a unique opportunity for the railway workers. After the Wilberforce Report but before the miners had balloted, the *Guardian* noted that 'the precarious state of coal supplies…has given a powerful new weapon to the railwaymen. If they wished they could call selective strikes designed to cripple power stations.' After all, they had 'refused to allow coal into the power stations over the past six weeks'.[8] The *Economist* realised that they 'would…need to use their muscle before coal stocks were rebuilt', and later suggested that the government's first reaction was 'to buy them off' by allowing British Rail to gradually increase its pay offer,[9] from the pre-Wilberforce norm of 8 percent to 11 percent, 'the bonus the miners had earned for their colleagues'.[10] The negotiations were 'protracted—deliberately so, it may be suspected'.[11]

By the time that official industrial action was eventually announced 'coal stocks…[had] been gradually rebuilt'.[12] But as almost all power station coal was moved by rail there was concern in the *Financial Times* over 'how much…will get through' and 'what effect intensive picketing, the real key to February's power crisis, might have'. The *Guardian* felt that electricity supplies were safe 'unless the railway workers follow the miners' example and picket power stations'. The *Economist* urged the government to invoke the Industrial Relations Act's 60-day cooling-off period as 'it would finally deprive the unions of what has been their strongest card: the vulnerability of the coal stocks…after the miners' strike'.[13] But this assumed that court orders would be obeyed.

Industrial action

The pattern of industrial action in the rail industry prior to 1972 did not suggest that an all-out strike would be likely. Since nationalisation in 1948 there had been only two official strikes—a 17-day strike by ASLEF train drivers in 1955 over differentials and a one-day strike in 1962 by NUR members in protest against railway workshop closures. But the NUR probably held the record for national strike threats that had led to last minute settlements or the establishment of committees or courts of inquiry—there were five examples of this between 1953 and 1966 alone. In the last case leading cabinet members and prime minister Harold Wilson were involved in persuading the union executive to call it off.[14]

As with many other public sector pay negotiations, the continual round of incomes policies from the mid-1960s removed or greatly reduced the flexibility (and cash) required to broker settlements. In 1967 ASLEF undertook a national work to rule. The following year the NUR did the same, and added a ban on overtime, Sunday and rest day working. The union's historian noted that 'the railway system, particularly in the south of England, was completely disrupted'.[15] This tactic was found to have some distinct advantages. The industrial relations academic Hugh Clegg, for example, argued, 'A railway strike causes a great deal of initial disruption, but within a day or two most individuals and organizations have made alternative…arrangements. An overtime ban or a work-to-rule causes considerable disruption and delay without turning the customers away'.[16]

While there had been a tradition of localised unofficial action on the railways it had been very limited.[17] But, as in many industries, national official action (or sometimes even the threat of it) can breathe life into local union organisation and make workers realise their power.

Derrick Fullick, ASLEF rep at Waterloo, later argued that the railway workers' action in the miners' strike 'did us the world of good. It flexed our muscles and prepared us for our own claim'.[18] It also reminded many railway workers that they could act independently of official guidelines.

Given the strategic position and the craftist attitudes of many train drivers, ASLEF (which represented most of them) was used to acting alone. Apart from its 1967 action, it had run a national work-to-rule and overtime ban for ten days (including the Easter weekend) as recently as April 1971.[19] While the miners were still on strike, on 22 February 1972, a call for a series of one-day strikes starting on 1 March was defeated on the ASLEF executive by only two votes.[20] Then, early in March, drivers on the important Southern Region threatened industrial action if there was no satisfactory settlement of the national wage claim by 10 April.

On 9 March a meeting of ASLEF members in the Eastern Region came within two votes of a majority for an immediate strike. The union's executive then agreed to call a stoppage from 16 March if pay talks had not restarted. This decision was reversed and a few days later only the casting vote of the chair stopped the union from starting a work to rule and bans on overtime and rest day working from 27 March. At the end of March the ASLEF executive again agreed on action. Six hundred of its members based at Stratford in east London had already voted on Thursday 30 March to begin a work to rule after Easter, on Tuesday 4 April. The executive stayed its hand yet again while further meetings took place with Marsh, until eventually the three unions decided on Wednesday 12 April to take joint action.[21]

The continual delays in calling national action clearly suited BRB management and the government as coal stocks were rebuilt. The eventual decision to act was clearly affected by the start of the unofficial action, arranged for Monday 10 April, on Southern Region. It took the form of a work to rule, an overtime ban, a withdrawal of cooperation, and double 'manning' of all trains without periscopes in the guard's van. The huge volume, and the accompanying problems of coordination, of London commuter traffic made it particularly vulnerable to any industrial action. Some 450,000 passengers arrived at London terminuses between 7am and 10am each morning on 900 trains—out of a daily national total of 3 million passengers on 17,000 trains.[22]

Action on Eastern Region led to 29 trains being cancelled in the evening rush hour on Tuesday 11 April, 45 on Wednesday, and 53 on Thursday and Friday (one quarter of the service). Southern Region cancelled 33 in the Monday evening peak period, increasing to 86 on Thursday and 182 on Friday evening. There were similar percentage reductions in trains available for morning peak travel periods through the week.[23] At the beginning of the unofficial action on the Monday ASLEF leader Ray Buckton had appealed unsuccessfully to his members to work normally until the official action was due to start.[24] Anxious, however, to keep some control over its militants, the ASLEF executive even debated the possibility of one-day strikes on top of the agreed official sanctions, but this was lost by one vote.[25]

The three unions had agreed that 'from 00.01 hours' on Monday 17 April there would be a work to rule, and a ban on overtime, and Sunday and rest day working. They felt that such tactics might avoid action against them under the Industrial Relations Act though, according to one source, contingency plans had been made for selective strikes.[26] Recourse to arbitration was unavailable as the post of chair of the Railway Staff National Tribunal was currently empty. But on 15 April the BRB chairman met the union leaders at the Department of Employment and told them that it was possible to get them all 'off the hook' as the government had made more money available.[27] As the *Economist* later explained, this change of heart had been guided by stronger reasons than the threat of inconvenience to railway commuters:

> What all industry, from the Government and Confederation of British Industry downwards, was almost too frightened to speak of, was a repetition of the sort of industrial blacking that took place towards the end of the miners' strike, should goods and passengers be switched on any scale to other forms of transport.[28]

Further evidence that this sentiment was shared at the time comes from Cecil King's diary entry: 'The newspapers say the Government is determined to stand firm over the railway strike. After their defeat by the miners it is hard to see how they can effectively do so. If there is a stoppage of power stations can this Government send in the troops?'[29]

But 'the government could not contemplate another Court of Inquiry after Wilberforce and the miners'.[30] The suggested device, in the absence of arbitration, was to appoint an independent person who would mediate, that is hear both sides and recommend an award. Alex Jarratt, managing director of International Publishing Corporation, was chosen as he had worked on a report on the railway workers when he was an official with the National Board for Prices and Incomes a few years earlier. ASLEF representatives made sure the terms of reference did not make the award 'binding' (perhaps they were taking a leaf out of the miners' book). The mediation took place on the Sunday, the day before the industrial action was due to start. While more money was available, it was not enough to satisfy the unions.[31] As Marsh himself later noted, '...it became clear that all the unions were on a roundabout which they desperately wanted to get off but did not know how to. The coal-miners had broken the barrier with a massive increase in pay, and my [sic] unions had little alternative but to try to match it'.[32]

The political commentator John Torode summed up the situation at the time:

> Attempts to impose the notorious 'N minus one' formula...have failed. By attempting this formula the government was boasting that logic and justice were not part of its industrial vocabulary. Ministers would use brute force to beat down wage inflation. It was an open invitation to the unions to use brute force in return...
>
> Above all: why accept the 'final' offer made by the chairman of any nationalised board these days? The dustmen, the electricity supply workers, the miners, all demonstrated one surprising truth about the Heath Administration. In spite of its...tough talking it had usually given way to good old-fashioned industrial action... [A] dispute leads to more money magically being found, even by bankrupt boards.
>
> If Sid Greene and Ray Buckton had both accepted Richard Marsh's 11-per-cent 'final' offer they would have been laughed out of court by their members. So, too, if they had accepted the Jarratt package without first trying a bit of disruption. The entire wage strategy of this government might have been designed to encourage workers to 'have a go'.[33]

The significance of the rail union leaders' rejection of Jarratt was not lost on the TSSA historian who noted that 'for the first time since 1926, the NUR, ASLEF and the TSSA were in agreement that industrial action was necessary'.[34] It was also almost the first occasion since 1926 that TSSA had taken any industrial action.[35]

Early in April the employment secretary, Robert Carr, had been removed by Edward Heath (someone had to be sacrificed for the humiliation of the miners' victory) and replaced by Maurice Macmillan (son of the former Conservative prime minister Harold Macmillan).[36] Anxious to make an impact, Macmillan summoned the three rail union leaders and their negotiating committees to his offices at 1am on Monday 17 April, just as their industrial action was getting under way, but failed to intimidate them by threatening use of the Industrial Relations Act. Later in the day he tried a different tactic and called over Vic Feather along with any available TUC General Council members.[37] In the event, 15 General Councillors, Feather and four other TUC officials met him at St James's Square at 5pm.

Macmillan hoped that the General Council would 'use their best endeavours' to persuade the railway unions to hold a ballot on the Jarratt 'award'. But those present decided that this was a matter for the rail unions, and warned that 'if a ballot was taken and the membership endorsed the unions' attitude—as they probably would—it could rigidify the situation'.[38] It was eventually agreed that the TUC's Finance and General Purposes Committee (F&GPC), its 'inner cabinet', would mediate, but three of its members (including Jack Jones) were at the Scottish TUC and Macmillan agreed to charter a government aeroplane to fly them back.[39]

Macmillan then had to report to the cabinet before meeting Feather and two other TUC leaders at 10pm that evening. He told them that the government wanted 'constructive suggestions to resolve the dispute, *provided that these did not involve any further monetary concessions*' (added emphasis). The following day, Tuesday 18 April, an emergency meeting of the F&GPC was held with the leaders of the railway unions at 2pm. During discussion 'the view was expressed that the dispute was developing from an industrial dispute affecting only three unions into a political confrontation between the trade union Movement and the Government'. Some committee members argued that there was room for bringing forward the date at which the Jarratt award might be implemented.[40]

Meanwhile the official sanctions were proving very effective. As expected, the main disruption was to London commuter services. In the Monday morning peak period only some 127 trains (less than a quarter of normal) operated on the Southern Region, increasing slightly to 167 on Tuesday and 177 on Wednesday. On Eastern Region 31 trains out of 162 ran on the Monday morning, rising to 54 on Tuesday and 65 on Wednesday. At other London terminuses on the Monday, 50 percent of commuter trains arrived at Euston and 40 percent at Marylebone. Off-peak services to and from London were less seriously disrupted, as were services outside London.

On the Wednesday, however, only 20 of the normal 200 daily freight trains were moved in the Midlands. This particularly affected car manufacturers. More ominously for the government, coal deliveries to West Midlands power stations had been cut from 25,000 tons a day to 2,000-3,000.[41] One small power station in Lancashire even had to close 'because coal supplies had failed to get through'. One general problem for bulk freight users was the supply of empty wagons for reloading. On the Monday apparently only 800 wagons had been 'turned round' compared to the normal 25,000. 'Unmanned' signal boxes had also led to temporary line closures.[42]

The 'cooling-off period'

The government then decided to use the emergency powers available to it under the Industrial Relations Act. Sensing that this would probably happen, a *Financial Times* editorial explained why these had not been deployed during the miners' strike:

> Given the degree of public support for the miners, who were absolutely determined to fight to the bitter end, court orders aimed at ending their strike would almost certainly have had no effect and might well have only brought the new Act in particular and the law in general into disrepute.[43]

The railway workers were believed to be an easier target.

On the night of Monday 17 April Macmillan assured a Tory backbench transport committee meeting that the government wanted a ballot—on a statutory basis if the unions would not do it voluntarily.[44] Bagwell claims that Feather was instrumental in persuading civil servants to advise Macmillan not to go for a compulsory ballot at this point, on the grounds that it would tie the hands of the union negotiators when they needed flexibility. The *Economist* suggested that civil servants were also concerned that any compulsory secret ballot would support the unions, which was the position suggested by the Donovan Report in 1968.[45] Late on Tuesday evening, after having consulted cabinet colleagues, Macmillan told Feather that there would be no compulsory ballot.[46]

The following morning Macmillan went to the cabinet and got its approval to apply for a 21-day 'cooling-off' period from the National Industrial Relations Court (NIRC) if the TUC had not persuaded the railway unions to call off their sanctions by noon that day. Ian Aitken of the *Guardian* commented that this deadline represented 'high noon in every sense of the phrase'.[47] The TUC F&GPC met at 1.30pm. Hugh

Scanlon spoke with particular defiance, arguing that 'the conciliatory line which had been proposed yesterday did not now meet the situation'. The railway unions should be reminded of TUC conference policy of non-cooperation with the agencies established under the Industrial Relations Act, especially the NIRC. As a result of such arguments the three unions were advised not to attend the court hearing.[48]

TSSA general secretary Percy Coldrick speculated on the workings of the court:

> The Secretary of State for Employment presented his application for a…'cooling-off period' to the National Industrial Relations Court at 12.45pm… By 1.25pm, ie 40 minutes later, the NIRC officials had read the lengthy application; had satisfied themselves that it complied with the terms of the Industrial Relations Act; had written and had typed and checked a covering letter to the three Trade Unions and had delivered the necessary documents to Walkden House [TSSA head office].[49]

When the court met at 4pm that afternoon, railway union leaders were absent, though some NUR executive members attended as observers.[50] Sir Geoffrey Howe QC, the Solicitor-General (a government position), put the government's case. Among his arguments were the vulnerability of bulk commodities—cement, steel, iron ore, chemicals and fertilisers. The problem of coal was accentuated by some pits being only able to move coal by rail, and some power stations could also only receive it by this means. Of particular concern was that half of industry could be vulnerable to shortages of fuel oil within a fortnight.[51] The government was only granted a 14-day period, however. Presumably the NIRC wished to assert some independence from the government.

A messenger of the court later tried to deliver the cooling-off order to the night porter at the NUR headquarters, but he refused to accept it and had to threaten to call the police before the messenger left to serve it the next morning. The caretaker at TSSA headquarters was woken at 12.55am on the Thursday and served with that union's order.[52]

The cooling-off order was a 'two-stage legal landmine'. First it required the unions to withdraw their instructions on industrial action 'forthwith'. Sir John Donaldson, the NIRC president, defined this as 'with the utmost possible speed in all the circumstances'. Second, the unions had to take all reasonable action to secure discontinuance, and Donaldson made it clear that each 'union will be accountable for the actions and omissions of those who serve it'. It appeared that the unions had, in practice, until midnight on the Thursday (20 April) to call off their action to meet the first requirement of the order.[53] Minds were then concentrated by the NIRC's decision during that Thursday to impose a second fine (£50,000) on the Transport and General Workers Union (TGWU) for contempt of court by failing to get the Liverpool dockers to remove their unofficial blacking of certain haulage companies (see Chapter 5). The government was ready to instigate similar contempt proceedings if the railway unions ignored the court order.[54] A figure of £10,000 per union per day (a total of £210,000 per week for the three unions) was later suggested.[55]

Thursday was a 'day of anguished talks with lawyers'.[56] One account has Buckton claiming that the ASLEF executive initially decided not to call off its work to rule, but changed its mind to preserve unity with the other two unions. However, the same source also suggests that 'any thoughts the railway unions might have had about defying the court were abruptly ended' with the TGWU fine.[57] It appears that there was a three-hour joint meeting of the three union executives on the Thursday evening. The railway unions' decision to comply with the NIRC's orders was seen as a 'watershed' by the *Financial Times*.[58] The permanent secretary—the senior civil servant—in the Department of Employment recalled:

> The application was a gamble. There was no reason to assume, in view of the trade union policy of non-co-operation, that the unions would comply with the court order to instruct their members to return to normal working or that their members would obey the instruction. The unions did, however, comply...and ministers enjoyed a brief spell of euphoria over the success of the Act.[59]

That night the NUR sent circulars to its 695 branches and 25 district councils to cease all sanctions. But its instructions were accompanied by a second circular, which partially nullified the first:[60]

> This union does not accept that any court order can force our members to disregard British Railways Board rules, for the breaking of which so many have been severely disciplined and also for reasons of general safety.
>
> Neither does this union accept that any court order can be so contrary to the contract of employment under which our members accepted employment with the BRB as to place a legal compulsion on any member to work excessive hours of duty, work on their rest days, work on days shown to be free from duty, or on days which are without the guaranteed week.[61]

The next day, Friday 21 April, most railway workers stopped the work to rule but did not work overtime, thus disrupting weekend services. On the Southern Region, the drivers continued their work to rule unofficially. Cliff Rose, a divisional manager claimed, 'This is not working to rule. It is sheer bloody-mindedness.' In fact on the Friday conditions on Southern Region commuter services were described as *'far, far worse than anything earlier in the week'* (added emphasis). [62]

The region's general manager, David Binnie, threatened that unless normal working was resumed (which included working 'hours in excess of standard' to get the trains back into position) drivers would be sent home.[63] One was at 3am on Monday 24 April: '...by mid-morning 284 drivers had either been sent home, walked out, or had not turned up for duty. Charing Cross, London Bridge and Victoria were closed for several hours...and, with a full stoppage threatened, pressure was brought to bear and...[the] instructions withdrawn'.[64] Macmillan had advised Marsh to 'persuade' the manager to withdraw his action.[65]

ASLEF officers then toured the Southern Region's 40 depots to persuade drivers to cooperate, in order to comply with the second part of the court's order. Some officials complained that 'their task of eliminating the last pockets of resistance' had been made more difficult by management's actions. On that day it was estimated that 900 of the region's 1,400 drivers had worked normally, providing about 45 percent of the service. Yet even in the evening peak period only 13 of 45 suburban trains ran out of London Bridge and three out of 31 from Cannon Street.

The *Times* editorial looked for explanations for Southern Region militancy. It found that these train drivers earned a much lower mileage bonus due to shorter trips, and that a shortage of drivers meant often having to work overtime or rest days. Also, as most London passengers were commuters rushing to or from work, the drivers' limited contact with them was often fraught. There were some signs of resistance elsewhere—for example, the ASLEF Scottish district council had initially voted to carry on the action, as had a joint union committee in Carlisle.[66] Eventually, at 6pm on Tuesday 25 April, Macmillan confirmed to the NIRC that industrial action had stopped (for the first time in 16 days) and that the cooling-off period could begin.[67]

By this point the TUC General Council was on the brink of compromising its opposition to the Industrial Relations Act. As early as Friday night, 21 April, Feather, confronted with the crisis posed by the

NIRC's actions against the railway unions and the TGWU, 'gave a strong indication that…he was ready to abandon the TUC's current policy'. The *Guardian* called this a 'tactical turnabout'. The *Times* summarised his argument that 'had the three railway unions given evidence to the court they would have hacked Sir Geoffrey Howe…to pieces'.[68] Tom Bradley, TSSA president and a Labour MP, concurred that 'by boycotting NIRC all we are doing is spitting in the wind'.[69]

The main crisis, concerning the TGWU's fine, will be discussed in Chapter 5, but the railway unions' plight was intertwined with this. The TUC F&GPC met on Monday 24 April and considered a letter from ASLEF. This argued that the union's legal advice claimed that if it had appeared in court it 'would have been able to present an excellent case, and could perhaps have prevented an Order being made against' it. The committee then voted five to three to prepare a document setting out the circumstances 'in which unions should be permitted to defend themselves' at the NIRC. Scanlon was critical of the railway unions for having complied with the court order.[70] At the full General Council on 26 April, NUR leader Greene made an 'impassioned speech' also to the effect that the government might not have gained its cooling-off order if the railway unions had been able to defend themselves in the NIRC. There was a vote of 19 to 9 not to overrule Monday's committee decision, and Feather urged 'speedy consideration' of new guidelines.[71] Greene's argument for appearing in court was soon proved spurious. When the railway unions faced further court action in May they not only lost the case, but also lost their appeal.

Despite general secretary Buckton's left wing reputation, the ASLEF monthly journal subsequently attacked 'ill-informed criticism' of the railway unions, arguing that there was no alternative 'but to accept the court ruling'. It even claimed that once the cooling-off order had been imposed 'the TUC should have realised that a boycott of the National Industrial Relations Court would be an act not of non-co-operation but of co-operation'.[72]

On Monday 1 May the F&GPC then recommended that unions should be able to defend themselves in the NIRC without even having to seek permission from the TUC. This was agreed at the next General Council meeting on 4 May and became policy from that date.[73] The official boycott of the NIRC had collapsed.

Meanwhile the cooling-off period 'proceeded uneventfully…the railways continued to run and the power stations to receive their coal'.[74] As the government made no more money available, only about four hours of talks took place—over restructuring the pay package.[75] The permanent secretary at the Department of Employment has since argued:

> The application for a cooling-off period could…be criticised as disingenuous. The purpose…was to allow moves to be made to secure a settlement, but the government was not yet ready to agree to any advance… The time gained did not remove the dilemma.[76]

To extend the cooling-off period the government had to apply before midnight on 8 May. While ASLEF wanted to reimpose sanctions immediately the cooling-off order expired, the unions collectively agreed to delay announcing any further action until after 8 May, as that would deprive the secretary of state of important grounds for an application for an extension. Accordingly the unions waited until 9 May to declare the restart of their sanctions on Friday 12 May.[77] The NUR's instructions included 'strict adherence to eight-hour shifts even when rostered for nine' (the ninth hour being paid at overtime rates).[78]

It has been suggested that the government had dithered and left it too late to apply for a new cooling-off period or an extension to the existing one. But as so little had happened in the 14-day period even the interventionist NIRC would have been unlikely to agree to an extension. The cooling-off period had been designed to buy time. It stopped the immediate industrial action, it allowed coal stocks to built up further, and it could also test whether the railway unions were able to turn their action on again. When the cabinet agreed on Thursday 11 May to apply to the NIRC for a compulsory strike ballot, the other emergency procedure open to it, this could be seen as fulfilling the same function.[79]

The ballot

As noted above, Macmillan had always wanted a ballot. As early as 24 April, even before the cooling-off period had officially started, BRB had sent a list of all employees entitled to vote to the Commission on Industrial Relations (CIR), the body that would oversee any ballot. This was known to the union leaders, who observed, 'It appeared as though British Rail was not looking for a settlement'.[80]

Marsh, however, had warned ministers, including Heath, that a ballot would be a mistake:

I then consulted the five regional general managers…and the chief executive… The unanimous advice…was that if a ballot was held in an effort to go over the heads of the union leaders, the membership would vote overwhelmingly in support of the union leaders… I sought yet another audience with the Prime Minister and repeated to him…that to ballot the railwaymen would be disastrous… I learned afterwards that the Cabinet…had discussed the advice which I had given, compared it with conversations that they had had with their friendly neighbourhood ticket collector, and had come to the conclusion that they were right about how railwaymen would react in these circumstances and that, not only I, but all the senior railway managers were wrong.[81]

The government's application for a ballot was filed at 5.45pm on Thursday 11 May, and the hearing was arranged to start at 8.30pm that evening. The ASLEF head office was telephoned by a NIRC official at 5.55pm and the NUR at 6pm. The railway unions were now represented in court following the TUC's change of policy. The unions' legal counsel complained of the lack of time that they had been given to prepare themselves. But NIRC president Donaldson suggested that the three general secretaries should assemble their executive committees to postpone for 24 hours the industrial action that was due to start at midnight that night. Shortly after 11pm the hearing was adjourned until the next day, when Donaldson accepted that the executives had dispersed for the night and would anyway be unlikely to agree to any postponement of the industrial action.

On the Friday, 50 percent of trains ran on the Southern Region, with 266 cancellations out of 529 services due to run between 7am and 10am. Because of the ban on Sunday work, BR decided then to shut down all rail traffic for 32 hours from 10pm on Saturday to 6am on Monday. Trains that could not reach their destination by 10pm on the Saturday were also cancelled.[82] The NIRC judgment in favour of the compulsory ballot was finally given on the evening of Saturday 13 May. The unions' lawyers immediately applied for an appeal but, unsurprisingly, they failed to persuade the NIRC to allow the unions to continue their industrial action until the result of the appeal was known.[83]

An appeal had been expected although it took place under unusual circumstances. Lord Denning, senior judge in the Court of Appeal, noted, 'It is the first time we have sat on a Sunday.' The *Times* reporter commented, 'No precedent could be found to contradict him, either from the oldest living precedent-encrusted memory in the High Court, or from the learned law books…that congest the gloomy walls of Number Three Court'.[84]

The hearing took four days and was lost by the unions. Meanwhile on the Sunday night, 14 May, the TSSA executive, meeting at the union's conference, sent telegrams to branches instructing members 'to work normally forthwith'. ASLEF instructions followed on the Monday morning, but the NUR could not act until a sufficient quorum of its executive was present. As a result its instructions did not arrive until early evening. Four London terminuses—Victoria, London Bridge, Charing Cross and Holborn—were 'all but shut down in the mid-afternoon [and] remained closed during the rush hour'. At Waterloo, ASLEF drivers joined the unofficial action after 6pm. On the Eastern Region both Liverpool Street and Fenchurch Street were operating roughly only one third of normal services in the evening peak period.

ASLEF again sent officers to meetings to persuade drivers to return.[85] Derek Fullick, ASLEF rep at Waterloo, explained his members' militancy, '…the lads were looking for an excuse to say, "Up your pipe". That sort of thing's never occurred in this industry. The footplatemen [drivers] used to be puddings'.[86] While there were some cancellations in the Tuesday evening rush hour due to drivers attending a meeting in Croydon, rail services were by then back to normal after four days of chaos.[87] At this point, however, 600 drivers in Ayr in Scotland had been on strike for four days in support of two men sent home for 'declining to carry out normal duties'.[88] General secretary Buckton admitted that 'before the Act was used, there were "big areas" of ASLEF, let alone the other two unions that didn't want industrial action. Things changed quickly, with the Waterloo depot in the lead'.[89]

The wording on the ballot paper was a source of some controversy. It was the 'forceful advocacy' of Howe, the Solicitor-General, 'that persuaded the NIRC…that a no-nonsense, no-compromise, open-and-shut question should appear on the ballot paper'. It asked, 'In the light of the BRB pay offer (about which you are being informed by the BRB) do you wish to take part in any further industrial action?'[90] 'As one Conservative backbencher commented, if you ask a silly question you will get a silly answer'.[91]

The government, 'having felt that it was rather bold to call for the ballot, kept mum during the voting'.[92] By contrast, the unions campaigned hard for a yes vote.[93] The TUC's policy of non-cooperation with the act had included advice that in the event of such a ballot 'the union is free to use every effort to persuade its members either to boy-cott the ballot or to vote for…action'.[94] But given the TUC's change of policy towards the NIRC, no one seems to have seriously consid-ered boycotting the ballot. ASLEF rep Fullick argued:

> [I]f we had abstained, only 1,000 of the 180,000 railway workers would have needed to say 'No' to further industrial action for them to win. The press would say it was apathy on the part of all of the rest rather than militant abstentionism. The men reckoned that to ignore it would be to be defeated.[95]

Incredibly even the administration of the ballot itself was affected by industrial action. First of all, rail workers on the Waterloo and City line in London walked off the job for the day on 23 May and marched off to collect ballot papers that had not been sent to them.[96] Then some members of the CIR staff responsible for counting the papers were not entitled to overtime pay over the spring bank holiday and 'refused week-end work because they were dissatisfied with the proposed arrangements for time off in lieu'.[97] The result was therefore not announced until Wednesday 31 May.[98]

Railway workers' ballot			
	Yes	*No*	*Abstain*
Union			
ASLEF	23,436	1,043	108
NUR	80,894	10,695	719
TSSA	21,581	10,321	633
Members of more than one union	261	46	-
Not declaring union affiliation	3,269	1,076	107
Total	129,441	23,181	1,567

Out of 172,444 asked to vote, there was an extremely high return producing an overwhelming majority in favour of continuing in-dustrial action. On a near 90 percent turnout, some 85 percent of those voting had supported further action. The 'ballot [had] turned into a boomerang'.[99] As Macmillan observed, 'Putting it mildly, it would appear to be a vote of confidence in the union leadership'.[100] Howe later wrote that it had been a mistake—'as should have been clear at the time'—to order a ballot, and that government ministers were 'wrong to believe that we had to use...both [emergency procedures] in quick-fire succession in the same dispute'.[101] But once the official action had resumed there was an awful logic to events, and the decision to ballot was predicated on 'a model of industrial relations behaviour which assumed that an apathetic rank-and-file membership was being misrepresented by a more militant union leadership'.[102]

Importantly for all concerned, the industrial action 'was now legitimated in the government's own terms'.[103] While ASLEF wanted to start sanctions again, Greene of the NUR argued that 'an "ominous silence" from the railwaymen's leaders would be as menacing as an open declaration of hostilities'.[104] When the order for the ballot had been given several weeks before, the *Economist* had speculated whether sanctions would be reimposed if the ballot was won, and had smirked even then that 'the power stations, which could have been the railwaymen's trump card...are no longer as vulnerable'. It had been incensed that what it considered the small sum dividing the two sides could prolong the dispute, and tried to incite retaliation: 'If British Rail's chairman...took the bit between his teeth and ordered a lockout, it would only take five days for the railwaymen to lose money this year even if their claim was met in full'.[105]

Following a meeting on 6 June Marsh announced that money for a suggested lump sum payment was not available. The unions then agreed on 9 June to start action again from Wednesday 14 June, allowing plenty of time for further concessions to be made.[106] Having now exhausted its legal weapons against the railway workers, the 'government decided its priorities: the dispute must be settled'.[107] After all, 'the Government could not plunge the nation into chaos (again) for the difference between an offer of 12 per cent and a claim for 13 per cent'.[108] Payments from 12 to 13 percent plus a lump-sum were agreed (over one year compared to the miners' bigger increase over 16 months), and the threatened sanctions were cancelled on Tuesday 13 June, only six hours before they were due to resume.[109]

The action taken by the railway union members was very modest compared to the miners. Yet the government's wage policy had been heavily defeated again. The special assistant to the Chancellor of the Exchequer later conceded, 'In economic terms the railway settlement was less important than that of the miners, but it was equally humiliating for the Government. It clearly signalled the end of "N minus 1".'[110]

As the whole dispute had rumbled on for over two months, the low wages of many railway workers had become public knowledge, further weakening the government's authority. While official sanctions had only occurred for two very short periods, the unofficial action, mainly by drivers on the Southern and Eastern Regions, was critically important. Macmillan told parliament that 'it would have been easier to obtain a settlement if the negotiating committees had not been so concerned to keep the unity of the three unions, which to some extent depend upon accepting the more demanding claims of parts of the ASLEF membership'.[111]

Despite the usual protestations, the government's hands were all over the dispute. Marsh recalled, 'Bert Farrimond, the BR Board Member for Industrial Relations, and I, had between us sixty or seventy meetings with Ministers at different levels, some in the middle of the night, some in the private houses of Ministers and some at the Employment Ministry... Ministers were telephoning almost hourly'.[112] One commentator described the denouement: 'When...Mr Macmillan realised that defeat was inevitable, he put ludicrous pressure on Mr Richard Marsh and his British Rail colleagues to settle... One moment they were being urged to stand firm; at the next, Mr Macmillan was hammering on the door of Mr Marsh's flat, where he was in bed suffering from a virus infection, to tell him to get down to the office to meet the unions'.[113]

With the government's use of the emergency provisions of the Industrial Relations Act, the railway dispute had two contradictory outcomes. Losing the ballot so decisively was a salutary experience for the government, and neither it nor the cooling-off period was used again. In one sense the government's 'first attempt to use the Act had been a humiliating failure. It established an impression that the Act was accident prone'.[114]

But the railway unions had obeyed court orders and the TUC General Council had agreed that unions should be allowed to defend themselves before the NIRC. As Heath told parliament, '...the trade unions themselves are now co-operating in working the Act and in appearing before the Court and putting their views to it'.[115] Government ministers were grateful for that, though neither they nor the TUC leadership were to know that it would turn out to be only a fleeting victory.

Chapter 4

Engineering sit-ins in Greater Manchester

On the day that the railway workers' official action started, 17 April, workers at some 25 engineering factories in the Manchester area were sitting-in—a movement without parallel in Britain before or since.

Like the miners and railway workers, the engineering dispute arose from a national pay claim. The similarities end there. The miners and railway workers faced one employer and one set of wage negotiations. In the miners' case only one union had negotiating rights. As was recognised in an editorial in the *Times*, 'Engineering could hardly be more different'.[1]

Industrial relations in engineering

Engineering was a vast sprawling sector of the economy, consisting of a conglomeration of separate industries making widely different products—from nuts and bolts to cars, from kettles to power station turbines, from telephones to machine tools, from specialist instruments to pipelines. While a significant proportion of the workforce was apprentice-trained, some sectors were dominated by the semi-skilled.

Its industrial relations were a mix of formalised national agreements, covering minimum pay and conditions and disputes procedures, and systems of workplace bargaining that ranged from highly-developed to almost non-existent. The variable nature of much engineering production—along with short runs and a preference by the employers for forms of piecework payment—encouraged workplace bargaining. Engineering was the heartland of the shop steward system, which had developed massively in the First World War, nearly disappeared in the inter-war slumps and depressions, but re-emerged particularly with full employment from 1940 onwards.

It was particularly the subject of the Donovan commission and epitomised the three 'problems' identified by most industrial relations commentators: unofficial and unconstitutional strikes (respectively, without union support and in breach of agreed disputes procedures); 'restrictive' practices (mainly initiated by workgroups rather than unions); and wage 'drift', whereby the gap between actual earnings—including piecework payments, overtime and shift pay—and nationally agreed minimum rates was not only increasing, but was rising faster than productivity growth (see Chapter 1).

At the pinnacle of the formal system of engineering industrial relations was the largest private sector employers' association, the Engineering Employers' Federation (EEF), which had a tradition of national lockouts of union members. Its historian, Eric Wigham, argued that '...the success of the general lock-out used to depend on bankrupting the unions and starving out the workers'. He was more sceptical of its efficacy in 1972: '...the workers, relying on social security payments and income tax refunds, can endure a long dispute without strike pay and without going hungry...as the miners did in 1972'.[2]

But at least one local association official believed that 'the prime purpose of the Federation is...the handling of industrial relations, which [still] remains a matter of battle and conflict, and the need is for the Federation to be a war horse able to fight its battles'.[3] One of its weapons, almost from its inception in 1896, was an arrangement for paying subsidies to firms involved in 'approved disputes'. Money was raised from member companies and a fund set up in 1914. The subsidies from the 'Indemnity Fund' were cut back after the large calls made on it during the wages explosion of 1970 (see below). But in 1972 they still amounted to £5 per week for every male worker on strike and £2.50 for females and juveniles, with proportionately less for action short of a strike.[4]

EEF member firms, directly affiliated to local associations, employed over 1.3 million manual workers in 1971—about 60 percent of the total in the industry. These were spread over some 5,600 separate establishments. In total there were over 24,000 establishments in the sector, but half of these employed less than 25 workers. Nearly 75 percent of all engineering establishments employing over 250 workers were federated (members of the EEF), about 50 percent in the 100-249 size range, less than 25 percent for 25-99, and about 5 percent of establishments employing less than 25.[5]

The Confederation of Shipbuilding and Engineering Unions (CSEU) was the unions' equivalent of the EEF, and existed to coordinate the policies and actions of unions nationally, to a lesser extent at district level and sometimes in the factory. It was dominated by the engineering section of the Amalgamated Union of Engineering Workers (AUEW) with over one million members.[6] This union was perceived to have one of the most democratic systems of government. A small 52-strong lay member National Committee (NC) met for a fortnight every year and decided the union's policy. This was then carried out by an executive council of seven full-time officers representing geographical areas and a president elected by the whole of the membership. All full-time officers were subject to election and regular re-election.

The voting system for elections encouraged political factions. If no candidate secured an overall majority the top two went to a second ballot, with all voting carried out at geographically-based union branch meetings (usually with low attendance). The right wing was in the ascendancy in the union at the beginning of the 1960s, with only about one quarter of the 160 full-time officers' posts held by the left. These included only one on the executive council and one of the two assistant general secretary posts. By 1973 some 62 of the 180 posts were in left-wing hands, including the president, three executive councillors and both assistant general secretaries.[7]

The senior official was the president, who chaired the executive council and the NC. The general secretary, while influential, had no voting rights and generally no negotiating responsibilities. From 1956 to 1967 the president was Bill Carron, made a papal knight (of the Order of Chivalry of St Gregory the Great) in 1959, knighted in Buckingham Palace in 1963 and ennobled in 1967 as Baron Carron of the City and County of Kingston upon Hull:[8] '[H]is views on leadership were closely attuned to his views of papal infallibility. Once the leader was chosen it must be left to him to take the decisions'.[9]

The anti-Communists in the union had started 'to organise seriously' in about 1952, and Industrial Research and Information Services (IRIS) was founded by them in 1956. 'The "broad left" coalition began…with the publication of *Voice of the Unions* in 1963, after the collapse in 1962 of the Communist… Engineering and Allied Trades' Shop Stewards' National Council… and its paper, *The Metalworker*.' *Voice* campaigned particularly on the reform of the 'status quo' clause in the engineering national procedure agreement (see below). *Engineering Voice*, associated with Amalgamated Engineering Union (AEU) assistant general secretary Ernie Roberts, 'the Prisoner of the Pope of

Peckham',[10] appeared in 1965. It was 'assisted by the reaction against the three-year "package deal" which Carron had put forward [and then negotiated with the employers], and against proposals for rule book changes [especially on branch organisation] made by [Jim] Conway, the general secretary'.[11]

John Tocher, Manchester AUEW divisional organiser and leading Communist Party (CP) member, recalled:

> Here in Manchester I think we led the way in developing what is now termed a broad left...we were seeking to set up a forum in which all people from centre to left or extreme left could come together and voice their opinions... It was a real forum for bouncing around different ideas... [T]here was a general consensus that there had to be a change. We were all agreed that we should organise not just on the factory level, but also on the electoral scene.[12]

Eddie Frow, another CP member and Manchester AUEW district secretary from 1961 to 1971, explained:

> We had a Broad Left Committee of 3 or 4 officials and 3 or 4 conveners or stewards, all District Committee members... We had Broad Left sub-committees in each area...[who] would also have a list of shop stewards and conveners in the area who were sympathetic. But their first job was to compile a register of voting nights. Then when the shop stewards were contacted, it was up to them to persuade the lads in the branch to attend and vote... In some case we had buses and cars waiting outside important factories on branch nights.[13]

The culmination of this work was mobilising the vote for left-winger and ex-Communist Hugh Scanlon in the 1967 presidential election to replace Carron, who had retired. Scanlon's majority over the right's candidate, John Boyd, was 6,367. He won a majority in only nine of the union's 26 divisions, but these included four of the five with the highest poll. In the Manchester division alone, with a turnout of 26 percent compared to the national average of 11 percent, his majority was 8,011.[14]

The union's policy-making body, the NC, was generally under the control of the right, though it became more evenly split in the early 1970s. With the increasing success of the left in elections for full-time positions, delegates to the 1970 rules revision conference narrowly supported the introduction of postal ballots (to start in 1972), believing that it would counter the left's organising in the branches. Challenges to this policy, from the left in 1971 and later, in 1975, also failed by the narrowest of margins.[15] But the Broad Left's preoccupation with elec-toralism meant that it could not counter the potential disadvantage of postal ballots, where media interference could favour right-wing can-didates. It continued to pursue the electoral road with diminishing re-turns, rather than build mass support in the factories for left-wing policies through, for example, an industry-wide stewards' movement.

The 1971 claim

The last national settlement in engineering, the 1968 three-year 'pack-age deal' forced on Scanlon (see below), was not inflation-proof. When prices rose sharply in 1970 and there was a general 'wages explosion' that year with the breakdown of the Labour government's incomes policy, many engineering workers took action on wages themselves: 'Local claims multiplied, many ignoring the agreement's productivity clauses, and were often accompanied by immediate threats of indus-trial action. The numbers of strikes reached record levels, although in many cases employers offered little resistance'.[16] The AUEW leader-ship was determined not to negotiate another long term deal.

When the AUEW NC initially decided on a pay and conditions res-olution in 1971 it did not include a reduction in the working week—and this is significant given later developments. This was added when the CSEU drew up a joint claim on behalf of all its affiliated unions.[17] According to Danny McGarvey, president of the Boilermakers' Soci-ety, 'We threw in Uncle Tom Cobley and the kitchen sink in the broad claim'.[18]

The claim specified a 'substantial' general increase. This had always been a selling point for national action in the past, as everybody would receive such an increase. However, the EEF had made it clear in the spring of 1971 that it would not concede any general increases in the future.[19] It had reluctantly conceded small general increases in the 1968 manual workers' package deal. But in 1971, first with the draughtsmen's union DATA, which became AUEW-TASS that year, and then with the clerical unions, it had successfully resisted them. In December 1971 CAWU and the white-collar sections of the TGWU and NUGMW finally agreed with the EEF that there would be no more general increases for clerical workers at national level, and that companies should take this into account in domestic salary negotia-tions. The EEF's 'basic motive was to stop double increases'—national 'new money', unrelated to individual firms' circumstances, on top of domestically negotiated rises.[20]

Increases in minimum rates were welcomed by the relatively small percentage of workers whose hourly rate was below the new minimum but only affected premium payments (overtime and shift premiums) for everyone else. Scanlon was particularly anxious to drive these rates up.[21] At the 1971 NC he stated that the aim of lifting all basic earnings was so that stewards could then 'put the flesh on the skeleton of what we have created nationally'.[22] On television, he confronted an engineering employer, asking, 'And you're proud of the fact that your industry offers a labourer £15 a week?'[23] Skilled workers' basic rate was £19 per week. The claim asked for these two rates to be raised to £20 and £25 respectively.

While a second week's paid annual holiday (plus six bank holidays) had been agreed in 1951, it was not until the two long-term deals of the 1960s that any progress was made on this, the 1964 agreement phasing in two extra days and the 1968 package a further three to make three weeks annual holiday.[24] More holidays on their own would not provide sufficient reason for taking action, but they were seen as permanent and inflation-proof gains unlike wages.

Along with extra holidays, a shorter working week without loss of pay also had a general appeal. The 44-hour working week agreed in 1947 had remained unchanged until 1960, when it was reduced to 42 hours. Under the 1964 package it was reduced to 41 hours in 1964 and 40 in 1965. The claim for 35 hours was more of an aspiration (it became CSEU policy in 1962).[25] While equal pay for women was in the claim, employers were anyway bound by the limited terms of the Equal Pay Act of 1970, which required equal pay for equal work by 1975.

Having met the unions in August 1971, the EEF made its first offer in November. As the final increase under the 1968 package deal was not due to take effect until 6 December 1971, the employers proposed that any new agreement should operate only from July 1972. They also indicated that it would last for one year, which removed the threat of yet another long-term deal. But the offer was only on minimum rates—£1.50 for skilled workers and lower for other grades. As Scanlon aptly put it, 'Never in the history of industrial conflict has so little ever been offered to so many'.[26]

Scanlon admitted that in informal talks with the employers in December the unions had been asked 'was there any question of compromise?' The CSEU executive committee (EC) had then made clear that:

> [A] reduced working week…was a campaign which must be started, but whether it could be realised in the present political and industrial atmosphere was open to considerable debate. We also knew the difficulties in arguing…for the four weeks' annual holiday. We were equally mindful…of improving earnings by way of local activity. So, we suggested we should have some realistic discussions on what the offer from the Engineering Employers' Federation would be on basic rates.

When the employers then asked the union negotiators whether they were firm on their demand of £20 for labourers and £25 for skilled, they replied 'yes'. At the same time they picked up 'a hint…of a possible improvement in the [number of]…statutory holidays'. Cuts in the working week were clearly not on the agenda.[27] A similar version of events comes from the EEF's historian: 'Scanlon hinted informally in December that other claims were negotiable if a £25 minimum was accepted, but the Federation had no mandate to offer that amount. When told this, Scanlon abruptly broke off the talks'.[28] The unions formally rejected the employers' offer on 15 December 1971.[29] Some form of industrial action was now inevitable.

Previous national disputes

National wages and conditions claims in engineering since the war had sometimes been accompanied by forms of national action—such as one-day 'token' strikes and threatened bans on overtime. The biggest national dispute was in 1957. Initially the AEU NC had voted for a two-day strike in the event of a breakdown in the engineering talks. But the shipbuilding negotiations stopped first and the CSEU shipbuilding committee proposed an indefinite strike, which was then agreed by a conference of union executive committees. The engineering unions followed suit. A total national shipbuilding strike (from 16 March) was followed by a staggered national engineering strike. Concern about the response of engineering workers was one factor tipping the balance against an immediate all-out strike. Instead, ten districts came out on 23 March—the eight shipbuilding areas, where the shipyards were already stopped, and the well organised Manchester and Sheffield CSEU districts. These were followed one week later by the enormous London district. Everybody else was due to strike in a further week's time, but by then both the shipbuilding and engineering strikes had been called off to await the outcomes of separate courts of inquiry.[30]

During the 1957 strike workers in non-federated engineering firms were expected to come out even though they were not directly affected. Engineering maintenance workers were also called out in non-engineering establishments in Manchester, causing some inter-union problems. The local CSEU district secretary at the time, AEU divisional organiser Hugh Scanlon, reported that an emergency committee 'is in continuous session during the dispute, and all areas are operating their own strike committees, pickets, etc'.[31]

The last experience of national action had been in 1968. Following an 'insulting' offer, there was a national one-day strike in May. When talks eventually broke down, the NC of the then AEF (Amalgamated Union of Engineering and Foundry Workers) voted 31 to 30 for a total unlimited stoppage to start late September. This was endorsed by the CSEU, which postponed its commencement. A right-wing AEF district secretary then served writs, claiming that the foundry workers' representatives on the NC should not have voted on the engineering negotiations. This removed the majority for a strike. Despite the AEF executive's unanimous rejection of the employers' final offer, a series of votes of the engineering NC members refused to back any action—'to everybody's surprise', according to the EEF's historian, who also referred to it as 'almost a miracle'.[32]

The Industrial Relations Act

The Industrial Relations Act cast its shadow over the 1971 claim, and its provisions undoubtedly affected the tactics adopted in the dispute—though in a number of ways that were not always obvious at the time.

The first influence was the effect on union funds. Unregistered unions were liable to unlimited damages if they fell foul of the act. So the AUEW set about separating its assets—into protected and unprotected funds. The latter would contain about £1.5 million plus any subscription income. This obviously made the funding of any national dispute problematic. Scanlon told the NC that 'if we take industrial action, it will be in the knowledge that this Union cannot finance it...whether you take national action or any other form of strike action!'[33] In practice, of course, few unions have paid benefit out for any length of time when a significant proportion of their members was in dispute. But this was clearly an attempt to remove the idea of national action from the union's deliberations.

The second factor was the Secretary of State for Employment's power to use emergency provisions in a national dispute, as demonstrated during the railway workers' industrial action. This fear was voiced by Scanlon when later addressing the NC in April 1972: 'It would be the easiest thing to go along the lines of a national stoppage,' but that would make the union liable to the emergency provisions of the act (as was happening to the railway unions as he spoke) and then in contempt of court if it refused to obey. He wanted a strategy that would 'best preserve the fabric of this union'.[34] One can plausibly speculate that Scanlon and the executive were doing their best to avoid a possible confrontation with the act.

A third consequence of the introduction of the Industrial Relations Act was that it affected the ongoing discussions on revising the existing national procedure agreement in the industry. The main impetus behind the unions trying to alter this was the controversial issue of 'status quo'. The unions wanted any proposed change affecting wages or working conditions to be put through procedure before it could take place. The existing agreement allowed the employer to introduce changes at will, and the unions could only retrospectively challenge them through procedure while having to work the new system.

As early as November 1970, after the Conservative government's 'consultative document' on industrial relations legislation but before the bill was published, the EEF made the following statement to the engineering unions:

> If...the Government were to include provisions [in the Industrial Relations Act]...allowing national procedure agreements to be referred by any of the parties to the NIRC [National Industrial Relations Court] for consideration by the CIR [Commission on Industrial Relations], the Federation would have no intention of using these provisions, *unless* in the future the new national procedure agreement is so disregarded as to make such action necessary; only then would the question arise whether or not the procedure recommended by the CIR should be made *legally enforceable*.[35] (added emphasis)

A legally enforceable procedure agreement would mean that any time union members broke the procedure (a not uncommon occurrence) their union was potentially legally liable. As Scanlon argued at the meeting with the employers in September 1971 where he gave

them notice, on behalf of the CSEU, to terminate the national procedure agreement: '...our real fears began to develop when the Government issued its Industrial Relations Bill... After that date, we were
never...able to get back to the realistic discussions which we thought
we were having'.[36]

National procedure agreements had first been introduced into many
industries in the 1890s, usually following national lockouts. As Hugh
Clegg explained, the new national employers' associations 'forced the
unions into industry-wide conflicts in place of the favourite union strategy of picking off one group of employers at a time'.[37] The price of peace
and national recognition was to accept agreements that outlawed industrial action until a long-winded procedure had been followed. Now,
from the end of 1971, there were to be no stages of procedure external
to the individual workplace. Once factory managers had rejected a
formal claim from their shop stewards, any industrial action taken to
pursue it could not be judged 'unconstitutional' and thus possibly subject to punitive action. It therefore opened the possibility of pursuing
a different kind of industrial action on a national claim.

Plant bargaining policy and strategy

In the summer of 1971, even before the unions had submitted their
claim, the EEF was speculating what might happen 'if the unions fail
to reach an agreement at national level and pursue a policy of picking-
off key firms'.[38] And later the *Times* argued that if talks broke down the
unions 'will presumably follow the draughtsmen's pattern'. Given the
depressed state of the industry and the unions' problems, 'a national
strike is virtually impossible and a co-ordinated national campaign will
be almost as difficult'.[39]

The draughtsmen's union had broken off national pay negotiations
with the EEF in March 1971 to pursue its demands on a plant by plant
basis—a tactic they had used before to good effect.[40] 'By that time the
Federation had completed their preparations for a struggle.' These
make interesting reading in light of what happened to the manual
workers in 1972:

> At first it was suggested that every firm should be expected to with-
> stand a strike in support of excessive demands for at least four weeks
> before conceding improved terms, but the idea of a minimum time
> was later dropped because of the different circumstances of different

companies... Some associations established 'action committees' to
advise firms and some arranged for regular meetings of the larger employers of draughtsmen... Special emphasis was also placed on 're-
taliatory escalation'. This meant sending home workers taking part
in action short of a strike until normal working was resumed.[41]

Only limited industrial action occurred, but the employers were im-
proving their own organisation.

Following the breakdown of national talks for manual workers, a
special three-day policy meeting of the full executive of the four sections of the AUEW (which included the draughtsmen) unanimously
recommended a policy of plant bargaining.[42] This was put to a recalled
engineering section NC on Monday 10 January, the second day of the
miners' strike.

Scanlon explained why the executive ruled out a national stoppage.
Under the union's rules the NC could only call a strike 'when there is
not time to ballot the members'. But given that any new agreement
would be unlikely to start much before July 1972 'we have an obliga-
tion' to ballot. Further an AUEW proposal for a national stoppage
would mean that 'most of the other unions within the Confederation
will demand a ballot of their members'. Then 'would there be the continuing delays that we had ad nauseam' in 1968. Finally, with one million unemployed—the post-war peak at that time—including significant
redundancies in engineering, there was concern that members might
be reluctant to take action. If the union did ballot, 'What would be our
position if the answer was "No"?' It 'could only mean that we accept
what has been offered'—and that would be humiliating.

The executive council recommendation was that district committees should advise stewards to put the full claim to their employers 'and
reach settlements on such items...that the Shop Stewards and District Committees...recognise as being acceptable in all the circumstances appertaining at that particular factory'. Where offers were
unacceptable the executive would 'make those disputes official
and...support any action which District Committees may recommend'.
However, and this is critical:

> ...we hope that District Committees could be a little selective at the
> outset and decide that they would take on firms A,B,C and D, and that
> they—once the decision was authorised—could take a ballot of the mem-
> bers in the locality for a levy... On the example of those firms, other and
> perhaps more difficult firms, could be taken on once the barrier is broken.[43]

After a proposal for a national strike ballot had been heavily rejected, the plant bargaining policy was carried by 47 to 4 with one abstention.[44] Thus there was the unusual situation of both the executive council and the NC being almost unanimously in favour of the same position. But the executive was driven by not wanting to risk national industrial action under the Industrial Relations Act. The right on the NC was, as usual, against any national action while the left was loyally supporting Scanlon. It was only a paper unity but could be exploited by militant action in the districts.

The AUEW position was accepted by the CSEU on 13 January. It now read:

> Affiliated unions are…urged to initiate negotiations with individual employers, through District/Area Committees and Shop Stewards on the understanding that, where acceptable to District/Area Committees and the members concerned, settlements may be concluded *on all or part of the claim*. In the event of there being no domestic settlement, individual Unions are recommended to give official recognition to any dispute which is supported by District/Area Committees.[45] (added emphasis)

The *Financial Times* noted that 'the unions have turned their backs on national industrial action and have even bypassed having an overtime ban or a nominal one-day strike'.[46] The *Economist* later acknowledged that 'a national overtime ban would have been ineffective against work-short bosses'.[47] It was left to Eric Wigham of the *Times* to grasp the significance of the unions' decision. In an article entitled 'The Danger Of History Repeating Itself', he argued that this represented, in 1972, a reversion to 1872 when there was no national recognition of unions or a procedure agreement in the industry. Policy was largely determined by district committees: '…it now seems to be intended to restore to them the power to decide when disputes against individual firms should be supported'.[48] This was precisely how it was understood in Sheffield and Manchester.

A special conference of the executives of all unions affiliated to the CSEU was held on 7 February and endorsed the plant bargaining policy. At a CSEU EC meeting three days later strategy was discussed. Reports vary. According to the *Financial Times* 'the strategy would include members in areas of strong union organisation supporting those in a weaker bargaining position.' Incomes Data Services, a specialist organisation, suggested: 'Shop stewards and local negotiators will be advised to pick one company or plant in each area where strong trade unionism offers the prospect of a satisfactory agreement to act as a "model"… Unions will then attempt to achieve the same terms at other plants, by industrial action if necessary.'

Scanlon and CSEU general secretary Jack Service were empowered to draw up guidelines to be issued through unions and district committees to shop stewards.[49] These were sent out on 21 February but seem either not to have been disseminated or to have been openly ignored.[50] There was substantial disquiet in the AUEW over the ruling-out of national action, and the union was forced to hold a special national conference of full-time officials on 29 February and 1 March (with consequences, as we will see below).[51]

Scanlon tried to publicly justify his position: 'We are picking our own arena for struggle and are not being provoked to fight on the Employers' ground [ie national level]… We are to challenge them at home base—in the factories'.[52] But the AUEW leaders in the large Sheffield and Manchester areas had decided that their 'best chance of success lay in demonstrating union solidarity at district level'.[53]

Sheffield

The local Broad-Left-led AUEW in Sheffield had seen the potential in the abandonment of national action. On 19 January the AUEW district committee (DC) decided to press for a £6 increase and a 35-hour week. It also called a meeting of shop stewards to be held on 30 January and agreed that the CSEU district committee, which was convening a meeting of all full-time officers on 24 January, should draw up plans for industrial action.[54] Four hundred stewards met and were addressed by their region's AUEW executive councillor (and CP member) Les Dixon. They agreed to meet a fortnight later to plan a campaign.[55]

It had been intended to give employers until 24 March to reply to individual factory claims, followed by a stewards' meeting in April to decide on action. However, because of the state of emergency called in the miners' strike, the 800 stewards at the 13 February meeting decided to give employers only until 24 February to reply. Some stewards called for 'a co-ordinated campaign…uniting all the confederation districts in the big industrial centres'. A recalled stewards' meeting three days after this would discuss a strike recommendation for Monday 28 February if the offers were not satisfactory—with possible exemptions where employers met certain minimum demands. Identical claims to employers produced identical replies from them that they were not prepared to deal with the national claim individually. This 'closing of ranks' by the employers led to a delay in possible action.

On 27 February, the day before the victorious miners returned to work, about 700 stewards met representing 150,000 workers in over 250 factories in the CSEU district covering Sheffield, Chesterfield, Barnsley and Doncaster. They agreed to hold factory meetings prior to a district-wide mass meeting at a football stadium in Sheffield two weeks later at which up to 50,000 workers were expected. A strike proposal would be put to this mass rally.[56] But this militant position faded from public view fairly quickly. The *Financial Times* reported that Sheffield stewards 'now appear to be having second thoughts'. The *Morning Star* was a little more informative, suggesting that the 'change in tactics' leading to the postponement of the mass rally had followed a conference in London.[57]

This conference of AUEW full-time officials, held on 29 February and 1 March, had ironically been called in response to the lack of enthusiasm in most districts over the plant bargaining strategy.[58] While they were in London the Sheffield officials must have been told, either publicly or privately, that they could not hold a district strike without a district ballot. Apart from the executive's concern about right-wing members taking the union to court for not following its own rule book, it did not want district strikes.

Scanlon has since argued that 'successful' district action could make the workers 'much stronger…than individual factories coming out'. But the 'possibility of stultifying, of no action at all' was seen to be greater 'in our [the executive's] view' by 'the actions of Sheffield and Manchester than it was by individual claims'. His concern was particularly with high-earnings factories not being prepared to take strike action on a district basis when they would benefit little from it directly: '…once you get that prevalent within a district you're half-way to being defeated'. As a result Scanlon and other national leaders did not use the militancy building up in Sheffield as a battering ram against the national employers. Rather than facilitating conformity to the union rule book, they were prepared to stifle the militancy.

Scanlon admitted, 'I think I lost more friends on this than when I accepted the peerage and that's saying something… But, on balance… I think we were right in saying to districts "No".'[59]

Greater Manchester

In Manchester district-wide industrial action was already taking place on unemployment. Just before the national meeting in December 1971 that formally rejected the employers' offer Scanlon had received a telegram from district secretary (and CP member) Bernard Panter on behalf of the Manchester AUEW DC urging national strikes. It also informed him that the DC was recommending that its 33,000 members should ban overtime from 1 February 1972—mainly in protest against growing redundancies, but that it could also be used in support of the national claim.[60]

On 6 January 1972 a special meeting of 450 AUEW shop stewards in the Manchester district voted for this, with only 30 against.[61] It was later agreed that some overtime could be allowed, subject to DC control, in factories where recruitment took place. Over 40 membership meetings took place in January to explain the DC's policy and by early February some 100 jobs had been created. The district overtime ban continued into March.[62]

Stewards and officials from CSEU-affiliated unions then met on 8 February to discuss the wage claim. They decided to call a stewards' meeting on 24 February to finalise demands to submit to individual factory managements, which would then be given ten days to reply. Manchester unions were complying with the plant bargaining policy but were 'also seeking to preserve their solidarity'.[63] Significantly the 8 February meeting in Manchester came before the 10 February CSEU national meeting from which emerged a strategy of how each district should act. Hence, as with Sheffield, the initial decision on district-wide action preceded formal national instructions on how to operate it.

The meeting of nearly 700 stewards during working hours on 24 February agreed some form of industrial action but did not specify what. The claim was for a £4 pay rise 'with special consideration for women leading up to equal pay', a reduction in the working week and four weeks holiday. As Tocher later explained, 'Quite frankly, we here did not see…that you could go and rally people around 13 points.' This was submitted to individual employers on Wednesday 1 March—there were hundreds of federated firms in the area and slightly more non-federated ones. It was agreed that industrial action could be taken on an area-wide basis if necessary, and that there could be action to support workers pressing the claim in small firms.[64]

In reply, the federated companies, 'in what even employers' association officials regard as an unprecedented degree of solidarity', told their stewards that they were not prepared to negotiate at all and that they should tell their union leaders to resume national talks.[65] The local employers' association director, Michael Fuller, remarked, 'I have never known our membership in the Manchester area so solid on any issue.'

The South Lancashire, Cheshire and North Wales Engineering Employers' Association was a recent amalgamation of associations covering an enormous area—the Manchester conurbation, Merseyside, Cheshire and North Wales, as well as Blackburn and Burnley. In Lancashire only the areas around Preston, Bolton, Rochdale and Wigan were outside it. After London and the West Midlands it was the third largest association in the EEF.[66] Its remit covered a much bigger area than CSEU district number 29, which only included the AUEW districts of Manchester, Stockport, Ashton and Warrington, and so it could draw directly on greater resources than the local unions.

Member firms were organised into 16 groups, with between 20 and 40 factories in each, and association officials met them to discuss tactics. At this stage stewards had hinted that selective strikes might be used to 'pick off' firms that resisted. The *Guardian* believed that 'the employers intend to combat selective strikes with "group lockouts" and a widespread stoppage of work could develop'.[67] The *Financial Times* suggested that the next mass stewards' meeting had to decide whether to accept the employers' challenge.[68]

On Monday 13 March there were calls at the 900-strong stewards' meeting for immediate strike action, but these were withdrawn on the advice of full-time officers. The latter were no doubt chastened by the Sheffield experience and not prepared to risk a similar result. Instead it was decided to implement a district-wide work to rule and ban on piecework (whereby workers could still earn their basic rate of wages) from 27 March, and to extend the Manchester AUEW district's existing ban on overtime. This recommendation would go to plant mass meetings over the next few days.[69] At the meeting, while there was sharp criticism of the abdication of leadership on the part of the national unions, 'not one speaker' supported either the employers' suggestion of referring the claim back to union national executives or the CSEU strategy of 'fragmented action in individual factories'. Only a handful voted against the district programme of action.[70]

One factory jumped the gun and inadvertently set the pattern for many others. At the GKN-owned James Mills steelworks at Bredbury near Stockport the stewards were concerned that the company had been shipping out twice the normal number of consignments to steel stockholders. At a report-back meeting at the plant the day after the district stewards' meeting the workers voted to start sanctions on Wednesday 15 March.[71] The convener, Alan Wells (in the NUGMW, which represented the majority of the workforce), was then given five minutes notice that all 900 workers would be suspended, pending dismissal, at midday on that Wednesday if the piecework ban was not lifted. The workers immediately occupied the plant, though not the offices or 'a rolling mill worked by men not involved'.[72]

Reacting to this, a meeting of 120 stewards under the auspices of the unofficial Stockport Area Engineering Shop Stewards' Committee agreed to bring sanctions in their area forward a week to Monday 20 March. Workers at some 12 firms responded—the AUEW estimated 5,000 members involved, with a similar number from other unions.[73] Following the Stockport stewards' decision to start sanctions early, the employers' association publicly declared that 'managements will either suspend all workers who take part in the campaign *or announce that the men concerned will only be paid for work done*' (added emphasis).[74] This appeared to be a partial retreat from their public face of belligerence.

Also on 20 March it was announced that a new company was being formed to take over the Fisher-Bendix factory on Merseyside, thus vindicating the earlier occupation there: '…the lesson was not lost on the Manchester engineers'.[75] At its weekly meeting on Tuesday 21 March the AUEW executive then gave official support to its 300 members involved in the Bredbury sit-in. A jubilant Tocher greeted this action as 'the biggest breakthrough' so far in the Manchester dispute', and announced, 'If there are widespread lockouts there will be widespread sit-ins. Some of the largest factories in the area will be taken over by the workers'.[76]

Given this encouragement, two more sit-ins began on Thursday 23 March. Workers at Laurence Scott had also started sanctions early and were threatened with suspension if they did not work normally from clocking-on time that morning. Panter addressed a mass meeting in the car park: 'We don't take kindly to lockouts.' When suspension notices were distributed, the workers announced a takeover and 'held a further meeting inside the factory at lunch time to work out a rota system'.[77] At Davies and Metcalfe of Romiley workers sat in when suspension notices were sent out. After two days it was reported, 'They have camp beds in the works, plus a TV. The occupation is round the clock with a rota for cleaning the plant.' But 'supervisors are still coming in'.[78]

In the week before the official start of sanctions on 27 March there were several other developments that also shaped the course of events over the next few months. One of these, according to Graham Chadwick, was that 'without a doubt most firms would have been willing to settle at this point on a purely cash basis and many made offers approaching the full cash claim'. Some money-only agreements were made before the CSEU district committee refused to ratify them in future.[79]

Another feature was that while some companies did make agreements with concessions on money, holidays and hours, most such agreements, now and throughout the whole dispute, were with non-federated companies.[80] Neither the EEF nor the local employers' association had any control over such companies, but commercial sanctions could be exercised: 'Statements attributed by the press to the…Employers' Association indicated even threats of trading sanctions against employers who have made agreements which do not align with the employers' policies'.[81]

The most publicised early deal was that of a federated firm—textile machinery manufacturers Ernest Scraggs, with factories at Macclesfield, Oldham and Altrincham. The 500 workers gained about £3 on the basic rate, three extra days holiday and a 38.5-hour week.[82] This may have been the agreement seen by Paul Ferris, with the daily starting time changed to 8.18am from 8am—'a trifling benefit when it's spread so thin'.[83] The company was asked to resign from the employers' association or, more likely, unceremoniously kicked out. The local association chair remarked, 'In any battle there are bound to be casualties, but if they are caused by self-inflicted wounds I propose to let them lie where they fall and not to recover the dead. We are better off without them'.[84] The immediate consequence was that when Tocher made a satisfactory agreement the same week with another federated company he refused to reveal its name.[85] This secrecy would backfire as, in the absence of open information, rumours (especially of poor settlements) could flourish. There was the added drawback that such a policy isolated factories from each other—instead of a united district campaign there was fragmentation.

Another incident that affected the tenor of the campaign was the events at Sharston Engineering, a small non-federated company in

Cheadle Hulme. Nineteen workers occupied the factory on 23 March following the laying-off of four of them. They then added the demands of the district claim. The owner, Mrs Isabella Dubost, went to court for an eviction order. The judge ruminated that 'if it were a big factory you might want 2,000 police with tear gas'. As Dubost claimed to have dismissed (rather than suspended) the workers, the judge felt able to grant her the order: 'It would be possible for a small number of people to get them out… I want to make sure that any order I might make can be enforced'.[86] Yet the police were unable to serve the writ on 30 March. Following a meeting between Dubost and union officials (including Tocher) the men were reinstated and took down their barricades. Within a fortnight the factory was shut and the workers dismissed.[87] For whatever reason the union officials had decided not to fight the eviction. In the event no other legal attempts were made to evict workers sitting-in elsewhere, but that could not have been predicted.

In fact most employers tried not to be too provocative. The *Financial Times* reported that before the unions' district-wide application of sanctions the employers were 'first of all trying to win the support of their workers and to discourage them from taking militant action'. Chadwick suggested that nearly a quarter of all factories decided 'on a show of hands' not to take any action on 27 March or after.[88] Workers at Mather and Platt, for example, had voted by a small majority in a secret ballot not to impose sanctions, and Panter then held a meeting outside the factory on Tuesday 28 March. Edward Morton, the company's personnel director and the chair of the local employers' association, 'made a brief appearance, but he left hurriedly to a storm of booing'. A second secret ballot was held which was overwhelmingly in favour of sanctions. These were operated from Tuesday 4 April. Sanctions also started on that date at Simon Engineering, another firm that had initially voted against them.[89]

Official sanctions

On Monday 27 March union officials claimed 'nearly 100 per cent support from their 200,000 members' according to the *Morning Star* and 85 percent according to the *Times* and the *Guardian*.[90] Among the federated companies the almost daily lists of figures suggested that workers in only a minority of federated firms were taking sanctions, but this depended on what they chose to understand by sanctions. Tocher claimed on the second day that the employers' association was 'whistling in the dark… The sanctions are being applied in all major factories and the only exceptions are a few small places where we have little or no union organisation'.[91] The picture was more patchy than that.

Many employers were determined to retaliate where action did take place. On 27 March, workers at E Peart & Co decided to sit-in 'following a dispute over how much money they would be paid while working to rule'.[92] At Mirrlees Blackstone (part of the Hawker Siddeley group) the management 'gave notice that all payments would cease at 2.30pm on Monday. At 2.31pm the occupation commenced.' A system of 24-hour shifts, one day on, three days off, was devised 'to save the members' money on travel'.[93] On Tuesday 28 March Serck Heat Transfers workers sat in.[94] British Steel (Openshaw) management announced, 'Unless you return to normal working by 3.10pm Tuesday, your services will not be required.' A mass meeting voted for a sit-in, and a committee was elected to organise rotas and other matters.[95]

On the same day the AUEW executive agreed dispute benefit at three more sit-ins (making four in total). But 'it is not likely to back any more because of the financial burden this would entail. The idea of a district-wide levy to support those who are not working is now being canvassed.' The *Financial Times* suggested that the executive did not want this district dispute to 'escalate any further', and that it was 'unhappy that Manchester has embarked on such a widespread confrontation'. The *Guardian* ran a similar story.[96]

But the same day that these reports were published saw a sudden increase in the number of sit-ins. At Ruston Paxman Diesels (part of the giant GEC group) in Newton-le-Willows, the workforce had already voted on Tuesday 21 March to sit-in if management retaliated when sanctions were imposed. The management demanded a written assurance that the workers dissociated themselves from the claim by 4.30pm on Wednesday 29 March or they would 'cease to pay'. A mass meeting of both day and night shifts voted on the Wednesday morning by 1400 to six to sit in from 4.30pm.[97] At another GEC factory (GEC-AEI Switchgear of Openshaw) workers were given an ultimatum, also on the Wednesday, of either work normally or be suspended. A mass meeting of 900 voted, with only 30 against, to sit-in.[98]

By Thursday 30 March, 12 factories were occupied.[99] The employers were clearly taken aback by the workers' response to the campaign. Three days earlier Fuller of the local employers' association was 'believed…[to be] holding a private meeting with employers at a Stockport hotel'.[100] This was significant, as Stockport workers had started industrial action the previous week. As early as 6 April Fuller admitted that member firms were exerting pressure for a resumption of national talks. The *Financial Times* argued that neither the EEF nor the unions 'will want it to appear that they are showing weakness by making the first move'. The *Economist* later suggested that nothing came of this approach because 'the EEF wants the unions to sweat it out'.[101] Association chairman Morton had earlier pronounced that the north west of England had become the 'battleground for a trial of strength', but he had not seen fit to suspend his own workers at Mather and Platt when they belatedly started to operate sanctions.[102]

Over the Easter break of 31 March to 3 April full-time officers and stewards held a number of meetings, and decided to step up the pressure. This is shown in the increase in Chadwick's estimate of the number of sit-ins: 5 April, fifteen; 6 April, sixteen; 7 April, seventeen; 8 April, twenty; 10 April, twenty one; 14 April, twenty four; 18 April, twenty seven.[103] At the peak of the movement there were up to 30 taking place, involving perhaps 25,000 workers.[104] All sources on the engineering sit-ins admit that the situation was difficult to track exactly. This was made more awkward by the existence of different sets of figures— those from the employers' association, which referred only to federated firms, and union figures that included non-federated companies.[105]

But not all suspensions of workers were met by sit-ins. At the largest engineering factory in the area, GEC-AEI in Trafford Park, the 3,500 workers faced the same threat as at the other GEC factories in Openshaw and Ruston Paxman. If they had not lifted sanctions by 4pm on the Thursday before Easter they would not be paid. The stewards decided to recommend that the workers refuse to report for work on the Easter Tuesday and claim a lockout. One said at the time, 'We have had instructions from the union…not to turn up for work today'.[106] This factory was to play a significant role later in the dispute.

After the Easter weekend, the *Times* suggested that payment of dispute benefit in Manchester 'might not be possible if thousands become involved in future disputes'.[107] It seems likely that there was no executive council meeting on Easter Tuesday, 4 April, which, conveniently for the AUEW, avoided the question of further extension of national support. But on Monday 10 April two sit-ins ended because of settlements, and at a third—Serck Heat Transfers—the workers left the factory and picketed it from the outside. Their dependents were not entitled to social security because of the sit-in, and the workers were not getting dispute benefit.

This appears to have been one factor forcing the AUEW executive the next day to give official support to, by then, a total of 24 factories where workers were sitting-in or locked out. An estimated 10,000 AUEW members were among the 12,750 workers affected by then. The following day the NUGMW agreed to pay its 1,500 members involved.[108] The AUEW executive decided that the tactics in Manchester 'were succeeding', which emboldened it to argue for 'a more stringent claim than that originally recommended by the Confederation'. This was carried at the CSEU EC on Thursday 13 April, with all claims at plant level now having to include £5-£6 on basic rates, the 35-hour week, extra holidays and equal pay.[109]

On the evening of the same day, Thursday 13 April, Scanlon attended a hastily convened CSEU district shop stewards' meeting in Manchester. He argued that the campaign should spread until it became 'nationwide' and brought the employers back to the conference table. About 400 stewards were present at the meeting,[110] which incredibly was the first since the industrial action began. The *Greater Manchester Engineer*, an International Socialists (IS) bulletin, noted that the meeting did not discuss the conduct of the dispute to date and decide on future action. Instead 'those stewards who actually got an invitation were treated to a series of speeches from union officials under the glare of TV lights'.[111] They were also 'asked beforehand not to let the side down'.[112]

According to the *Greater Manchester Engineer*, Scanlon 'said he had come to defend the national leadership against charges that they had failed to put up a fight'. He outlined the unions' national strategy of letting the strongest factories fight the claim, 'which would have avoided the Manchester problem of weak factories being thrown into the struggle'. The *Greater Manchester Engineer* objected that 'he didn't say why this was the first we had heard of the plan'.[113] What is clear from the union's own records is that this strategy did exist but, as Scanlon himself complained later that month at the NC, no district was operating it. In a *Greater Manchester Engineer* special leaflet to the 13 April meeting an even more devastating criticism was made:

> The original Manchester plan, voted at a mass stewards' meeting, was to fight for the claim *as a District*. There was talk of strong factories helping the weak… But the plan has not been followed. We have not

had a *District* fight, but plant-by-plant bargaining in one district—a very different thing. (original emphasis)

The leaflet also argued, 'The policy of secrecy about settlements must end. Some officials and right-wing stewards are using the secrecy at present to mislead many workers and stop them fighting for the full claim'.[114] Since early in the dispute, the *Greater Manchester Engineer* had campaigned against secrecy, but it did not publish secret settlements as 'we would never do anything to undermine the unity of the TU movement'.[115] Whether in retrospect this was appropriate is open to debate. By contrast, the *Morning Star* approvingly noted that 'union officials have done their utmost to protect employers who have conceded the demands'.[116]

Regarding the claim itself, Scanlon apparently told the meeting of his earlier offer to the employers to drop the demand for a shorter working week.[117] The reinstatement of the hours demand that very day as being central to the claim was clearly a move with two intentions— to persuade the employers that the union's overall campaign was very much alive and to counter internal dissent regarding the union's strategy. Scanlon and the rest of the AUEW executive were preparing for strong criticism at the annual meeting of the union's policy-making lay-member NC.[118]

AUEW national committee

In his presidential address on the opening day, Monday 17 April, Scanlon first reiterated the decision taken by the recalled NC in January:

> The strategy we hoped would be adopted was for District Committees to select certain firms with whom we could reasonably anticipate a more realistic approach to that of the Federation, or where we could organise to compel such a realistic approach. In the event of there not being a satisfactory settlement…industrial action should be undertaken and District Committees would then use the rules of our Union, with a view to organising a levy to give financial support to those members who were undertaking the struggle on behalf of all others in the area.

While acknowledging that some action had taken place, he was scathing that:

> …no District has even considered, much less operated, the strategy originally envisaged… There seems to have been little initiative by

the officials or District Committees to implement this policy, and one can hardly be critical of Shop Stewards where such initiative is lacking.

He continued with a swipe at both left and right within the union:

> What is even more surprising is that many of the so-called 'militant' Districts have been reticent in either effecting settlements or seeking to challenge firms from which reasonable offers are not forthcoming.
>
> Other Districts, famed for their lack of interest in national negotiations due to their ability to negotiate high earnings levels within their own establishments, have merely continued with their past practice, and have apparently done nothing to challenge the miserable basic rates and holiday entitlements which continue in the Engineering Industry.

Yet the executive council's position was that:

> ...to seek agreements with separate member firms was the only viable alternative to the insulting reply by the Federation, and might compel them to think again and to reopen national negotiations... To talk of a renewed approach to the Federation, without establishing a basis in a substantial number of areas in the country, would only invite the same insulting treatment.[119]

Later, right-wing executive councillor John Boyd suggested that a return to national bargaining at that point might produce only 50p more on the pay offer.[120]

On Wednesday 26 April the NC debated the policy and voted 28 to 23 against ending it and returning to national talks. The *Guardian* saw it as a 'narrow defeat for the right wing'. Left-wing NC member Len Brindle suggested that to return to national bargaining would be to commit hara-kiri. In the debate Scanlon repeated the fact that not one area, including even Manchester (which had a form of district bargaining), had followed the union's strategy. Nevertheless 'the executive will not condemn them because they are the only district that is doing anything at all to bring about a realisation of our policy'.[121] A resolution was then passed which 'reaffirms full support' for the plant strategy and 'congratulates and gives full support to our members who are taking action on this claim'.[122]

Other than Greater Manchester, there was significant action in only two other districts. In Leeds officials representing 14,000 workers gave one week's notice on 10 April of a ban on piecework and overtime. This was intended to affect some 30 of the 90 federated companies. It produced a lockout, a sit-in and a one-day strike, but in most companies sanctions were either never implemented or were rapidly removed to allow negotiations.[123]

After having been stopped in their tracks earlier, the Sheffield unions now only sanctioned industrial action in individual factories after a strict procedure. Meetings with managements were to be held during the week 20-24 March at the 13 biggest engineering works—selected, according to Bill Owen, CSEU district secretary, 'because they represented a third of the workforce in the Sheffield area in plants where shop stewards and trade unions were well organized'.[124] But by early April sanctions were only operating in one firm, leading to a sit-in there. The call by 700 shop stewards for a May Day strike was only supported by 4,000 workers in four factories.[125] The campaign gradually built up, however, and at its peak in June there were 15 strikes, including a couple of sit-ins, and piecework and overtime bans in several other factories.[126]

To elicit more general support, a meeting of all AUEW engineering section full-time officials in London on 24 May was followed by national officers addressing stewards' mass meetings in the main engineering areas—but to little effect.[127] In fact by as late as 29 June only 49 percent of federated firms nationally had even had the claim submitted to them.[128] Why were Scanlon and his supporters unable to enforce even this? National action in engineering had historically united the otherwise disparate sections of the industry. The most significant post-war national action was to be over the shorter working week in the summer and autumn of 1979, with a series of one-day and two-day strikes.[129] In 1972 the emphasis on individual factory claims, particularly on basic rates, was divisive and was seen by many as an abdication of leadership. It has been suggested that as Manchester and Sheffield 'featured regularly between 1960 and 1973 as the areas with some of the lowest average earnings (less overtime) in the union...[they] had most to gain' from taking action. Elsewhere 'the rank and file were in a position not only to put hostile motions but also to refuse to implement the national policy'—mainly because they did not believe that it could work.[130]

Greater Manchester again

Mid-April to mid-May

The four weeks following Scanlon's visit to Manchester were relatively quiet. A few sit-ins finished and others started. One reporter was surprised that nationally the 'militant action by the engineers' in Manchester had received 'surprisingly little by way of publicity' and pointed out that 'Like the Yeti, it has rarely been photographed'.[131] Cecil King, the diarist, recorded that the sit-ins were 'a menace seldom referred to in the papers'.[132] Yet the *Guardian* had pointed out very early in the Manchester events that 'the sit-in tactic has been used as an industrial dispute weapon for the first time'.[133] Perhaps the simultaneous entanglements of the dockers and the railway workers with the Industrial Relations Act diverted attention away from what in almost any other year would have been heralded as a major development in industrial militancy.

Chadwick was later to write that the 'Manchester sit-ins broke new ground in one important respect. They were not defensive but offensive.' He marvelled that 'they happened so very easily' and that the workers involved 'saw quite clearly that the occupation of the factories…in which they were employed was a perfectly logical and legitimate action to take'. He contrasted this with 'the heartsearching and ultimate inhibition which prevented the GEC workers on Merseyside from occupying their plants in 1969', and concluded, 'We would be blind if we were to overlook such an Olympian leap in consciousness'.[134]

At the same time the employers were engaging in a tried and tested tactic—the use of the Indemnity Fund. There was public acknowledgement in mid-April that the EEF had sent over £1 million to Manchester and Stockport firms. The *Financial Times* called it 'an unprecedented move'. Tom Carlile, EEF president, praised 'the admirable solidarity of member firms when under local attack'.[135] Another £1 million followed in late May.[136] When workers at Ruston Paxman took over their factory's offices, they discovered precise details of the EEF payments. The £5 per man, and £2.50 per woman and apprentice was doubled after the first week. In total £2,378,319 was paid out of the Indemnity Fund that year.[137] Tocher also claimed that 'Manchester engineering firms were getting all sorts of concessions on delivery dates and so forth'.[138]

By contrast, the unions were disorganised. The CSEU special conference of union executives in February had agreed that dispute benefit would be the responsibility of individual unions.[139] This led to problems in practice. For example, the Boilermakers' Society, due to other calls on its funds, only paid £1 per week strike benefit.[140] At the end of May, in a closed session of its national delegate conference, the Manchester district delegate (full-time officer), Chris Gollaglee (who was also chair of the CSEU district committee), estimated that some 700 of his members had been on strike, locked out or sitting in: '...members threatened to go to the home of the District Delegate and remove the furniture and pawn it'.[141]

The AUEW, which did pay full dispute benefit, argued that districts should hold levies to support members. But this was a cumbersome procedure. In Greater Manchester the four district committees of Manchester, Stockport, Ashton and Warrington agreed in early April to ballot their membership on this. But the Manchester result was not reported to its DC until the middle of June—2,390 for, with 819 against.[142] It was not clear whether this decision was ever operated. There was, however, a late donation to the CSEU district of £2,000 from the Vibrator works in Leningrad.[143]

As the CSEU strategy had been based on its individual districts, there was limited contact between them. However, the neighbouring Oldham area, to the north east of Manchester, did take action which contributed to the scale of events in the region. A shop stewards' meeting on 15 March had agreed a similar claim to Manchester and, the day before Scanlon's visit in April, a meeting of some 200 stewards agreed to ban overtime and piecework, and undertake one-day strikes. Three Ferranti factories were in the Manchester CSEU district and three in Oldham, but the unions in the five plants nearest to each other seem to have coordinated their actions to some extent, even if the management tried to split them.[144]

What appeared at the time to be a major breakthrough for the unions occurred at Fairey Engineering of Stockport when 800 manual workers settled on 17 April for, among other things, a 37.5-hour week from January 1973. A company spokesman 'was unwilling to confirm that it provided for a 37½-hour week, but a union official said: "There is no doubt that this is what is meant by *staff conditions* for manual workers"' (added emphasis).[145]

Yet this success was outweighed by the difficulties the unions were having with some other large factories. When the Gardner workforce accepted a deal with no concession on hours or holidays, the CSEU district committee refused to ratify it. Tocher arranged to address a lunchtime meeting of Gardner workers in a local bingo hall on Friday 21 April, but the company's solicitors threatened that they might use the Industrial Relations Act against him. He went ahead and convinced the 1,000 workers present to repudiate the agreement, despite their having already received the £2 wage rise in their pay packets. He argued that foremen giving out ballot papers had invalidated their initial vote.[146] While it appears that no sanctions were reimposed at Gardner,[147] Tocher's defiant attitude had an impact on how Mather and Platt management prepared for a similar situation.

At a special meeting on 18 April the AUEW DC had refused to approve an agreement with that company, made four days earlier (and approved by secret ballot), that included the following clauses:

> Both parties agree that working conditions, such as hours of work, holidays, etc, are matter for national negotiation and agreement... The stewards reaffirm their authority to conclude this agreement...without reference for ratification to any body external to Park Works [the district committee].[148]

Scanlon pronounced, 'I am sure the executive would consider we are still in dispute with the firm,' and Tocher attacked the shop stewards for 'prostituting the mass movement' by using it to get a rise they would not have got otherwise. A spokesman for the stewards then countered, 'We were told by an area official that if we decided to go for money alone there was nothing they could do to stop us and that's exactly what we've done'.[149] The convener and all stewards were summoned to another special DC on Friday 21 April, at which they agreed to withdraw the settlement pending a mass meeting to be addressed by district officials.[150]

The stewards went to Morton, the personnel manager, who claimed that they 'said "We've been instructed by the district committee to unsign that agreement"...and I said, "Sorry, mate, once it's signed, it's signed".'[151] A mass meeting at the plant was eventually organised during the lunchbreak on Monday 24 April. Morton decided that district secretary Panter should not be allowed into the plant, and he was forced to use a loudhailer from outside, the *Morning Star* suggesting that 'it is believed the shop stewards had meekly accepted this restriction'. Only about 100 of the 2,000-strong meeting voted for his appeal to reject the cash-only settlement and reintroduce a work to rule. Apparently Panter said, 'But don't you see? You are only getting the money.' The reply was, 'And that's what we want.' However, 50 patternmakers at the plant refused to accept the deal and continued sanctions.[152]

The next day the 3,500 workers at GEC-AEI Trafford Park returned to work after three weeks of lockout. A formula had been agreed which would allow negotiations on the claim while the overtime and piecework bans were reimposed. At the time the unions saw this as a major breakthrough for their strategy and a possible means of settling the other stoppages.[153]

By the end of April the number of settlements was slowly increasing, but the propaganda war between employers' association director Fuller and Tocher for the CSEU continued, disputing how many agreements were cash only, and how many included holidays and hours.[154] The divisions between factories within the same combine, particularly marked in the case of GEC, were further demonstrated by the Hawker Siddeley experience. Two thousand workers at the Chadderton (Oldham) factory had held three weekly one-day strikes before accepting an offer in a ballot and returning to work on 8 May. At the same company's Woodford plant 1,200 refused to ballot on the same offer and continued their sit-in.[155]

The centre cracks

In the wake of the policy-making NC in April, the AUEW executive eventually circularised all branches and district committees on 9 May urging further action on the claim. This accused the EEF of urging its member companies to 'adopt a policy of maximum possible escalation when faced with industrial action…making the action as costly to the unions as possible, as quickly as possible'. It then claimed that the EEF had insisted that 'sectional actions or go-slows should not be tolerated but management should react in such a way that the unions turn it into full strike action'.[156] The employers' policy was obviously working, though they had not anticipated sit-ins. But while the union's original tactic was again confirmed, there was a major retreat on its demands:

> Due to certain Districts reaching settlement on wages alone, the original tactics envisaged by National Committee and Executive Council were reiterated, ie that certain federated firms would be selected and attempts made to reach agreement on *at least* three minimum conditions: 1. Substantial improvement in basic rates. 2. Improvements in the number of holidays. 3. General all-round increases.[157] (original emphasis)

Incredibly, there was no mention of hours. Tocher's immediate reaction was that the union executive's decision would not change the Manchester situation.[158] But the big companies seem to have taken advantage of the change in the union's national position to force a crisis in Manchester. On Friday 12 May the Ferranti group (which had witnessed a number of one-day strikes in support of the claim) shut three of its factories following the start of a go-slow by 3,500 workers—the workers sat in. But GEC-AEI's threat to close its Trafford Park factory, warning of a 'protracted stoppage', precipitated a vote by the shop stewards of 92 to 20, also on 12 May, to drop the hours demand (now that it was no longer national policy) and call off the work to rule if talks could be resumed.[159]

Jim Arnison in the *Morning Star* put a strangely positive gloss on the GEC stewards' decision. It showed how the CP's support for the AUEW national leadership's policies led its daily paper to legitimate the actions of the leading right-winger in the district. Arnison suggested that the continuation of the overtime ban (which was still district policy because of unemployment) somehow would 'bring scant comfort to the Manchester Engineering Employers' Association':

> The attitude taken up by the convener Bert Brennan and his fellow shop stewards is emphatic. If the employers will not at this stage concede shorter hours they must not expect the workers to extend the working week beyond 40 hours.

Arnison's reporting ignored sentiments such as Chadwick's description of 'the widely hated James Brennan, OBE, right wing leader of the Trafford Park AEI stewards'.[160] Brennan was such a good servant of the company that it let him stay on as convener until he retired in 1977, aged 72![161]

The GEC-AEI decision was critical as the plant was seen to be a 'pacesetter' regionally. The Manchester campaign had insisted on cuts in hours and was 'clearly thrown into considerable confusion by this softening in the [national] AUEW line'. The *Guardian* mused, not for the first time, that the Manchester campaign was 'a source of acute embarrassment to the AUEW', costing it at that point in the region of £100,000 per week'. Tocher stated that the 'whole question…will be discussed on Monday and we will then decide what tactics to pursue'.[162]

By the Monday, 15 May, in the light of the change in national policy and the GEC-AEI vote, Manchester district union officials met in an emergency meeting of the CSEU district committee and accepted the new policy.[163] Later the same morning there was a CSEU district meeting of 600 shop stewards. This followed the GEC-AEI position and voted that where concessions on pay and holidays were won then piecework sanctions and work to rules would end, but that there would continue to be a complete overtime ban where there was no cut in working hours. Tocher described it as a 'change of tactic'. The *Guardian* called it a 'tactical retreat'.[164]

Jim Arnison in the *Morning Star* reported under the headline 'Engineers Adopt New Tactic To Win Claim', in which he quoted Tocher:

> We have achieved 43 settlements on the three points [wages, holidays, hours], but we have now taken into consideration certain *settlements reached locally and in the shipbuilding industry, together with circulars received from some unions* and claims that have been submitted in other industries without reference to ours. (added emphasis)

Panter tried to be even more positive: 'It means that those factories where agreements have been reached on the first two points of the claim can be *brought back* into the struggle for the shorter working week' (added emphasis).[165]

There was opposition to this change at the stewards' meeting. IS member John Deason of Ruston Paxman moved an amendment that the shorter working week should be kept as one of the basic demands and this gathered the support of one third of the meeting. It appears that the GEC-AEI stewards lifted their sanctions after and not before the Monday morning meeting which changed the Manchester policy. This would explain their heavy representation at the meeting—'two coach loads' during working hours. According to Deason, the 'majority [in the meeting] were delegations of stewards from plants who…had already made secret settlements'. By contrast Ruston Paxman, still sitting in, only had five stewards present.[166]

While there are doubts about the legitimacy of the decision-making process (though in truth there was no agreed system of representation at any of the mass stewards' meetings), the greater problem lay at the centre of the union. The national leadership had initially supported the Manchester sit-ins, but once a stalemate situation had occurred the financial cost of that support was considered too great.

In an interview several years later Tocher bluntly suggested that 'we wouldn't compromise on the demand for a shorter working week—until the Executive instructed us to'. He added, 'We could have settled for money and holidays weeks before on very generous terms if we'd forget the hours issue'.[167]

Scanlon has tried to justify his position as follows:

> It wasn't an easy decision…don't forget these lads…Benny Rothman, Johnny Tocher, Bernard Regan, all those people, they were responsible

for me being president and they felt considerably let down. But when you're faced with...negotiations that are dragging on...[and] there seems nothing other than calling the whole thing off, then you've got to consider is there some other tactic you can adopt... We were saying a partial settlement is better than no settlement at all... It was tactically correct to do what we did.[168]

From the position that a reduced working week was not, and never was (in the minds of most national union leaders) a central part of the claim, Scanlon was undoubtedly right. But the main factor sustaining the action in the Manchester area was precisely the hours question. The local full-time officials had gone to great lengths to keep that at the front of everyone's mind and had refused to ratify settlements not including concessions on this. They had been left stranded just like the stewards and the membership. One commentator observed that 'John Tocher in the divisional office had sharp differences of opinion with the head-quarters, just as workers at factories had sharp differences with the divisional office'.[169] But as a leading CP member, and therefore a key supporter of the Broad Left in the AUEW, Tocher himself was trapped by, and unable to break with, the CP's policy of uncritically support-ing left-wing union leaders.

On Tuesday 16 May a special meeting of the Manchester AUEW DC adopted the new policy.[170] GEC-AEI Trafford Park immediately lifted their piecework sanctions and accepted a new deal on the Friday on pay and holidays. Elsewhere little changed immediately. On the day following the district stewards' meeting a mass meeting at Bred-bury Mills, the first of the factory sit-ins, rejected a company offer, and Ferranti shut down two more factories employing 1,800 workers be-cause of their go-slow, precipitating further sit-ins.[171] But this pro-vided only temporary respite. On Wednesday 17 May shop stewards were meeting management in several factories.[172] The *Economist* sug-gested that 'at least 10 disputes were in the folding-up stage by Thurs-day night'.[173] For example, Bredbury workers were threatened with redundancies on 17 May and resumed work six days later.[174]

Excluding the final flurry of Ferranti sit-ins, workers at some 16 federated factories were still sitting-in on 17 May, and workers at nine factories were 'laid off'. By 25 May this was down to six longstanding sit-ins plus six at Ferranti. At the beginning of June the *Economist* gloated that 'the campaign finally collapsed with the overwhelming vote by three of the six Ferranti factories to end their sit-ins'.[175] The others in the group followed almost immediately.[176] While the evidence on non-federated companies is sparse, it is likely that most of their remaining sit-ins also folded during the second half of May.

By the end of the first week in June only five workforces were still sitting-in their factories. Yet after 11 weeks of action at the Metal Box factory at Timperley, the stewards won a vote against a company offer by 74 to 41. The senior steward 'was amazed'. One worker who had been in the industry for 35 years voted not to go back, saying:

> He had been learning things this year. He had learned there were similar factories within twenty miles where the rates were better than at Timperley. He had thought, for the first time in his life, about how much money he was entitled to… 'I thought, perhaps I'm worth more than I am getting. I don't want to be given a rise just because the cost of living has gone up'.[177]

However, at Viking Engineering in Stockport, employing about 100 workers, the sit-in was continued because of the earlier dismissal (on 14 April) of Kevin Horner, the convener, for alleged obscene language.[178] Some sit-ins were sustained into July and one even into August. The 47 workers of Bason and Son of Stockport were one of the last groups to sit in (on 28 April) but they did not finish until 11 August, days before the national settlement.[179]

Even with the ending of sanctions on the pay claim there was an attempt to maintain some district discipline. On 4 July, the Manchester AUEW DC discussed the problems of meeting orders in companies still banning overtime and agreed to approve up to 30 hours a month where absolutely essential. This was reaffirmed at a special district shop stewards' meeting with 100 present on 17 July.[180]

Sit-ins or occupations?

The *Morning Star* was clear that this 'great sit-in movement…has brought a new dimension to the class struggle'.[181] Individually each sit-in was a direct challenge to the property rights of the employer. Collectively they briefly invited comparisons with much larger movements in other countries. Yet in very few cases were there full-scale occupations where management was locked out of the site, and this relative timidity both by workers and union officials meant that the full potential of the tactic was never realised. As *International Socialism* put it 'they were occupations more in form than in content'.[182]

Right at the beginning of the movement the *Economist* noted, 'Most of the [first] eight sit-ins are being looked upon as simple strikes. The managements have turned off the light and heat, and left the men to it.' The next week it argued, 'The sit-ins are purely nominal (a representative sample of men in an unheated, unlighted factory) and amount to a strike'.[183]

By contrast, Jim Arnison in the *Morning Star* noted that 'at some occupied factories, the employers have shown a marked reluctance to follow the "get tough" line of their association and have helped to ensure a smooth-running sit-in by providing lighting, heating, telephone and canteen facilities'.[184] Peter Hildrew in the *Guardian* was even more positive: 'Arriving in shifts and loaded with sleeping bags, sandwiches and packs of cards, the men seem convinced that they have an effective new tactic'.[185]

At the first sit-in, Bredbury:

> …after a 12-hour night shift without light, heat and water, these services were restored and the men began to organize. Factory attendance was split into nine shifts [of eight hours] which meant that all workers spent two days at home and one in the factory. Those at work were organized into gangs to deal with cleansing, sanitary arrangements, outside picketing and so on. The firm's conference rooms were taken over for meetings.[186]

But even after this one observer described it as a 'damp, cold and largely unlit factory'. Members of the steel workers' union, covered by a different set of negotiations, were still working at the adjoining strip mill. This union had been expelled from the site's joint shop stewards' committee because its members were working on machinery serviced by scab labour.[187] While management and customers tried to shift material they failed, and 'nothing was allowed to pass through the gates without the strict permission of the stewards'.[188]

At Barlow and Chidlaw in Salford AUEW shop steward Jim Regan reported when the sit-in started on about 7 April, 'Management threatened to turn the light off at night. The men said they wouldn't let them back in the morning to turn them on, thus stopping the computers and office staff from working. The management soon backed down'.[189] However, by mid-May 80 workers at Archibald Edmeston in Eccles had been sitting-in since 4 April 'without heat or lighting'. The management brought in 'a crate of beer as a bribe. They seem to have forgotten that alcohol is strictly forbidden on the premises'.[190]

Two of the sit-ins in the Warrington area were reported early on as 'only sat-in 8 hours a day and not at weekends' but 'the stewards think even this is an advance'.[191] When workers at Chesterfield Tube in the Sheffield CSEU district sat-in, they took their spring holiday week as normal before returning.[192] In some factories there was a more militant attitude. At Linotype in Broadheath workers who had sat-in since 7 April chained and padlocked the main gates in the middle of May 'to prevent any movement of traffic in or out'.[193] When sanctions began at Hawker Siddeley in Woodford management started 'collecting in any keys they know to be held by the unions and…a lot of new locks and bolts have been appearing about the plant'. A sit-in started on 5 April and the 'first attempt to turn the sit-in into an all-out occupation' took place a few days later. 'New padlocks "appeared" on all the gates overnight', and the workers tried 'to keep out anyone they didn't want in the plant'. Eventually 'the management cut off the offending locks but not before the staff workers had been delayed 1½ hours'.[194] By late April the strikers were:

> …picketing staff workers each day—causing big delays and traffic jams… The pickets insist on speaking to everyone who comes in. Result: traffic snarl-ups, especially the morning after two-ton concrete blocks mysteriously appeared at the gates by night! So far, police have left the pickets alone, but there are now dozens of them in the mornings sending staff cars round and round the airfield until the pickets let them in.[195]

Mass picketing of the gates was still occurring in early June with staff being delayed up to four hours every morning.[196]

At Metal Box in Timperley, on the edge of Manchester, early in the sit-in (which started on 7 April) there had been a 'confrontation between workers and managers, both sides using chains, padlocks and bolt-cutters to fasten the gates shut (the workers) or open (the managers). Police watched…while men snipped away and lengths of broken chain accumulated.' There was also an incident 'when management cut off the electricity and locked the lavatories. The management people got locked in as a punishment; one of them was there for, it was thought, eighty-nine hours.'

The 140-strong workforce was divided into shifts to occupy the plant round the clock. The senior shop steward, John Roylance, enthused about the sit-in, 'It's fantastic, what we've done, what we've gone through… There's one of the lads, normally he can't get to work by a quarter to eight… Now he gets here at six. It's in the blood, you can't get it out'.[197]

At Ruston Paxman the hourly paid lodge men joined the sit-in in late April, forcing the foremen to do gate duty. Among the shopfloor workers:

...the attendance rate, working 12 hours on and two days off has been very high. The few who went 'on the club' [off sick] to avoid their turn have been turning up since the stewards made it clear a strict register was being kept, to be studied closely at the end of the dispute.[198]

In the eighth week of their sit-in workers at Ruston Paxman fully occupied the factory: '...the ejection of management followed...the provocative moving of spares by junior management in brief cases, car boots etc'.[199] Ruston Paxman, Metal Box and Redpath Pearson in Trafford Park were the only three that were ever fully occupied.[200]

A correspondent on the *Times* wrote towards the end of May that the Manchester sit-ins:

...have been thoroughly gentlemanly affairs with very few incidents on picket lines and, indeed, little outward evidence that they are taking place at all. Workers go into the factories, keep them clean and tidy, observe safety regulations, make their own catering arrangements, amuse themselves with television, radio, cards, darts, bingo sessions and occasional concert parties... When management men go into the plants they usually...go out of their way to avoid any sort of abrasive contact with the men... It is the sort of situation that they might have made into one of those Ealing comedy films, just after the war.[201]

In many ways the sit-ins were an advance on pure strikes. One steward explained, 'With a sit-in you don't have to worry about scabs. There is no need to chase lorries. Nothing gets in or out. We are in control'.[202] Another steward called it 'inside picketing'.[203] A third, John Doherty, AUEW convener at Mirrlees Blackstone, said, 'It's really an inside form of picketing.' In his factory there were four teams of 200 workers who did 24-hour shifts from noon to noon: 'We need to have 200 there, so that if they try to keep us out we can gather at the gate and all push our way in together'.[204]

Yet in practice the sit-ins were more passive than strikes with external picketing. As Chadwick argued at the time:

Each group of workers in each factory was fighting in effective isolation from each other group of workers. When the employers at one factory retaliated...it was up to the men at that particular plant to work out for themselves their own tactics. Most trade union full time officials worked extremely hard during this period; addressing factory gate meetings, talking with employers and cajoling recalcitrants but they were hamstrung by their situation and by their traditional *modus operandi*.

Those areas with strong traditions (and with a stronger and more articulate political perspective) such as Stockport and Openshaw set up joint shop stewards' committees to try to co-ordinate their own very local activities. But no district-wide official news-sheet was published and no 'shock troops' were mobilized... A district team of experienced and well briefed union activists operating in a similar way to the building workers' flying pickets of a few weeks later would really have frightened the employers and have hoisted flagging morale at those firms where a siege mentality was developing...in those cold, silent factories.[205]

There was an attempt by the IS to get a joint occupations committee. An appeal went out on 1 May in the *Greater Manchester Engineer* and a meeting was held on 10 May at which 11 factories were represented. A resolution was sent to the CSEU district committee but got overtaken by the decision to drop the hours claim.[206] Yet it demonstrated that those actually sitting-in were anxious for a more coordinated and militant approach in the district, even if they did not feel confident enough to act independently of the union officials.

The settlement

In mid-August the EEF and CSEU met again at national level and settled at a level slightly above what the shipbuilding employers had agreed with the same unions three months earlier—two extra days holiday (one in 1972 and another one in 1973), along with minimum rates of £25 for skilled workers and £20 for labourers (implemented in two equal stages—August 1972 and August 1973).[207] In the AUEW monthly journal, it was headlined 'New One-Year Agreement', and much was made of this and the fact that the NC claim on minimum rates had been fully conceded (albeit in two stages) 'perhaps for the first time'.[208] It was a significant advance from the very low original offer but a small return for all the industrial action.

The AUEW general secretary, the right-wing Jim Conway, used a very public opportunity within the union to rubbish the final settlement: 'I would confidently state that...less than 10 per cent and in all probability...around 5 per cent...of our members working a 40-hour week actually take home a larger pay packet arising from the Agreement.' He also attacked the amount of dispute benefit paid out to achieve this.[209] Such a response was hardly surprising since the same man had written that 'in the long term we have gained nothing from strikes' in the union's monthly journal—which he edited.[210]

Conway's attack on the settlement was reprinted in the journal. In the same issue there was an executive council report:

> [A]ttempts are being made to under-sell this...settlement and, whilst Executive Council are the first to recognise that the original claim was, by no means, achieved, they would remind all members *and particularly officials at every level*, that the AUEW, almost unaided, bore the brunt of the struggle, including very high sums paid out in Dispute Benefit. It is, therefore, completely erroneous to equate the amount thus spent with the settlement achieved.
>
> Executive Council trust that all members recognise that strikes often need to be undertaken in order to prevent employers from acting irresponsibly in the future.[211] (added emphasis)

Tocher loyally agreed: 'We wouldn't have got the employers back round the table without the sit-ins'.[212] But Scanlon's insistence on a 12-month settlement could not stop the EEF delaying the start of the next national wage agreement until April 1974.

Conclusion

After the settlement, the *Times* editorialised, 'The determination of the employers, concerting their resistance as they had not done for many years, surprised both the unions and many observers'.[213] Paul Routledge wrote that the plant strategy failed 'because the employers saw it coming, and prepared for it...they met union militancy with employer militancy'.[214] The *Economist* was positively triumphalist: 'The employers resisted by adopting trade union tactics; a £2m strike fund, daily briefings to keep wavering employers in line and even expulsion from the bosses' club, the EEF (six were actually booted out)'.[215]

In fact many of the factories that had experienced sit-ins, lockouts or strikes belonged to some of the largest employers in the EEF nationally. GEC (with at least six factories affected in Greater Manchester and Oldham, and others elsewhere) was the second biggest in the EEF; Hawker Siddeley (with three) the fourth; GKN (with one) the seventh; Ferranti (with six taking sanctions in Manchester and Oldham) the seventeenth; and British Steel (with four) the eighteenth.[216] At the large but non-federated Metal Box (with one of the few genuine occupations), the management eventually admitted to the stewards that 'meeting their demands would mean conceding the claim in all fifty of their factories'.[217]

The large companies had the resources to bide their time. Arnold Weinstock, the boss of the giant GEC, confided in mid-April that he was 'inclined to hold out'.[218] Tocher was aware that it was the big companies in the EEF 'who held out come what may'.[219] This problem highlighted the question of union strategy. The *Economist* pointed out that 'Mr Scanlon is one of the union movement's most able tacticians',[220] but ignored the fact that his ideas had not been implemented. Scanlon wanted factories systematically targeted and then other workers levied in support of any industrial action taken. But this did not happen as neither he nor the AUEW leadership as a whole was able to dictate to the union's own districts,[221] let alone to the multi-union CSEU district committees.

In 1989 the CSEU was able to surmount this same problem by nationally selecting a limited number of factories to strike for a shorter working week and building up a huge fund by levy to finance this, but this only occurred because the EEF had by then abandoned national bargaining.[222] Yet even in 1972 there were opportunities as was shown forcefully in the late summer by the national building workers' strike. In this dispute something akin to the Scanlon strategy of selective strikes on a regional basis was actually operated, but when it became bogged down local multi-union action committees escalated it into a series of local all-out stoppages and forced a much higher national settlement. One important difference was that in the building workers' dispute CP activists were an important part of the rank-and-file movement against the established right-wing leadership of the main union. The Broad Left in engineering had a temporary ascendancy within the AUEW and was anxious not to attack the national leadership, especially Scanlon.

Despite such loyalty the Manchester Broad Left found itself leading a militant campaign, but one very different from that envisaged by Scanlon. The sit-ins were not only unprecedented in scale, they were also 'the first instance of planned action of this type being applied to a district through union channels'.[223] Yet, as the *Greater Manchester Engineer* pointed out, it was not a district fight but plant-by-plant bargaining within a district. This was reinforced by the early policy of secrecy on settlements, which might have secured better individual deals in the short term but at the expense of the wider struggle. The local AUEW officials were doing what they knew best—exploiting negotiating possibilities. But the scale of employers' resistance required a different type of leadership. After the flurry of enthusiastic district stewards' meetings held before sanctions started there were only two more—one hurriedly called to give Scanlon a platform from which to defend his position and the other to force through the dropping of the hours demand.

The Broad Left and CP politics of the local officials meant that they were not prepared to further challenge the national union's left-wing leadership over the conduct of the dispute. The leading Broad Left stewards were also more oriented on union structures than on shopfloor organisation and were unable, and unwilling, to challenge the district officials. Tocher admitted that 'there was a lot of disillusionment after the sit-ins… People had sacrificed a lot, many of them got nothing.' He was due for re-election later that year and 'only won by 200 odd votes out of 17,000'.[224] Panter failed to get re-elected the next year.[225] The Broad Left never recovered nationally from the 1972 setback, and the adoption of postal balloting reinforced the increasing ascendancy of the right wing in the union. Despite Scanlon's continuing radicalism over the Industrial Relations Act, he ended up supporting Labour's incomes policy, the 'Social Contract' (see Chapter 7). The sit-ins were a missed opportunity for the left.

Miners' pickets blockade the Ollerton pit in Nottinghamshire

A Kent miners' water-borne picket patrols the River Thames opposite parliament

Striking miners mount a mass picket outside the Saltley coke depot
in Birmingham

Miners' pickets (including Arthur Scargill on the left) thank
Birmingham engineers for their solidarity action

Solidarity strike action to free the five jailed London dockers swept the country

A mass demonstration of dockers and their supporters demanding the release of the jailed dockers

137

The Pentonville Five: Derek Watkins, Bernie Steer, Vic Turner,
Cornelius (Con) Clancy and Tony Merrick

The released dockers are greeted by triumphant supporters outside
Pentonville prison

Building workers set off on a 'flying picket' to stop those sites still working

Victory celebrations outside the huge World's End building site in west London

Des Warren and
Ricky Tomlinson,
two building workers
later imprisoned for
'conspiracy'

Merseyside dockers
show their support
for the Shrewsbury
building workers

Chapter 5

The dockers and the Industrial Relations Act

(written with Fred Lindop)[1]

For the second time in just over 20 years, dockers' unofficial action was responsible for ending anti-strike legislation in Britain. In 1951 it had been Order 1305, the wartime regulation that allowed strikers to be prosecuted. Within months of the dockers' action and the ensuing court case against their leaders this provision for outlawing strikes had been removed by Attlee's Labour government.[2] In 1972 the dockers' long traditions of unofficial organisation at both port and national level again sustained them against court orders and continuous attempts by the Transport and General Workers Union (TGWU) to stop their action. The dramatic events surrounding the imprisonment of five dockers were the decisive factor in holding most trade unions to the Trades Union Congress (TUC) policy on deregistration under the Industrial Relations Act. Simultaneously the industrial and political crisis caused by the reactions to the jailings seriously damaged the credibility of the act, in the eyes of both employers and government ministers. Repeal was delayed (until a few months after the election of a Labour government in February 1974) but it was rarely used from that point.

Dock work and union organisation

By the beginning of the 1970s British dockers faced a revolution in cargo-handling techniques, in particular the use of containers. By an accident of history, the dockers' unofficial rank-and-file campaign in 1972 against the effects of containerisation on job opportunities coincided with the full implementation of the Industrial Relations Act. This meant that although the campaign was *industrial* it unleashed a train of events which inevitably became increasingly *political*, and which ended by inflicting another humiliating defeat on the Conservative government.

Dockers' workplace union organisation was formed under the long-standing system of casual employment that, until 1947, required men to report at the dock gate and wait to be hired for an hour or half-day depending on the fluctuating requirements for labour. The men who were hired would often remain employed until the end of the particular loading or unloading operation was completed. Those who failed to get hired either wandered the dock area looking for employment or went home until the next hiring later that day or the following morning. Employers thought that casualism was the only appropriate method of meeting the labour requirements. Constant fluctuations in trade, caused by economic booms and slumps and seasonal imports and exports, were exacerbated on a daily basis by the tide and the weather. The dockers offered themselves for hire to a vast number of small and medium-sized employers. With the pool of labour generally well in excess of the combined maximum daily requirements of all employers in the port, underemployment and fluctuating wages were the inevitable result.[3]

The 1945 Labour government, in an attempt to provide some security for a casualised workforce and to strengthen labour discipline, introduced the National Dock Labour Scheme. Every docker was now 'registered', as were the employers, and only registered dockers could perform dock work, as defined by statute, in those ports which were included in the scheme. If dockers attended work but none was available they were paid 'attendance money' and a guaranteed weekly wage if earnings plus any attendance money fell below a nationally agreed minimum. In return for greater security of income and employment, dockers were required to attend work on a regular basis and accept whatever work was available. But in practice the 1947 scheme simply regularised the casual system by introducing local Dock Labour Boards as 'holding employers' of dock labour, interposed between the docker and the 'operational employers'. Neither working conditions nor the system of hiring changed much, and as a result the conflicts and insecurity engendered by casualism lived on.[4]

However, the post-war economic boom and tight labour market did strengthen the dockers' bargaining position, and gave them the opportunity to turn their casual employment arrangements, combined with the dominant gang piecework system of payment, against the employers to steadily improve the pay for particular jobs. It also allowed a significant degree of independence and autonomy in the actual organisation of work tasks and practices. The absence of a system of shop stewards (employers and union officials had agreed that the casual system made this impossible) led to workplace union organisation that was totally unofficial. The ban by the TGWU on Communist Party (CP) members holding union office (1949-68) added a political dimension to the situation because it confined Communist dock workers to a mainly unofficial outlet for their industrial activity. The existence of competing unions in the major ports of London, Liverpool and Hull, with differing traditions of internal democracy, was another factor that made for an unusual degree of rank-and file-independence. The majority TGWU, seen by many dockers as centralised and bureaucratic, had constantly to be aware of the danger of loss of members to the localist and fiercely democratic National Amalgamated Stevedores and Dockers Union (NASD).[5] The latter was only recognised by the employers in London but had significant membership in both Liverpool and Hull following a major exodus from the TGWU in the mid-1950s.[6]

With a multitude of employers in the ports, the industry was not only highly competitive, but there was a distinct lack of cohesion and cooperation on the employers' side. Furthermore, the port operator was under constant pressure from clients to turn vessels around as quickly as possible, as in port a ship became simply a floating warehouse accumulating costs and earning no revenue. The result was that the docks were one of Britain's most strike-prone industries, with 70 percent of all post-war dock strikes lasting only one day or less.[7] With the country heavily reliant on overseas trade, dock strikes became a major concern for successive Labour and Conservative governments, and led to the declaration of a state of emergency on several occasions. Official inquiries abounded, leading to the docks being dubbed 'the most inquired into' of all industries.[8]

The most prominent inquiry was that under Lord Devlin in 1964, set up by the Labour government with TGWU support. The Devlin Report led to the decasualisation of the docks via a two-phase modernisation programme.[9] Phase One ended casual employment in all registered ports from September 1967 by instituting permanent employment and a higher guaranteed wage (while retaining piecework in most ports, 1967-70). Phase Two provided for port-by-port agreements that were intended to end various 'restrictive' practices, tighten work discipline and establish fixed wages, with productivity agreements to be negotiated according to locally agreed timetables (1970-71). A shop steward system was also introduced into the various docks and ports in 1967, and Jack Jones, who became TGWU general secretary in 1969, played a leading role in setting up the stewards' organisation, thereby establishing his own and the union's credentials among the dockers.

The Devlin reforms did not bring the various unregistered ports under the National Dock Labour Scheme. There also continued to be a steady loss of jobs in the registered sector. The introduction of the first part of Devlin was met with a rash of strikes as dockers in ports up and down the country resisted various terms of the decasualisation programme. In Liverpool there was a six-week strike to demand a major revision of piecework rates. Although Jones failed to get the strike called off, he managed to persuade the prime minister, Harold Wilson, to send in the government's 'troubleshooter', industrialist Jack Scamp, to negotiate with the unofficial committee while the strike continued, eventually conceding most of the men's demands. Meanwhile in London unofficial attempts to call a port-wide strike against Devlin in September 1967 failed to win much support, although an unofficial port workers' liaison committee brought out the Royal Docks and part of the West India Docks over a 'manning' grievance. The strike lasted eight weeks in the face of unprecedented criticism by union officials and the media but numerous efforts to spread it to the majority of the port's workforce failed. The Royal Docks returned to work with their solidarity unbroken, but the divisions between sectors of the port left a legacy of bitterness and mutual suspicion which undercut attempts to create a port-wide shop stewards' committee.

Notoriously, some London dockers went on strike in April 1968 and marched on parliament in support of leading Conservative MP Enoch Powell's 'rivers of blood' speech calling for an end to black immigration into Britain. It has been suggested that this reflected the dockers' concern with the rundown of their industry under a Labour government that was seen as not protecting their interests. In despair and anger they looked to Powell instead. In fact, only about one third of London dockers took part in any strike action and only a few hundred went to Westminster. Housing, rather than job insecurity, was the main concern of many dockers with racist sentiments. The opposition by the CP and others to the strikes was not well coordinated, and was complicated by the dockers' traditions of respecting strike votes.[10]

Over the next few years, although Devlin led to progressive doses of voluntary redundancy, wages rose dramatically. In fact national average earnings of dockers increased by more than half between 1967 and 1970, and they were more successful than most in bypassing Labour's pay restraint policies.

Although the introduction of a shop steward system had been seen by Devlin as a means of curtailing stoppages of work the number of disputes actually shot up, as stewards fought to improve dockers' pay and conditions.[11] On Merseyside (Liverpool and Birkenhead), a port shop stewards' committee developed within a year of Devlin, strongly committed to 'Broad Left' policies (the CP had long had an influence in the Liverpool docks). By the end of 1969 the stewards' committee had taken the local official machinery of the TGWU over completely. By contrast, in Hull, the weakness of the CP and the continued existence of the 'Blue Union' (as the NASD was known) as a significant force meant that the Hull stewards' committee, which had become established by 1968, remained entirely independent of, and frequently at odds with, TGWU officials.

In London a joint union stewards' committee linking all sectors of the large (23,755 registered dockers in 1967) and geographically far-flung (with docks and wharves spread over 35 miles of river) port did not emerge until 1972. Not only did the Blue Union retain the allegiance of a substantial minority who were very critical of the TGWU, but the notable CP tradition, which provided the main focus of militant activity, was relatively weak outside the biggest sector of the port, the Royal Docks. This was compounded by the widespread and divergent nature of the various sectors of the port, reflected in strong currents of parochialism and inter-sector hostilities. The left in the Royal Docks had rendered ineffective the ban that the TGWU officials had initially attempted to impose on Communists standing as stewards. But the overall weakness of the shop stewards' movement in London meant that full-time officials and lay committees of both unions retained much greater influence over policy than in Liverpool and Hull.[12]

The campaign against the effects of containerisation

By the beginning of the 1970s it became clear that the major threat to dockers' jobs and working practices came not from the formal modernisation scheme but from the employers' exploitation of changes in cargo handling techniques. The most important was containerisation, which drastically reduced the number of times that goods had to be handled and raised the spectre of large scale redundancies among registered dockers. Between 1966 and 1972 about 20,000 registered dockers' jobs had been lost, nearly one third of the register, and many more were threatened.[13] Containerisation also made it possible for employers to escape the legal constraints of the National Dock Labour Scheme by moving the 'stripping and stuffing' of containers away from ports to inland container depots and cold stores. Here fewer workers unloaded ever larger cargoes, under poorer conditions and at lower rates of pay than dockers could command, at sites where union organisation was far weaker or non-existent. Container depots began to appear in all parts of the country, as far inland as Cambridge and Birmingham, as the employers used the new transport technology as a weapon to break the National Dock Labour Scheme and reorganise the ports industry to their advantage. In this process the container depot workers were pawns in the employers' strategy.

The dock unions had been aware of the threat that containerisation posed in the 1960s, but the Labour government ignored union pressures until an unofficial strike in November 1969 against the closure of Hays Wharf spread to most of the port of London. Within a few days the government had established the Bristow committee, which recommended that work previously done by dockers should be defined as dockwork, within a five-mile corridor each side of the River Thames. But the government did nothing to implement the report, in spite of a national one-day strike in March 1970. The wharves stayed closed and 2,000 men were transferred to other sectors of the port, while Hays Wharf developed container and cold storage facilities at Dagenham.

Such developments spurred on the emergence of a national ports shop stewards' committee despite hostility from full-time union officials. The first national unofficial meeting of stewards had taken place in 1969, dominated by stewards from Liverpool and London (which effectively meant the Royal Docks), and by the CP. They met again to support the call made by the Liaison Committee for the Defence of Trade Unions (LCDTU) for a national protest strike against the Industrial Relations Bill in December 1970. This call was supported by most dockers. But the weaknesses in the shop stewards' position in the years 1969-71, compounded by the divisive effects of the port-by-port negotiations over the second stage of the Devlin scheme, were highlighted during the official national docks strike in July 1970. The militant stewards proved unable to shift the issue of pay to the defence of jobs, and the strike remained firmly under the control of full-time officials. It was settled by a deal between Jones, the employers and the newly elected Conservative government.[14]

When the economy started faltering in the second half of 1971, the crisis over jobs in the ports intensified and led to moves to reconvene the national stewards' committee in December 1971, with representatives from London, Liverpool, Southampton, Preston, Hull and Manchester.[15] The stewards launched a campaign to make the introduction of containerisation operate for the benefit of dockers (improved pay and conditions) rather than for the employers (who were looking for lower labour costs). They demanded a reduction in the working week, early retirement, no redundancies, and for all unregistered ports to be brought into the National Dock Labour Scheme. They also insisted that the 'unattached register', the labour pool in which dockers regarded by employers as being 'surplus to requirements' were provided with half pay, be purely temporary for dockers in transit from one employer to another. The stewards' first move was to call a one-day unofficial national strike on 26 January 1972, supported by over 25,000 dockers. The TGWU leadership refused to recall the union's docks delegate conference, the body that could formally decide on official strike action in the docks.[16] On 7 March up to 14,000 London dockers took unofficial strike action to support some 50 men whose jobs were under threat, against a background of a huge growth in the unattached register. But Liverpool and other ports resisted London proposals for an immediate national strike.[17]

While the unattached register dominated the national docks scene early in 1972, in Liverpool the container issue blew up into a major dispute when dockers' unofficial action came into direct conflict with the Industrial Relations Act. An unofficial joint TGWU committee of dockers and lorry drivers which met in the TGWU offices in Liverpool gave transport firms until 20 March to sign a document giving guarantees on drivers' terms and conditions, and on container loads. After this date the committee mounted an unofficial blacking campaign at the docks of road haulage companies that handled containerised traffic using unregistered labour.[18] Heaton Transport, a firm based in St Helens, sought redress from the National Industrial Relations Court (NIRC). On 23 March the court instructed the TGWU to stop its docker members blacking Heaton's lorries, as it was an 'unfair industrial practice' and the union was responsible for the actions of its shop stewards. In line with TUC policy, the TGWU refused to attend the NIRC, and Jones insisted that the union would uphold the TUC policy of boycotting the working of the Industrial Relations Act. But Jones also instructed local TGWU officials to press for the blacking to be lifted:[19]

> I applied all the pressure I could to get negotiations going and to persuade our members to cool down…and I personally made appeals by telephone to shop stewards in the Liverpool docks. They listened to my views and in response told me that the dockers were at boiling point; the work was moving away from dockland 'like butter melting in the sun'.[20]

Most of the national media did not report the case for a week—it was overshadowed by the government's declaration of direct rule in Northern Ireland. But on 29 March that changed when the NIRC fined the TGWU £5,000 (suspended for two weeks) for contempt of court for failing to obey the court's order.

Jones now made desperate attempts to convince the government and the NIRC that the union was doing everything it could to end the blacking campaign. But Sir John Donaldson, the NIRC president, insisted that the union would be deemed to be implicitly endorsing the actions of its members unless those actions were specifically disavowed and the members disciplined. When the fine was not paid the union received the following letter from the NIRC, a classic example of legal jargon:

> You will note that in accordance with section 47(3)(a) of the Criminal Justice Act 1967 as applied to this Court by paragraph 28 of Schedule 3 to the Industrial Relations Act 1971, the Order specifies the Bow Street Magistrates' Court (South Westminster Petty Sessional Division), Bow Street, London WC2, as the Court for the purposes of collection, enforcement and remission of the fine. You will further note that *the Writs*

of Sequestration to be sued out are not to issue for a period of three weeks from
the date of the enclosed Order and that execution under any such Writ
is not to be proceeded with unless the amount of the fine payable remains unpaid after the expiration of such period.[21] (added emphasis)

Many dockers believed that Jones was supportive of their stance but
that he had to be seen publicly calling for the blacking to be lifted.
Nonetheless a 5,000-strong mass meeting of Merseyside dockers on
9 April voted to defy the court order and ignore the pleas of their
union officers.[22] When it became clear that the TGWU leadership
could not persuade the stewards to lift the boycott, Heaton went
back to the NIRC. On 20 April a further fine of £50,000 was imposed and the union warned that continued defiance of the court
could lead to the seizure of all its assets.[23]

Although some Liverpool stewards and dockers now called for an
immediate strike, the majority of stewards were still unwilling to escalate the conflict. For example, shop stewards' chairman Jimmy
Symes said on 21 April, the day after the fine, 'The dockers are in a
mood to strike… The shop stewards have exercised a restraining influence for about a fortnight, but today more so'.[24] The stewards feared
that a political fight against the Industrial Relations Act would mar-
ginalise the jobs issue. They also did not want to make an even more
explicit challenge to the authority of the TGWU general secretary.
Nonetheless the refusal of the stewards to call off their unofficial
blacking led them inexorably in this direction.[25]

The official TUC boycott collapses

There was widespread support in the Conservative Party and the
press for a 'showdown' with the unions in general and the dockers in
particular,[26] although the miners' strike had shown that a direct attack
on strongly organised workers was very risky. The developing railway pay dispute and the container issue both seemed to offer possibilities for demonstrating firmness. In the event, neither turned out
as prime minister Edward Heath and his cabinet colleagues had hoped
for.[27]

We have seen in Chapter 3 that when the TUC's 'inner cabinet',
the Finance and General Purposes Committee (F&GPC), met on
Monday 24 April in the wake of the railway unions facing a cooling-
off order it agreed that guidelines should be drawn up concerning

the circumstances in which unions could attend the NIRC. The same meeting discussed the TGWU fines and it was noted, probably by TUC general secretary Vic Feather, that:

> ...if the committee decided to support the T&GWU, the TUC might also become liable for contempt of court, and its funds, and the funds of affiliates, thereby put at risk. This might lead to a confrontation between the trade union Movement and the State, and it was a battle which the Movement was unlikely to win.

Despite this, the committee ambiguously recommended support for the TGWU 'in its actions'.[28] This was queried at the full General Council two days later. Jones argued that the union was 'prepared to face sequestration...if that was the wish of the Movement'. That he did not want that to happen was clear from his following comments:

> His interpretation of the [F&GP] Committee's recommendation would be that the General Council considered that the T&GWU should continue not to appear before the NIRC; would support the T&GWU in continuing that action; and would give the necessary financial aid... So that there was no misunderstanding about...[what] would arise if the Union were sequestrated...the Union had twelve hundred employees who would need to be paid wages...legal complications might arise...

Jones then tried to propose a motion on this that was ruled out of order. In the debate he argued that 'it must be clearly understood that if the T&GWU submitted to sequestration the TUC immediately became *absolutely and entirely involved*' (added emphasis). Despite this threat, the vote to refer back the F&GPC's support for the TGWU was only narrowly won by 16 to 14.[29] The committee met straight after the General Council and now advised the TGWU 'that the fine should be paid' as the union was 'faced by the possibility of sequestration'. It was feared that otherwise the TUC would itself be threatened by the law:

> If the TUC decided to support the T&GWU, the TUC itself might also become liable for contempt of court, and its funds, and the funds of its affiliates, thereby put at risk... It would be wrong for the TUC deliberately to court actions for damages by putting itself in a position where it was clearly contravening the law, just as it would be wrong for the TUC deliberately to encourage unions to break the law. It was therefore proposed that the T&GWU should be advised that the fines should be paid.[30]

Len Murray, the TUC assistant general secretary at the time, later explained:

> The TUC was pragmatic. Whenever we said we're going to stand up to the law...we never sought to destroy the law. That was always its whole attitude. Ultimately the bottom line was survival, continuity and respect for the law and acknowledgement of the democratic process as distinct to the revolutionary process.[31]

Although Jones publicly opposed the change in TUC policy, he dismissed the proposal, put forward by several members of the union's lay general executive council on 1 May, to defy the law by calling for a national strike of the whole of the TGWU's 1.75 million membership. Instead, after a statement from the union's lawyers that sequestration was now imminent, Jones managed to convince the executive to pay the fines, although this was only agreed after a four-hour meeting by the casting vote of the chair, Len Forden, following an 18 to 18 split.[32] Jones recalled, 'I knew what they [the dockers] were doing and I had a great deal of sympathy for them... But it would have been foolish for the union to say that it would declare full support for the picketing because that would have immediately brought down the new law, sequestration and all that followed with it'.[33]

Earlier the same day a specially convened TUC F&GPC had recommended that unions should have the right to defend themselves at the NIRC, without prior consultation with the General Council, 'where an offensive action is being taken against a union or its members'.[34] The TUC had started its retreat on the Industrial Relations Act.[35] At a full General Council meeting three days later a move against this recommendation was lost by the large vote of 21 to 5—only Lawrence Daly of the National Union of Mineworkers (NUM), Les Buck of the sheet metal workers and Hugh Scanlon of the Amalgamated Union of Engineering Workers (AUEW) were identified in the minority. Scanlon, who had not been present at several recent meetings, drew out the implications of the TUC decision:

> The AUEW understood Congress policy to be that no union should register or should appear before NIRC or participate in its proceedings, and that unions should act as though NIRC did not exist. That was Congress policy. The Trade Union Movement could not on the one hand have such a policy, and the General Council on the other deviate from it immediately they were faced with a crisis. The General

Council had now put the Movement on a slippery slope which would lead to co-operation with [the] NIRC.[36]

On the day that the TGWU executive was deliberating over paying the fines, Monday 1 May, Southampton dockers were on a 24-hour strike against the fine while Merseyside and Preston dockers struck to celebrate May Day.[37] At the May Day demonstration in Liverpool against the Industrial Relations Act and the Conservative government, Jimmy Symes, shop stewards' chair, remained defiant:

> There was obviously going to be a confrontation after the Industrial Relations Act and it just so happens we were the first in the firing line. It is a bad law and we, as good trade unionists, cannot sit by and let it run its course… We all like Jack Jones in Liverpool. But, without any hard feelings, we think Jack is wrong. We believe that a union is only governed by the members and we, as shop stewards, are the representatives. The fines on the T&G are merely sabre-rattling by the NIRC and we will not let them deflect us from what we believe is our right, that dockers must handle all container work.[38]

A few days later the TGWU was again threatened with sequestration by the NIRC, following a further complaint from Heaton about the continuing blacking action, unless the union could demonstrate that it would make a serious effort to implement the court's orders by disciplining its stewards and withdrawing their credentials:

> The union is accountable if its officers, officials, representatives or shop stewards do their union work in breach of the law. It is for the union to see that they do not break the law. If they persist in doing so they are unworthy of the union's trust and of continuing in office. The various officials who have given evidence may well be right when they say that the withdrawal of the credentials of the shop stewards…at this moment would be damaging to industrial relations. They may also be right that such action could lead to a strike and great damage to the economy. These…are short-term dangers. They must be faced in order that in the longer term we may have an orderly system of industrial relations… This will take leadership and courage in full measure. Surely the union has both.[39]

The union was given 21 days to comply with the ruling, but appealed against the judgment to the Court of Appeal, thus suspending the deadline.[40]

On May Day, the national port shop stewards' committee had extended the blacking campaign to two transport firms in each port across the country. In Hull this quickly led to another court case, brought by the firm Panalpina, against the chair of the Hull port shop stewards' committee, Walter Cunningham (who refused to attend the NIRC), and the TGWU (whose regional officer, David Shenton, did attend to argue the case). This was the first time a TGWU official, as opposed to lawyers acting for them, had appeared at the NIRC. He was credited with arguing that the 'chances of persuading the dockers to abandon the blacking would be very much reduced, if not permanently destroyed, if the union took punitive action against stewards'. The *Financial Times* commented that this was the first indication that the union was even considering this. One fear expressed by another union officer was that action against the stewards could result in TGWU members joining the NASD.[41]

Again the NIRC ordered the blacking to stop, and again Jones advised the dockers to resume normal working. But a meeting of 1,700 Hull dockers voted to continue the action, and Cunningham insisted that if the court were to fine him he would not pay it: 'If ultimately I am faced with going to jail, there are plenty of lads here ready to step into my place'.[42]

In response to the mounting crisis, union leaders and government ministers had discussions about offering a sufficiently high voluntary severance inducement to deal with the alleged 'surplus labour' in the registered ports. But the unofficial movement was totally opposed to this approach, and Jones had to insist publicly that defence of dockers' jobs was the key issue. In order to regain the initiative, a resolution had been agreed at the 1 May TGWU executive meeting on 'the need for leadership to be given to the Docks Membership in pursuit of the Union's official policy'.[43] A docks delegate conference was convened on 4 May, at which Jones proposed giving the employers 28 days notice of a national strike. This move did not impress the shop stewards' leaders, as the *Morning Star* reported:

> The...moves toward calling a national official strike...[were] criticised by rank-and-file militants as a 'sham'. They pointed out...that the docks' shop stewards have led the fight against the bosses' attacks on the DLBS [Dock Labour Board Scheme] with precious little assistance from the national officials of the union. Now, when the dockers were on the move, the union was stepping in officially. Stewards feared that the only purpose in calling an official strike would be that it would give the union's national officials the power to call it off.

They remember...1970, when the union called off the national docks strike.[44]

Following one postponement, hundreds of dockers massed outside the TGWU headquarters in Smith Square on 14 June and protested when the docks delegate conference (by 49 to 32 votes) again delayed the threatened official national strike for six weeks. This was to allow an inquiry into job security headed by Jones and Lord Aldington, a friend of Heath and a former government minister who was now chair of the Port of London Authority.[45] Although the call for national action by leaders of the TGWU was aimed at taking the initiative in the fight away from the stewards, the strike demand had now become one supported by the rank and file and the stewards. But Jones's attempt to upstage the national stewards' committee was immediately threatened by further intervention against the dockers by the NIRC.

Chobham Farm

With the unofficial national decision to extend the blacking of haulage firms, London stewards had selected Dagenham Cold Storage and UK Cold Storage, which shared the same site. They reinforced the existing blacking of Midland Cold Storage. But few drivers honoured the ban, and most traffic was diverted to other ports. The stewards decided to directly picket the depots and to black all firms using them. With this also not fully working, a group of young stewards from the Royal Docks took the initiative to picket the Chobham Farm site in Stratford, east London, where lorries turned away from Dagenham were being diverted. Although Bernie Steer and Vic Turner, secretary and chair of the London (and Royal Docks) joint union stewards' committee (and leading member and very close sympathiser of the CP respectively), initially argued against this move their objections were overruled in practice by the site being picketed again. A mass picket of around 1,000 gathered on 6 June. The number of lorries crossing the picket was reduced after a few days to a few hard-core offenders. After three weeks the firm indicated its willingness to accept a TGWU proposal to take on registered dockers and gradually phase out 'non-dockers' who were being paid considerably less. But the docks stewards insisted there should be no dismissals, as Turner explained:

> We wanted to stop the lorries actually going into the place. And we
> spoke to various people who worked there and said... 'Our object is not

to get you put on the dole queue but to maintain this as registered dock work... I ensure you that you will not be flung out of work, we'll see to that'.[46]

But the Chobham Farm drivers (also in the TGWU) and warehouse workers did not believe that the dockers would defend their jobs. Thus it was the Chobham Farm stewards, not the company, who now applied to the NIRC for an order to stop the dockers picketing the depot and blacking firms that used it. On 12 June the NIRC obliged, naming the shop stewards' committee of the port of London and three dockers (Steer, Turner and Alan Williams), but not the TGWU or the NASD. Donaldson made no attempt to include the trade unions in the order, clearly accepting that there was no point in proceeding against them.[47] When the ruling was announced, Steer defiantly declared:

> The shop stewards will continue to picket Chobham Farm—Donaldson or no Donaldson—until our men are in there doing work which we rightly claim is ours. No court will intimidate us to do otherwise. If we break the law defending our jobs, that's their problem not ours.[48]

On the same day the AUEW president, Scanlon, saluted the dockers, and attacked the retreat of the TUC General Council and appearances 'of certain affiliated unions' at the NIRC:

> The dockers up and down the country, who have consistently voted to continue blacking...are setting the finest possible example to the movement... They are carrying out the policy of both the Croydon special conference and the 1971 TUC Congress to the letter... [This policy] has now been over-ruled by the TUC General Council...[which had] taken this line under pressure from certain affiliated unions faced with injunctions and fines, who were not prepared to make a stand... The result has been that, at the first whiff of gunpowder, an undignified retreat has been made.[49]

On the following day, 13 June, the Court of Appeal unexpectedly upheld the TGWU's appeal against the NIRC orders in the Heaton and other cases, and set aside the fines, thereby compounding the government's problems. Lord Denning, Master of the Rolls (senior judge of the Court of Appeal) from 1962 to 1982, decided to quash the previous NIRC judgment on a number of grounds. The TGWU had done all that it reasonably could to carry out the court's orders, withdrawing credentials from shop stewards was unlikely to have any effect, and parliament had not specifically required that an unregistered union should be penalised for the actions of its stewards. It was therefore unjust for the union to be penalised simply because it was not registered under the act.

Denning's overriding concern was to defend the majesty of the law and strengthen public consensus about the 'impartiality' of British justice in the face of criticisms of the political bias of the NIRC.[50] But his ruling that unions were not liable for the behaviour of their shop stewards came, in the words of government minister Robert Carr, like a 'torpedo below the waterline', and effectively destroyed the basis of government strategy.[51] It opened the way to the very outcome that ministers had believed was impossible under the act—the 'martyrdom' of individual trade unionists—because redress could now be sought only from workers who were engaging in unlawful action. The judgment caused Heath to fume, 'This was exactly what the union militants wanted. Even though they had been using their strength to bully and blackmail the nation, they could now pose as the underdogs'.[52]

Geoffrey Howe, Solicitor-General, speculated on the reasons for this 'remarkable twist':

> Denning had, for many years, been giving judgments that were skilfully designed—so far as judge-made law could achieve it—to curb the excessive power of trade unions. Why then this tragic aberration? I suspect that he and his Appeal Court colleagues were…wary…of the novelty that was the National Industrial Relations Court. They felt the need to demonstrate in some way that, no less than the rest of the High Court, it was subject to their surveillance. There may even have been a touch of jealousy at the attention that was being paid to the crisp clarity of Mr Justice Donaldson's written judgments. Judicial prose of a quality to command the front page of the tabloid press had previously been Lord Denning's virtual monopoly.[53]

As the NIRC had already made an interim order against three of the stewards picketing Chobham Farm, Donaldson now altered this to one threatening them with imprisonment for contempt if they did not attend the court by 2pm on Friday 16 June and satisfactorily explain their conduct: 'No one likes or approves of all the law but we cannot pick and choose. Either we live by the rule of law and all the law or we abandon the way of life which we have known for centuries… Our duty is to uphold the rule of law and act as Parliament directed us'.[54] The national port stewards' committee met immediately and called for an indefinite national docks strike if any of the three were imprisoned, and unofficial strikes broke out at most ports across the country during Thursday and Friday involving about 35,000 dockers.

On the previous Saturday, 10 June, an LCDTU conference, attended by over 1,200 delegates from 500 union branches and shop stewards' committees, had already called for strike action if any trade unionist was imprisoned by the NIRC.[55] Messages of support with promises to strike now poured in from stewards' and union organisations in manufacturing, mining and transport. Car workers from a number of sections at British Leyland's Longbridge plant in Birmingham took strike action on the Friday, and the works committee, representing 25,000 workers, said it would propose factory-wide strike action to a meeting of the plant's shop stewards on the Monday.[56] The cabinet went into emergency session as the pound sterling, already weakened by rumours of higher inflation and fears of industrial conflict, came under greater pressure. The cost of government intervention to hold down the exchange rate within the limits set by the Common Market currency agreement intensified rumours of devaluation. A week later, after the panic had passed, the pound was allowed to float—in effect, a devaluation of the currency.[57]

The three stewards cited for contempt refused to appear before the court, and the union representing two of them, NASD, rejected offers from the TGWU to provide the services of the latter's lawyers if the three men would allow themselves to be represented in court.[58] Instead, on the Friday, the stewards and several hundred dockers formed a mass picket at Chobham Farm to greet the court tipstaff who was due to arrest the three men. But no arrests took place.

On the Friday morning there had been a meeting between Heath, Howe and the Attorney-General, Sir Peter Rawlinson.[59] It is quite possible that this started the train of events that led to the intervention of the Official Solicitor, an obscure functionary who acted for people unable to represent themselves in legal matters (such as children). Denning engineered a meeting on the Friday between the Official Solicitor and Peter Pain QC, who normally acted for the TGWU. This enabled the Official Solicitor to instruct Pain to apply to the Court of Appeal to set aside the committal orders due to a technicality, that the evidence fell 'far short of that required to deprive a man of his liberty'.[60] Labour Party leader Harold Wilson was moved to comment, 'Even Gilbert and Sullivan could not have envisaged the dramatic intervention in court of a good fairy in the unlikely shape of the Official Solicitor'.[61] Poking fun at the government was a lot easier for the Parliamentary Labour Party than supporting the dockers, however.

Denning later explained, 'We were influenced perhaps by the state of the country, by the realisation that there would be a general strike, which would paralyse the whole nation'.[62] Whatever the nature of the intrigue that lay behind the quashing of the contempt order, it could not alter the fact that the Court of Appeal had forced the NIRC into a direct conflict with individual stewards. It simply delayed a clash until a new case appeared. This duly happened a fortnight later.

Midland Cold Storage

The dockers' nationwide strike action in support of the three shop stewards threatened with imprisonment inflicted a major political setback for the Conservative government. It proved that militancy, solidarity and determination at rank-and-file level could break the union laws.

The Chobham Farm events and their aftermath were to give added urgency to TUC and government attempts to reach an accommodation. Thus on Monday 26 June, three days after the pound was allowed to float, the TUC General Council gave a clear signal that it was willing to reach an arrangement with the government on the economy, including being prepared to discuss an incomes policy. It called on the government to suspend the operation of the Industrial Relations Act (not to repeal it) on the grounds that this law was 'acting against *the national interest*' (added emphasis).[63] Like the Labour Party, the TUC believed in some classless national interest rather than in class interests.

At the same time the TUC F&GPC considered a document *Industrial Relations Act: Review of the Situation*, which stated the TUC officials' view that 'a policy of using industrial action to compel the present government to repeal the Act would not be effective'. It noted that 'there will be outbursts of industrial action and other hostile demonstrations, which neither unions themselves nor the TUC will be able to restrain'. But there was 'no evidence that the affiliated unions have reached the point where they would be prepared to hand over to the General Council the authority to use the strike weapon for what would in fact be a political purpose'.[64] The union leaders were clearly aware that events could get out of their control.

Meanwhile the dockers' unofficial movement scored an important victory when the Chobham Farm management signed an agreement with the TGWU to employ registered dockers to 'stuff and strip' containers, with an initial intake of 40 dockers. The existing workforce was found alternative jobs in security, vehicle control and other ancillary areas on the same pay as the dockers. It gave a further spur to the campaign, and picketing and blacking of vehicles was now concentrated at Dagenham Cold Storage and Midland Cold Storage. However, after the imposition of a complete black on Hays Wharf Transport, one of the largest firms in London, there was a marked deterioration of relations with stewards from the TGWU's Road Transport Commercial trade group when some of the blacked lorry drivers put up counter-pickets across the docks from 18 July.[65]

On 4 July Midland Cold Storage applied to the NIRC for an order to stop the dockers picketing. The court summoned seven named dockers (including Steer and Turner) to appear before it. When they did not comply it granted a temporary order restraining them from blacking or encouraging others to black lorries entering or leaving Midland's depot. The seven said that they would ignore the order and continue the picket. Turner remembers:

> We made sure that everybody knew that there would be a dock gate meeting every morning so we could give them an up-to-date state of the poll... You could always rely on about 3-4,000 turning up for a daily meeting... We had our meetings in the open air, we had nothing to fear... This is why the newspapers and television attacked me and Bernie Steer. They couldn't attack what we stood for because we were explaining to our members exactly what was happening and they were supporting us. So they tried the old personal attacks, but actually what that done was only strengthen things.[66]

Midland Cold Storage, which *Socialist Worker* spectacularly exposed as being owned by the giant Vestey Corporation, one of the world's largest meat companies,[67] returned to the court to ask that the seven be punished for not obeying the order. On Friday 21 July Donaldson issued warrants for the arrest of five of the dockers (the evidence against the other two was alleged to be inconclusive). Most dockers believed that the decision by Midland was not taken in isolation. They were convinced that the government had finally determined on an open confrontation, a view reinforced by the timing of the arrests. They took place at the beginning of the two-week summer holiday period in many of the important industries (including car manufacture, engineering and mining) where the dockers had been promised strike support. The government had also been making contingency plans to cope with a dock strike for some time. The dockers thought that the cabinet had decided that its overall industrial policy, and the success of the Jones-Aldington committee, required that the militants should be decisively defeated.[68]

Pentonville

Once the decision was taken to arrest the five dockers there were immediate stoppages of work across the port of London and a mass picket of over 500 dockers outside the Midland Cold Storage Depot. But the named stewards decided not to risk a confrontation with the police by resisting arrest. The four apprehended that day were placed in Pentonville prison, while the fifth was found picketing the prison the next day!

> Vic Turner suddenly appeared in the picket lines outside the prison…
> Turner, angry about newspaper reports that he had gone into hiding,
> refused to talk to reporters. But later, after speaking to senior police officers he relented… 'I have come down here to show that I am not in
> hiding. I am not a wounded animal or a criminal.' Mr Turner, wearing
> a smart grey striped suit with brown shirt and matching tie [sic], rejoined
> the…picket line but later he was arrested and taken into the jail.[69]

Immediately after the initial arrests on the Friday an impromptu meeting of dockers decided to shift the centre of picketing to Pentonville prison. This was to become the unofficial 24-hour organising centre of the dockers' movement over the next five days, as the small picket on Friday night was swollen by large numbers of dockers, and other trade unionists and socialists. The mood of the picket was set by the group of mainly younger dockers and stewards who had taken the initiative at Chobham Farm. Pentonville became a symbol of resistance to the Conservative government as Saltley gates had in the miners' strike five months earlier. Eddie Prevost, a TGWU activist and CP member who later joined the International Socialists (IS), recalled:

One of these stewards who read *Socialist Worker* said, 'Come on…we'll go and put a picket round the 'ville while they're in the nick'… We rushed down, put a picket round, and…the picket became the nerve centre of the strike, the focus of the strike. On the one hand you had the Industrial Relations Act and the Court, and on the other hand you had the picket line, and that was the place that delegations of workers from across the country offered their support. This began the politicisation of the workers on the picket line, dockers and others. It was an amazing situation.[70]

Although the NASD, three of whose members were imprisoned, made the strike official, Jones made it clear there would be no visits by TGWU officers and his two members were to be given no assistance. Nonetheless the unofficial strike of London dockers spread immediately on the Friday to Liverpool, Manchester and Hull, with the rest of the scheme ports following on the Monday, with near 100 percent support. According to the Department of Employment, some 40,000 dockers were on strike between 24 and 26 July.

Pentonville became a centre from which delegates and flying pickets were sent to call for secondary action in the form of strikes (very different from the secondary action asked for in the miners' strike) to force the release of the imprisoned dockers. The group of younger stewards decided that the first priority was to stop the national newspapers, then centred around nearby Fleet Street with over 25,000 workers,[71] knowing that this would have an immediate political and psychological impact. But the initial response was cool. Only the electricians seemed willing to stop work, but they were unwilling to act in isolation. The newspapers appeared the next morning and played down the significance of the jailings. Bob Light, a young IS member from the Royal Docks, explained:

On the first night the stewards very furtively, secretly, organised a couple of teams and went to Fleet Street, boldly to stop the presses— and they failed… They organised to go back on the Saturday, but this time they organised politically. So instead of…a small group of shop stewards, now rank-and-file dockers were positively invited to go and get in man-to-man arguments with printers about why they had a duty to their class to strike… We had a loud speaker and we went down Fleet Street that night marching from paper to paper in a procession of shouting and leafleting and cheering and arguing. We had a magnificent leaflet, printed by *Socialist Worker*, designed by Micky Fenn. It had five bars with the names of the five imprisoned, with the legend underneath: 'Five Trade Unionists Are Inside—Why Aren't You Out?' The attitude behind that kind of demand was total class defiance: 'Come out, it's a class battle'.[72]

Crucial to the dockers' eventual success in stopping the national newspapers was the existence of two different networks of socialists that existed within Fleet Street. First, there was the CP's network of members, which numbered about 100 including many 'fathers of the chapel' (FoCs, similar to shop stewards), with a significant base among the electricians.[73] Second, there was an informal London print workers' group that met in Fleet Street. Formed in 1968, it was a broad alliance of about 30-40 CP, Labour Party, IS and other left wing activists that produced a bulletin, the *Printworker*, which campaigned for militant policies on the basis of rank and file united action across the different union chapels.[74] Both these networks had been important in raising financial support for the miners' strike. They were now instrumental in ensuring that the delegations of dockers on the Saturday were able to meet virtually every FoC to put the argument for solidarity strike action. Micky Fenn, one of the rank-and-file docker activists, explained:

> It wasn't easy bringing out Fleet Street…but we went right up there and said to the FoCs, 'Look, your unions were always the ones at the front of the anti-Industrial Relations Act demos, and you know that if you were in the same position the docks would be out for you.' And they hung their heads low and had to agree.[75]

'Stop work' meetings were called at a number of newspapers in the early evening, resulting in some strike votes, and printers who had voted to strike then marched to other newspaper offices to urge support for the 'Pentonville Five'. The *Sunday Mirror* was the first to stop, and there was then a domino effect. John Mitchell, an FoC for the Society of Graphical and Allied Trades (SOGAT) on the *Sunday Express*, recalled:

> A meeting of all the FoCs was called in the King Ludd pub… The broad consensus was that we would meet again at midnight after we had held chapel meetings… Some chapels had dockers round, although we didn't. In the *Sunday Express* I convened a meeting, and I'll never forget it to my dying day. There was I, with all my perceived eloquence stating the case, and this little lad got up and said 'The way I see it these

guys haven't done anything wrong. They've done for their members what we expect our chapel officials to do for us. And it seems to me if they can do this to the dockers who's next? So I move that while they're in, we're out.' And out we went.[76]

Sean Geraghty, chair of the EETPU London Press branch, explained that the electricians proved crucial to encouraging action by other printers:

Basically the reason the papers shut down is because we shut them down. The electricians were the first ones to take action. Having made a decision to take action to support the five...we got around all the chapels...and we didn't have to put pickets up because once we switched off the machine there was nobody who would touch them. You had your particular role and responsibility and that was it.[77]

In the process, the National Society of Operative Printers and Assistants (NATSOPA) joint chapels' committee and its chair Bill Freeman (senior) endorsed the strike call. Only the *Sunday Times* was unaffected, while just a few editions of the other London-based Sunday papers were printed. Stopping the national daily papers proved a more difficult problem, although the momentum that had developed on the Saturday evening encouraged those printers who arrived for work on the Sunday to join the action. Richard Briginshaw, the NATSOPA general secretary, and officials from EETPU threatened disciplinary measures if their members took 'disruptive action'. But Vincent Flynn, the relatively new general secretary of SOGAT (who had close fraternal relations with IS in the early 1970s), issued an appeal to his members, and SOGAT chapels throughout Fleet Street voted to strike. NATSOPA and other smaller unions' chapels followed and, combined with the action by electricians, the national daily papers and the London evening papers did not reappear until Friday 28 July. This example was followed in many provincial centres, with no evening papers from Monday in both Manchester and Liverpool, for example. The impact inside the print unions was dramatic, as Mike Britton, NATSOPA convener ('Imperial chair') on the *Sunday Times*, explained:

By the Monday night it had become obvious we were going to have a major dispute on Fleet Street. I was summoned by Briginshaw and threatened with disciplinary action. But the fact that the lads had taken action without him meant he then had to get on the platform and say 'Right, I'm with you lads'. He saw it was the end of his era, because he didn't have that absolute control that he used to have… The membership of NATSOPA took control of our union, briefly for four days. The same was true in other unions, they took charge of their own destiny.[78]

On the Saturday morning a rally at Clerkenwell Green, which had been organised in support of a print workers' occupation against job loss at Briant Colour Printing, was swollen by the arrival of hundreds of enthusiastic Fleet Street printers, and a decision was made to march to Pentonville prison. IS member Ross Pritchard takes up the story:

> Bill Freeman [of SOGAT] had access to a flatback lorry and about 2,000 set off behind this lorry and marched to Pentonville. It was a wonderful day, just marvellous. We had taken the police completely by surprise… We set this lorry up as a permanent platform and we had a steady succession of speakers… We said we were going to stay there until the dockers were released. Of course, people went home to get some sleep, but the picket never dwindled to any great extent, we were always getting replacements and people kept coming back. We set up an ad hoc committee to run the picket. There was Bill Freeman and his son, John Lawrence and me. In terms of the dockers there was Eddie Prevost, Micky Fenn, Bob Light and others. And we managed to work politically together with the Communist Party within this network without any rancour.[79]

The closure of the national newspapers and the Pentonville mass picket caught the imagination of many trade unionists around the country. It has been estimated that at the very least 90,000 workers (including 40,000 dockers) were on indefinite strike by the time the five were released on the Wednesday afternoon of 26 July. As many as a quarter of a million came out for one or two days, with longer strikes threatened if the men were not released quickly.[80] In addition, the South Wales district council of the NUM gave overwhelming support to a recommendation from their executive to strike from Thursday unless the five were released. Most importantly, the joint executives of the AUEW voted to call members out on the following Monday, 31 July, and to call on the TUC to organise a general strike on that day. Many other union branches, district committees and shop stewards' committees called on their union leaders and the

TUC to hold an official national strike. All of this happened despite the action being totally unofficial, with strikers facing opposition or indifference from union leaders, and while many of the strongest unionised sectors were on holiday.

The wave of solidarity action reflected the influence of socialists, particularly CP members, and the activity of the dockers centred around Pentonville. The CP industrial organiser, Bert Ramelson, convened an emergency 'industrial aggregate' of the London district on Sunday morning at which he called on members to 'spread the strikes to force the TUC to call a general strike until the dockers were released'.[81] The LCDTU, which had played a crucial role in leading opposition to the anti-union legislation, sent a formal letter to affiliated bodies calling for the implementation of the 10 June conference decision to organise industrial action in the event of legal intervention against the dockers. Noting that there had already been a 'considerable response', it urged: '…what is essential is to extend it until it reaches the proportions of a general strike and the trade union leadership is compelled to make it official'.[82] What effect this letter had in the circumstances is debatable.

On Saturday 22 July the *Morning Star* stated, 'A call for the most widespread possible strikes in support of the imprisoned dockers was made last night by Kevin Halpin of the Liaison Committee.' The editorial noted, 'The time for words has gone. Emergency action is the order of the day.' A CP statement urged 'mobilisation of the whole labour movement including industrial action'. Because of the strikes the *Morning Star* was then not published until the dockers were released. Certainly the majority of workplaces and employment sectors that were affected by strikes were those in which the LCDTU and the CP (and much smaller left-wing organisations such as IS) had a significant influence on trade union activity.[83]

Among those who came out on indefinite strike from Monday 24 July onwards were many of the unregistered dockers in south east and Humberside ports; tugboatmen and maintenance staff on the Mersey; fish porters at Fleetwood, Grimsby and Aberdeen, followed by trawler crews from Tuesday and Wednesday; lorry drivers in Liverpool; workers at Covent Garden fruit and vegetable market, and Smithfield meat market; ship repair workers in London and Birkenhead; workers on some major construction sites around the Humber, the Mersey, Scotland, South Wales and the Thames, and on a smattering of building sites in London and provincial cities; several breweries and container depots in London; most of the factories on the Kirkby industrial estate on Merseyside; miners in several pits which were working in South Wales, Yorkshire and Scotland; maintenance workers at British Leyland; Shotton steelworkers; and even the lorry drivers at Midland Cold Storage, who had been counter-picketing the docks, struck on the Tuesday.

Those who struck for one day before the five were released included thousands of engineering workers and transport workers in London (including London Transport bus drivers), Sheffield, Lincoln, the west of Scotland and other provincial centres; ground staff at Heathrow airport; steel workers in Yorkshire; engine drivers and station staff at Waterloo; shipyard workers in Birkenhead; council workers in Tower Hamlets, Lambeth and Brighton; and many other groups. Moreover, when the five dockers were released on the Wednesday afternoon of 26 July the movement of sympathy strikes showed every sign of growing.[84]

Central to the dynamic of the strike movement were the delegations of dockers from Pentonville who were sent to different workplaces across London, often following personal contacts made through the CP or other left wing groups which played a crucial role in galvanising solidarity action. In many, although by no means all, cases there was a positive response, although usually this was because the ground had already been prepared by socialist militants. Bob Light recalled:

> I was a 22-year old docker, I'd been working in the docks for two years. And I turned up at the World's End massive building site in Chelsea rather sheepishly and knocked on this little wooden door to be greeted by Frank Campbell, one of the IS builders, who said 'Thank God, you're here now'. And I just stood at the door while Frank went inside and shouted 'There's a dockers' picket line, everybody out'. And they all came out...
>
> And the story I can never erase from 1972...was that sometime on Monday afternoon the shop stewards decided there was one significant workplace that we had omitted, Heathrow Airport. And so I was dispatched with another docker and an IS engineering worker. The three of us drove into Heathrow absolutely contemptuous of all the security guards, drove up to Terminal One, demanded to see their convener and two hours later there were no holiday flights from Heathrow [due to action by ground staff]. This was the sheer sense of adrenaline

that happens when a class is on the move, and the class was on the move in those hot heady days of July 1972.[85]

There was clearly a gap between the widespread sympathy for the dockers inside the working class movement (alongside passive hostility to Heath) and actually coming out on unofficial strike—strikes generally took place only where there were organised groups arguing for them. Yet a demonstration to Pentonville prison on the Tuesday attracted 30,000 trade unionists gathered behind the Royal Docks shop stewards' committee banner, which bore the slogan 'Arise Ye Workers'. Mike Hicks, a SOGAT member on the *Daily Express* and secretary of the Fleet Street CP branch, remembers:

> It was a sight I've never seen before, because London was buzzing at the time with building sites. As the march approached one building site, we stopped about 25 yards away and a chant started for them to stop work... I spoke to the builders and asked them to stop and join the march. And to see them all coming down the scaffolding and jump on to the march...was marvellous. I've never seen anything like it before or since. With the newspapers stopped everyone was aware that there was something happening.[86]

The importance of the strike wave was much greater than the actual numbers involved might indicate. The strikes challenged not only the authority of official union leaderships, but also that of the judicial system and the government. In the process they challenged the British labourist tradition of keeping trade union activity separate from politics. For example, on Wednesday 26 July in Hull a meeting of 300 workplace and union branch delegates from most of the larger factories and construction sites, and from local government, railways and the docks, not only called for an all-out strike from Thursday but also demanded that the TUC call an indefinite strike to bring down the government.[87] Nonetheless this conscious challenge to the legitimacy of the state was generally limited and cautious. The extent to which the TUC General Council was concerned to prevent industrial militancy being used for political ends is explored in some detail below.

Yet although the dockers' leadership in London and Liverpool was dominated by members of the CP, which was strongly committed to defiance of the act, the port shop stewards did not seek confrontation with the NIRC, or with Jones and the leaders of the TUC. In fact they saw the legal and political dimension that their campaign had acquired as likely to divert attention away from the defence of jobs to larger political concerns.[88] This had been reflected in Steer and Turner's initial attempt to keep the picketing in London to a minimal level. Turner, a very close CP supporter, explained:

> …we supported the protests over the Act and we saw it as a threat, but we didn't actually address that situation like other trade unionists did because we were so concerned about our campaign over the erosion of our work… It was the Industrial Relations Act confronting us, and not us confronting the Industrial Relations Act. We had started our campaign before the Industrial Relations Act and we carried on in spite of it.[89]

Although the CP had earlier condemned the TUC General Council's advice to the TGWU to pay the fines it did not criticise the TGWU leadership. Yet this union had abandoned its boycott of the NIRC, agreed to pay the fines and made a serious attempt to persuade its docker members to drop their blacking. Following the imprisonment of the Pentonville Five the CP refrained from any direct criticism of Jones's refusal to organise solidarity or even publicly be seen to be supportive of their action. As a national political party, the CP merely demanded that the TUC call a one-day general strike rather than an indefinite strike to free the dockers, although many CP members were already campaigning for such a stoppage. This was a graphic illustration of its disintegration as a centralised organisation. It also did not seek to fuse explicit political demands for the overthrow of the Conservative government with its call for solidarity with the imprisoned dockers.

Such a cautious approach can partly be explained by the CP's left social democratic politics, which essentially believed in changing British society through parliamentary means with a strictly subordinate role for militant workers' struggle from below. It also reflected the contradiction between giving a lead to unofficial rank-and-file militancy and trying to cultivate influence amongst left-wing trade union officials (such as Jones) and Labour MPs. Because of the Industrial Relations Act, the struggle against the employers and the government now involved spreading industrial action in defiance of even left-wing union leaders. But the CP's ability to provide a national focus for coordinating militant rank-and-file activity in an independent political direction was considerably blunted, despite the activities of many of its individual members.

Meanwhile the Labour Party leadership, while keen to make as much political capital as it could at the expense of the Conservatives, avoided giving any credence to accusations that it had encouraged and supported the dockers. Reginald Prentice, Labour's shadow employment spokesperson and a TGWU-sponsored MP, gained massive media coverage for his denunciation of the unofficial leaders shortly after the arrests:

> They are absolutely wrong to organise picketing and blacking which have not got the support of their union. They are even more wrong to defy the order of the court. They have been looking for martyrdom for weeks. I have no sympathy for them and I don't think they deserve the support of other workers.[90]

He also said, 'The Industrial Relations Act is a bad law, but it is the law and no-one can claim to be above it'.[91] This was the standard Labour Party response to a deeply unpopular law.

Legal manoeuvres and the TUC general strike call

On the Saturday, 22 July, the TUC general secretary devoted most of a speech to attacking calls for a general strike: 'No responsible trade unionist…is wanting to call for a general strike… General strikes are very harmful indeed—not only harmful to the country, but harmful also to the trade union movement itself'.[92]

By the Monday, 24 July, the growing momentum of the unofficial strike movement forced the TUC to call off its tentative talks with Heath on the economy. The TUC F&GPC met in a normal scheduled meeting that afternoon. Some members urged a one-day stoppage, arguing that 'if the General Council did not themselves take action of this kind unofficial bodies would assume leadership'. But no decision was made other than to attend a meeting at Downing Street that evening provisionally arranged by Feather.[93] Heath duly met the committee at 7.30pm. He was informed that 'at its [regular] meeting on Wednesday the General Council would be confronted with demands for action which might prove difficult to resist'.[94]

On Wednesday 26 July, after five days of escalating unofficial strike action, the TUC General Council voted for a one-day national stoppage the following Monday. On the same morning the Law Lords overturned the Court of Appeal's ruling and declared that the TGWU was reponsible for the actions of its shop stewards after all. The five dockers were freed from prison (and the Law Lords reimposed the fines on the TGWU). The threatened one-day stoppage was called off. It was a stunning victory for rank-and-file militancy, and reflected the working class confidence that followed the miners' success only five months earlier. A combination of factors expedited the men's release. Most important was the developing unofficial campaign of strikes. But we need to understand the legal manoeuvres that were required to justify this about turn, and the role of the TUC General Council's decision.

Heaton had appealed to the House of Lords (the highest court in the land) against Denning's judgment that unions were not responsible for the actions of their stewards. After all, the blacking was continuing. When the Law Lords started hearing the case on 11 July, it was believed that their ruling would come after the courts' normal two-month summer break. Even by the end of what was an unusually short hearing on 19 July the judgment was still only expected on 31 July at the earliest.[95] But the arrest of the dockers on 21 July and the developing strike movement changed everything. According to Gerald Dorfman, senior Conservative ministers were confident on the Monday, 24 July, that the Law Lords would reverse the Court of Appeal judgment on the Heaton case and 'thus open the way for the jailed workers to be released', although they did not know when.[96]

Fred Lindop has suggested that 'at some time on Monday night or Tuesday morning, 24 and 25 July, the timetable was changed and the process accelerated'.[97] We now know that Lord Hailsham as Lord Chancellor told the Lord Chief Justice, Lord Widgery, early on the Tuesday morning that the Lords judgment would be given the next day, and his diary entry noted that it was 'confidently expected' that it would reverse the appeal court ruling.[98] Dorfman interviewed Conservative MP Nicholas Scott on the Wednesday and wrote, 'Ministers heard [on the Tuesday] that the Lords would give their judgment in the Heaton case the following day…[and] also heard the rumour that the news would be "good".'[99]

The TGWU was extremely concerned about the conduct of the case and later produced three letters for TUC General Council members. The last quoted the *Sunday Mirror* of 30 July stating that the NIRC president had met the 'Appeal Judges' (presumably the Law

Lords) in private on the night of Tuesday 25 July.[100] In an important article published in the *New Statesman* several months later, John Griffith reiterated many of the TGWU's concerns. He noted that the Official Solicitor had unsuccessfully attempted to get the NIRC to reconvene on the Tuesday afternoon so that he could apply for the dockers' release, and 'was told to apply "not later than Wednesday afternoon".' This was significant as the Law Lords gave their judgment 'in the late morning of Wednesday 26 July', only seven days after the hearing closed. It was a single judgment, which was 'uncommon', and 'it was handed to counsel, shortly before it was delivered, not printed (as is usual) but duplicated and with typed and manuscript corrections'.

Griffith argued powerfully that the NIRC's argument on the Wednesday afternoon—that the Law Lords' decision had 'entirely changed' the situation—conveniently ignored the fact that the dockers had been jailed for contempt of the NIRC,[101] which contempt they continued to refuse to purge,[102] and not for blacking. Reflecting on the events, the *Economist* commented that 'the government's attitude…was remarkably relaxed and it was plain that Mr Heath had decided this was not going to be his general strike week. By Wednesday it was clear why. The House of Lords handed down its ruling'.[103] At the heart of Griffith's explanation was the way in which 'constitutional principle' had been sacrificed to extract the government from a threatening situation:

> A political and economic crisis of possibly considerable proportions was avoided by…the speeding-up of the delivery of the House of Lords' decision…and…the discovery by the NIRC that, because of that decision, they could release the dockers. It appeared very much as if the judicial system had bent itself to the needs of the politicians and that…the principles of the rule of law to which the NIRC earlier paid such respect had been sacrificed to the expediency of the political and economic situation.[104]

Significantly, however, there was no need to assume there had been a 'conspiracy' between the judges and government ministers:

> The community of rulers is a close and narrow community. Judges and politicians do not have to agree on the details of policies, they do not have to belong to the same political party. *There is no conspiracy because there is no need for a conspiracy.* All share the same fundamental premises.

And one of these is the desirability of avoiding widespread industrial unrest.[105] (added emphasis)

The TGWU was also working hard behind the scenes to accelerate the legal process in order to get the pickets released, using their legal advisers to make contact with the Official Solicitor.[106] There was therefore a coincidence of interests which led the government and both the TGWU and TUC to want to extricate themselves from the rapidly escalating industrial unrest.

It is difficult to judge how important the role of the TUC was in the release of the dockers. Its most recent historian writes uncritically of 'the freeing of the "Pentonville five" following the TUC's threat of a one-day general strike'.[107] And this view tends to be accepted in most works of history or politics that refer to it, though two of this chapter's authors have both recently challenged this.[108] We have seen that TUC leaders made a veiled threat to Heath on the Monday evening. But when the TUC General Council met at its normal monthly meeting at 10am on the Wednesday, it was reported early on that 'the House of Lords would, that morning, give their decision on the appeal, and following that the Official Solicitor would probably go to the NIRC'.[109] This gives substance to Peter Paterson's account that when the General Council 'decided on the strike there was no one in the room who did not realise that the Official Solicitor was about his benign and healing work, and that the dockers were likely to be released from Pentonville that very afternoon'.[110] A few years later, Michael Moran observed of Paterson's article that 'I have received independent assurances that this is an accurate account'.[111]

The General Council minutes reveal that those present were aware that if the intervention of the Official Solicitor secured the quick release of the dockers the motion for a one-day strike 'would become academic'.[112] Jones has even recently claimed that 'we moved what you call a general strike in the knowledge that it wouldn't be necessary'.[113] Murray has also admitted that the TUC strike call did not lead to the dockers' release: 'I wish I could claim…that we were so powerful'.[114] However, the principle of supporting such a strike was at stake, and the debate was probably conducted little differently than if those present had not had a shrewd suspicion of the legal outcome. What was probably different was the scale of the vote.

The minutes of the meeting reveal how both left and right leaders were extremely wary of allowing industrial militancy to be used for political ends to challenge the government. Scanlon moved that the General Council 'call on all affiliated unions to organise a one-day stoppage of work and demonstrations on Monday next July 31' for the dockers' release. Jones seconded the motion and proposed an addendum of 'and for the repeal of the Industrial Relations Act'. In the debate Lord Cooper of the general and municipal union, the NUGMW, argued that 'a one-day protest could lead to protest beyond a day and to a general strike', while George Lowthian of the builders' union, UCATT, argued that going for the act's repeal 'would transform a one-day stoppage…into a political strike'. When some others followed this line of argument, Jones withdrew his addendum. We can only speculate on his motives for having proposed this in the first place.

Roy Grantham of the clerical workers' union, CAWU, repeated the argument that 'for the General Secretary to call a one-day official stoppage of the whole of the movement…could lead to the possibility of a general strike'. He then raised points reminiscent of those by many union leaders during the 1926 General Strike:[115] '…the action proposed…would be regarded by any Government as a challenge to its authority, and as a challenge to…the right of Parliament to create legislation and to ensure that it was carried out'. Frank Chapple of the EETPU was more forceful: 'No doubt some people thought that, if a crisis was created by a one-day general strike and a complete general strike, the General Council would win. They might however lose… He would not wish the democratic form of Government of this country to be changed as a result of strike action.' He was repeating the points he had made at a critical moment during the miners' strike earlier in the year.

TUC general secretary Feather responded, somewhat disingenuously, that 'any suggestion that the one-day stoppage could be construed as a political general strike could be dismissed quickly. To organise a political or general strike would certainly take more than five days'. Replying to the debate, Scanlon pointed out that 'the motion was *not* seeking a confrontation with Government, or a *revolution, or a general strike*' (added emphasis). Unions 'would be able to differentiate between a strike and a one-day stoppage of protest… A strike and a protest stoppage were not the same.' He concluded, 'He was sure that the carrying of the motion would in itself ensure speedy action by the Official Solicitor towards getting the dockers released'.[116]

Thus even Scanlon, who had taken the most uncompromising position regarding cooperation with the act, distanced himself from an openly political stance. The motion was passed by 18 to 7, with six abstentions. The TUC circular informing affiliated unions and trades councils was headlined 'Protest Stoppages of Work' (as was the one announcing its cancellation), and did not use the word 'strike'.[117]

The TUC's call was an attempt to assert some authority over an unofficial movement that was threatening to get out of control. As Sean Geraghty, chair of the EETPU London Press branch, suggested:

> It was becoming infectious, the troops were mutinying... There was such a reaction that [for] the TUC general secretaries...the only way to assert control was to try and get back in front of the members. I don't think at the time anyone thought the TUC would [call a one-day strike], but it was a rational thing for them to do...
>
> It wasn't difficult to see that without...official backing the thing could have spread to a complete shutdown of the transport industry, that could have brought the country to a standstill. Particularly, as when you get people out on strike it's often much more difficult to get them back in because they start raising all sorts of other grievances.[118]

The TUC's strike call to its affiliated membership of nearly 10 million was important not just because it underlined the gravity of the situation to the government. It was also an admission that trade union action could legitimately be used for political ends, whatever the protestations of the union leaders.

The five dockers were released from prison on the Wednesday afternoon to tumultuous scenes as thousands of demonstrators gathered to greet them. Ross Pritchard, NGA printer and editor of the *Printworker* bulletin, described the mood outside the prison:

> Of course, when the dockers were released there was massive jubilation, and you felt it had proved something, that you could do *anything* if you like. You could sense the power of the working class, you had seen it in action, and you felt you could only go forward from there. Everybody suddenly realised that they had been involved in quite a historical thing. People began to think of how working class power can change things.[119]

Most of the press, which reappeared on Friday 28 July, openly accepted that the dockers' release was a serious defeat for both the government and the 'rule of law'. Among the popular papers, the *Sun* summed up the feeling in its editorial, headlined 'The Edge Of The Abyss':

> The Cabinet, the TUC and the Labour Party were yesterday cautiously groping their way back from the brink of the worst national crisis for nearly half a century... With television dominated by the carnival-like scenes outside Pentonville prison and reality blunted by the absence of newspapers, even some politicians took time to realise how close the nation had drifted to chaos in five hot July days.[120]

Pentonville was an incredible victory. Denning later acknowledged, 'The political consequences were immense. The Industrial Relations Act had been shattered. The Government had set up the Industrial Court to enforce the Act. Yet it had been shown by events to be powerless'.[121] Thus by the end of July 1972, in the wake of industrial action by the miners, the railway workers and the dockers, the Conservatives' policies on both pay and industrial relations were in disarray.

Official strike

Before the dockers had a chance to catch their breath they were on strike again. The day after the release of the Pentonville Five the TGWU docks delegate conference voted (with delegates from unregistered ports abstaining) against the union leadership's recommendation to accept a government-backed Jones-Aldington interim report. This report, co-authored by TGWU general secretary Jones, offered only limited assurances about the severe haemorrhage of jobs in the industry. An official national strike, which had been threatened since early June, was agreed and began immediately.

During the unofficial strike over the Pentonville jailings Humberside dockers had picketed a number of Trentside wharves that operated outside the National Dock Labour Scheme. When 18 pickets achieved no response on 24 July, the next day some 800 achieved a different outcome, stopping all the wharves (including one where the pickets had to force their way through the gates). With the start of the official national dock strike on 28 July, picketing took place again. Following the decision of workers at Neap House Wharf to work normally from 7 August, on several occasions hundreds of pickets confronted hundreds of police, with arrests and injuries. One commentator saw this as the second of the 'two moments of drama' in the 1972 dockers' struggle, and another observed that 'this time, the police seemed determined not to be seen to lose as at Saltley'.[122]

Elsewhere the blacking of Heaton and Midland Cold Storage continued. Douglas Hurd, Heath's political secretary, recorded in his diary on 27 July, 'Crash into another tunnel as dockers reject Jones-Aldington Report and strike. Clear now that we live under chaotic tyranny of tyrants [trade union leaders] not knowing they are such and vassals usurping the power of barons'.[123] A state of emergency (the government's fourth in two years) was declared on 3 August, aimed at preventing possible food shortages.

However, apart from Neap House Wharf the strike was relatively passive, with the leading shop stewards failing to involve the mass of dockers in picketing. And with Jones refusing to call for solidarity action by lorry drivers or railway workers it also remained isolated. The strike ended after three weeks, when Jones managed to persuade a majority of the docks delegate conference to accept a deal involving only slight changes to the original package:

> …many more dockers were represented by the 30 votes cast at the conference to continue the strike than the 53 to stop it—something like 30,000 to 15,000… North Cornwall, where 66 dockers are employed, sends one delegate to the conference; the Royal Group of docks in London, with a membership of 4,000, sends just two, a splendid example of disproportional representation in action. Nor are the delegates directly elected by the rank and file…but…by…committees.[124]

There was fierce opposition from the national port shop stewards' committee and an 8,000-strong dockers' protest meeting in Liverpool. But the CP's criticism of Jones was again muted, despite the furious reaction from hundreds of dockers outside Transport House when news of the delegates' acceptance of the 'peace plan' was announced. Following Jones's refusal to address the dockers, a group of them burst into a press conference, denouncing the back to work decision. Journalists were ejected from the room, Jones's documents were torn up and a jug of water was thrown over him.[125] Yet when criticism of the TGWU leadership over ending the strike appeared in the *Morning Star*, the notes of discussions by union leaders in the CP indicated their objection to the 'unfruitful aspects…of the attacks on Jones'. Some CP bodies even complained that 'insufficient consideration was given to the role of Jack Jones… There were fears expressed that there may be a pushing of Jones into the position of opposition to the party'.[126]

The outcome of the three-week national docks strike was a reminder of the limitations of trade union struggle, and of the role of left-wing full-time union leaders, even during a period of general workers' advance. Yet the success of Pentonville was not wasted as it helped to spur rank-and-file building workers to escalate their own industrial action.

Chapter 6

The building workers' 'great revolt'

From early August to mid-September 1972, the last six weeks of the building workers' strike witnessed a massive assertion of rank-and-file control over the running of the dispute. Even in an exceptional year this was outstanding. It was more than a strike. It was a revolt.

The official union tactic, which began in late June, of increasing each week the number of selective stoppages in every region had limited impact, and by the beginning of August the national union leaders were desperate for a settlement. But the groundswell of militant opposition to what was perceived to be a 'sell out' was by then so widespread and increasingly organised that the national officials were not only forced to retreat, but were rapidly marginalised. The workers escalated the dispute into an all-out strike involving mass and flying pickets in which many Communist Party (CP) members were prominent at local level. Although the strike did not directly involve the government, the widespread use of picketing to win the dispute in the wake of similar tactics by miners and dockers proved to be a further embarassment for the Conservatives' industrial relations policies.

As with the Manchester engineering sit-ins, there was limited press coverage, and both disputes seemed overshadowed by events in the docks. The *Financial Times* was aware that, as the second largest private sector group after the engineers, the building trade negotiations would 'have a significant effect on negotiations elsewhere'.[1] Like engineering, the concentration of the national union leaders was on raising basic rates, but this struck a very different chord in the building industry and was a demand that workers could unite around.

As the main building employers' association later noted:

> We had scarcely started negotiations proper when there came the miners' strike and the subsequent Wilberforce award. Neither of these could have been foreseen on anything like the scale in which they materialised; they changed the whole complexion of industrial wage bargaining.[2]

Industrial relations in building

The strike was over the renegotiation of the collective agreement made by the National Joint Council for the Building Industry (NJC). In the late 1960s this covered approximately 850,000 employees. Separate agreements existed in civil engineering construction (150,000 employees) and local authority building (then just under 200,000), but the NJC agreement exercised 'a considerable influence' on these two sectors. There were other agreements for small sub-sectors such as demolition, felt roofing, tile fixing and mastic asphalt. But only two significant sectors of the industry tended to be relatively independent of NJC rates—electrical contracting (55,000 workers), and heating and ventilating (32,000).[3]

The dominant employers' body in the building industry was the National Federation of Building Trades Employers (NFBTE), with its 13,600 member firms in 1968. The exact number of employers in the industry has always been notoriously difficult to pin down, due to the presence of so many tiny firms and self employed workers. But the National Board for Prices and Incomes came up with 46,800 employing two or more operatives, of which about 36,000 were engaged purely on building activities.[4]

Trade unions faced extraordinary problems on building sites:

> The trade union organisation of construction workers and the regulation of their conditions by collective agreement present difficulties of an unusual kind... Any given building site will be the scene of work only for a period of months or at the most two or three years. Moreover as the normal sequence of building operations proceeds the composition and balance of the labour force on any particular site change from week to week; those engaged on site preparation will be gradually replaced by those...constructing the shell of the building, and they in turn will be replaced by those who perform the joinery, electrical work and internal decoration...
>
> The trade union organiser...except on the largest sites cannot create any enduring site organisation or rely on site representatives with any assurance of permanence. To these inherent difficulties...must be added...that the industry...is characterised by a multiplicity of small employers, and that many men move between construction and other industries according to employment prospects.[5]

Allied to this was an employers' blacklist that kept men off sites for years at a time. One Liverpool activist explained:

> You go along to a job that is advertising for men. If it's not too well organised you see the foreman about a start, and if he needs you he will normally say, 'Come back for a start on Monday, but before you go just drop your name and address in at the office'. And that's the catch you see, your name and address. They...then run through the lists and you can be sure that if you have worked on certain sites or been a steward before that, that when you turn up on Monday for the start that all vacancies have been filled.[6]

Historically, building unionism had been dominated by craft unions. Declining fortunes caused the merger of four, including three of the largest—the Amalgamated Society of Woodworkers (ASW), the Amalgamated Society of Painters and Decorators, and the Amalgamated Union of Building Trade Workers (AUBTW, which organised bricklayers and had a substantial labourers' section) into the Union of Construction and Allied Trades and Technicians (UCATT) by 1971: 'Between 1955 and 1971 the unions that formed UCATT experienced a drop of membership of some 31 per cent.' George Smith, ASW general secretary, wrote that 'the mergers...themselves mainly took place because of...[financial] difficulties in the building unions'. The cost base of the unions could not be cut because of the high officer-member ratio necessary in such a casualised industry.[7]

UCATT's withdrawal from the long-established National Federation of Building Trades Operatives (NFBTO) caused the latter's disbandment. The same happened to its short-lived successor, the National Federation of Construction Unions. As a result UCATT (with the bulk of the former membership of the NFBTO) became the 'dominant' negotiator in dealings with the employers, and 'there was no hiding behind the NFBTO or other unions should...national negotiations fail to "deliver the goods".'[8]

Of prime importance to all the unions was the way the workforce was divided between 'bona-fide' and 'labour-only' (lump) sub-contractors. The former took on specialist work for a main contractor and supplied their own materials, equipment and expertise, as well as providing a workforce with holiday stamps, insurance cards, tax deductions and so on. The latter provided labour only to the main contractor under a system where the individual building worker became self employed. Under this arrangement, although workers were able to secure relatively higher wages than union rates they lost the right to unemployment pay and other benefits.

The term 'lump' derived from the practice of doing the job for a lump sum, as in piecework. The obvious advantage to the main contractor in using lump labour, and having a contract negotiated outside union control, was that they avoided paying the tax necessary for a direct employee and were able to undermine national union agreements on hours, safety and apprenticeship training. For the trade unions the lump nullified the guaranteed weekly wage and contained the potential of being a 'scab's charter' by preventing trade union organisation, since such workers were nominally self-employed.[9]

There was 'an inverse and causal relationship' between labour-only sub-contracting (LOSC) and unionisation: '...as demand for labour grew in the industry, so did LOSC. In turn, as LOSC grew, union membership declined'.[10] It was a classic vicious circle. Between 1965 and 1973 the number of building workers classified as operating some form of labour-only contracts grew from an estimated 160,000-200,000 to 400,000.[11] The impetus for this was provided by acute shortages of skilled and unskilled labour within a boom period for construction in Britain. But while such a tight labour market forced firms to pay wages well above the nationally negotiated union rate many building workers did not feel the immediate need for shop stewards or trade unionism because they were in a position to do their own bargaining. As a result, trade unionism was drained of its membership in a climate normally understood as ideal for union growth.[12]

The difficulties of being a shop steward in the industry tended to militate against all but the most determined in taking up the position. Therefore the presence of CP members was often crucial for providing active leadership at site level in many of the larger cities. For example, in Liverpool a number of young militants, especially many of those who took up the stewards' position, were recruited into the CP, which established a dominant presence within the industry in the city.[13]

During the mid-1960s joint shop stewards' committees had begun to coordinate activities between stewards representing a variety of trades on different sites. In London a Joint Sites Committee was formed in 1963 with strong CP activist involvement following limited regional official action over a national pay claim. Lou Lewis, an ASW shop steward and CP member, recalled:

In 1963 we were out on strike for a week in London, and then the leadership sold us out. There was a lot of bitterness that they didn't advance the basic rate and the dispute had a big effect dividing the rank and file from the national leadership. So the three principal organised jobs in London decided we were going to set up an unofficial shop stewards' network and...we had what we called a Joint Sites Committee... Its main thing was to initiate action, to encourage workers to take action around the bonus and everything else, to increase the earning rate.[14]

Similar organisation was established elsewhere. In 1966 the Merseyside Shop Stewards' Building Operatives Committee and the Manchester Building Workers' Forum were formed. Such bodies tended to function usually on the big organised sites over specific issues before collapsing because of the victimisation of stewards or official union harassment, only to re-emerge later. In 1967 the AUBTW argued that 'people who support unofficial bodies are acting against the interests of this union'.[15] Smith, the right-wing ASW general secretary, became infamous for his determination to attack CP shop stewards. Partly as a result of such official hostility, when disputes emerged in these cities they were often long, drawn-out and bitter.

The London Joint Sites Committee, influenced by CP members, made its first major impact in connection with a strike over bonus payments and sackings at the huge Myton's Barbican site in 1966. Smith refused to support the strike and described the shop stewards as 'little Caesars'. The union also refused to support a 13-month dispute over bonus payments at Sunleys' Horseferry Road site in 1966-67. The two strikes became the subject of a court of inquiry. Its report argued that any disciplinary action taken by the unions 'should be exemplary and effective in destroying the influence of the Joint Sites Committee on these sites'. It continued:

If the 'mischievous activity', as the TGWU [Transport and General Workers Union] has stigmatised it, of the irresponsible and subversive elements in these cases is shown to succeed and at the same time the unions are shown to be unable to control and suppress it, then a grave blow will have been struck at union authority in the London Region and for the future the power of the Joint Sites Committee will be greatly and dangerously enhanced.[16]

The Building Workers' Charter group

In April 1970 in Manchester shop stewards' representatives from the local committees in London, Liverpool and Manchester came together to form a national rank-and-file Building Workers' Charter group. Some 288 delegates from 50 union branches and a similar number of sites attended. The group, which was led by CP members, was prompted by the need to halt the decline in building unionism and the inability of the unions to control the employers' increasing use of lump labour. It was formed around demands that included a militant wage policy of £35 for 35 hours (with annual agreements), the abolition of the lump, greater union democracy and the establishment of one union for the building industry. It quickly became a broad rank-and-file grouping in the industry, uniting members of the CP, Labour Party, International Socialists (IS) and non-aligned union activists. Although its organisation and programme reflected its shop steward base, the Charter group attempted to galvanise support not merely on the sites but also within union branches. The case for a *Building Workers' Charter* paper was articulated by Lou Lewis, its first editor:

> Far too often at site level we have fought long and bitterly to establish decent wages and conditions, only to see the results of our struggles disappear with the completion of the contract, as we move off to fresh fields to struggle once more to establish these self same conditions— often with the same employer… The moral must be obvious. Isolated struggle is not enough—nor will it even be enough to establish any permanent change. Similarly within the trade union movement, isolated and uncoordinated attempts to change policy will prove just as futile.
>
> What is needed is to unite all building workers on a National Policy that can be fought for on every site and within every branch of the Trade Union movement… Our main task is to ensure that the Charter is fought for nationally. It is for this reason that we building workers need our own paper, so that it can carry our gospel to every part of the country.[17]

To gain credibility UCATT needed to campaign against the lump and for a wage claim that would substantially improve the national basic rate. As one shop steward put it, '…the only way to beat the lump was to equal and go beyond lump payments at site level'.[18] This was recognised by both the trade union leadership and the industry's rank-and-file movement. But in the two years after its formation it was the Charter group and not the full-time officials of the new union who provided the leadership on these issues. Lou Lewis, who was elected onto the CP's national executive committee, explained, 'The Communist Party was the catalyst for a lot of the organisation… In London there were about 200 party members in the building industry. The activists involved were mainly stewards and people who had been stewards'.[19] Sales of *Building Workers' Charter* reached 10,000 per issue in the first year of publication,[20] and its second conference in April 1971 attracted 500 delegates. In the process, the group stimulated increased CP strength on the UCATT executive and at its annual conference.

The group also achieved some notable successes, especially in Birmingham where the building industry was transformed. In January 1971 there were only two organised sites there, and only one steward had attended the Charter's founding conference. But there were enough stewards prepared to campaign against the lump, and a city-wide stewards' committee was formed. In October 1971 this committee 'was able to close down 20 sites and organise a 1,200-strong demonstration against the lump'.[21]

The stewards targeted the largest local building employer, Bryant, to eradicate the lump and for £1 per hour. In February 1972 UCATT organised an overtime ban and boycott of the bonus system at Bryant. The company retaliated by sacking Pete Carter (CP member and chair of the city stewards' committee) and another steward, and took out an injunction alleging damage and trespass. On Monday 7 February 600 building workers demonstrated outside the court (and then later joined the miners' picket at Saltley). On 16 February there was a 1,000-strong demonstration from 16 sites outside Bryant's offices. Before the end of the month the company had capitulated, signed a local agreement that gave a 50 percent increase on basic pay (up from £20 to £30 for skilled workers, and from £17.50 to £26 for labourers). It also agreed to encourage trade union membership on its sites, dropped the injunctions, and reinstated Carter and John Shortland.[22] This occurred as national wage negotiations had offered no more than £1.40 (7 percent) on the basic.[23] It vividly demonstrated that with militant organisation and leadership building unionism could go forward. Not surprisingly, Bryant was threatened with expulsion from the NFBTE[24] and then attempted to pull out of the agreement.[25]

Following a vigorous Charter campaign, UCATT was won in December 1971 to an official national claim for £30 for 35 hours. After initial negotiations produced the £1.40 rise mentioned above even less than the engineering employers had offered to their unions, 5,000 Liverpool building workers took unofficial action in support of the claim on 15 March.

The employers expected a boom in the industry in 1972 that would cause the demand for labour to well outstrip supply. In this situation they wanted the right to expand even further the use of lump labour, because any possibility of labour shortage (which the union could easily capitalise on) could not be allowed to develop. But this expansion of the lump required that the union rate be kept as low as possible. This meant a head-on clash with the new union could not be avoided. Following the employers' total refusal to negotiate on the claim, the UCATT negotiating committee even attempted to back down by abandoning the shorter working week and dropping the wage claim to £22.50, the difference to be made up by a guaranteed bonus.

This attempted climbdown was only halted following strong resistance in the regions where rank-and-file building workers, influenced by the Charter group, campaigned to put strength into the union's original claim. On 29 April a Charter national conference, sponsored by groups from 14 towns and cities, brought together 900 building workers on a delegate basis from across the country. It urged militant industrial action in support of the pay and hours campaign.[26] May Day marches across the country against the Industrial Relations Act involved many building workers demonstrating on their claim. In central London 2,000 workers marched to the NFBTE headquarters, and in Glasgow every building site in the city stopped work at midday with almost 2,000 joining a march through the city centre.[27]

On 22 May Peter Kavanagh (a CP member) staged a sit-in at the top of a crane above the Lovell site in Guilford Street, London, protesting against victimisation of himself and others, and the employers' use of the lump. He came down to join a 300-strong march from a dozen sites to the NFBTE offices on 31 May. From 30 May to 2 June, Alan Prior and John Mahon also sat-in cranes 120 feet above Birmingham city centre over Bryant's refusal to employ Prior, who was believed to be on a blacklist. They came down minutes before a judge was to consider the company's application for their breach of an injunction.[28] On 5 June every building site in the Edinburgh area was hit by a half-day token protest stoppage, and 2,000 of the strikers marched through the city.[29]

By the summer of 1972, building on such action, the Charter group had widened its base of support from London, Liverpool and Manchester. Birmingham (where it won a majority on the UCATT regional council) led the way, with other areas such as Glasgow, Leicester, Stoke and Southampton now represented. The main strength lay in the north west, with local groups in Liverpool, Manchester, Preston, Bolton, Wigan, Runcorn and Widnes. The last issue of the *Building Workers' Charter* paper before the strike reported the recent conference's call for 'mass national action' to win the claim: 'We need to put pressure on our leaders to take the necessary action. We are confident that the membership will respond'.[30] In many respects the prospect of strike action raised the real problem of establishing UCATT in the industry. Terry Austrin argued that the strike:

> ...had to take on...the lump, and because of that, it required an unusually high degree of organised activity in the form of picketing. The strike could not simply be a withdrawal of labour by an effectively organised workforce, for the building workforce was fragmented, riddled with the lump, and in many cases lacking any experience in industrial action. It was a workforce that in the main had not looked to the unions to solve its problems in the post-war period.[31]

In areas where UCATT had any strength the Charter group played an important part in providing leadership. Aware of this, the union leadership now refrained from attacking the unofficial movement and tried to exploit the success of its struggles and the local organisation of its activists.

The selective strike strategy

In May and June 1972 the employers made two increased offers, both of which were rejected by the four unions—UCATT (with 280,000 members), TGWU (with 80,000 members), the general and municipal workers' NUGMW and the furniture trades workers' FTAT (both with a relatively small construction membership). Early in May the building unions had started to consider selective strikes and a levy on everyone else. On 10 May they set up a national action committee along with regional action committees to select target sites. The UCATT conference agreed that at least one site controlled by each of the 39 major contractors should be included.[32]

The NJC had reached deadlock on 25 May and a special committee was set up. On 22 June, four days before the strike was due to start, the union members on the committee said that any settlement must include a minimum earnings guarantee and a threshold clause whereby wages rose after a certain rise in the price level. The unions argued that any delay in the earnings guarantee meant that they could accept nothing less than £25 for 40 hours for craft workers.[33]

The plan was to escalate the strike slowly through selective regional stoppages, with six extra sites belonging to the biggest companies being brought out every week in each of ten regions. A national levy of £1 per head was requested of all members who were not required to cease work (though they banned overtime). UCATT assistant general secretary Les Wood argued that in the building industry:

> ...a national strike...does not have the same dislocative impact as do strikes...[in] motor car manufacturing, electrical power...or in the docks. To be really effective a building strike has to hit the employers where it hurts most, and that is on those contracts where they stand to make the greatest profit. For this reason the dispute during its early stages was confined to luxury projects such as hotels and blocks of flats being built for private sale.[34]

The sites selected in London were the new television centre and five luxury hotels. In the north west region they included the new Bass Charington brewery in Runcorn, the teaching hospital in Liverpool, the Piccadilly hotel in Manchester, the hotel block and airport at Wythenshawe, Chester's telephone exchange and a new police station in Colwyn Bay. Midlands sites stopped included a shopping precinct in Sutton Coldfield and the shopping centre in Stoke-on-Trent.[35] The choice of sites, it was suggested, was concentrated on those where the contractors were subject to penalty payments for late completion.[36]

Before the strike started, the *Guardian* argued that 'selective strikes are hardly likely to worry the government or the large majority of the public'.[37] But the employers also believed that it would develop beyond selective action 'because in those areas where the militants are strong there will be unofficial action as well, in an attempt to widen the area of the dispute'.[38]

There was clearly a lot of enthusiasm locally. On the first day of the strike sites in Manchester, St Helens, Wigan and Skelmersdale were hit by half-day stoppages. Large rallies took place in Glasgow, Edinburgh and Dundee. A 2,000-strong demonstration in Birmingham on the second Monday, 3 July, rallied outside the regional NFBTE offices.[39] At the end of the second week the NFBTE president admitted in a circular to member firms that 118 sites were stopped (7,000-10,000 men) and a few civil engineering jobs had been 'affected'. But he suggested, possibly with some truth, that the unions were having difficulty getting some sites out, that picketing had to be used in odd cases, and that the overtime ban and levy were difficult to enforce: 'The efforts of Regions and individual firms to "control" [ban] recruitment from stopped firms are undoubtedly having an effect.'

He continued, 'Seeing it through is bound to take a little time. In wage disputes of this kind timing is vital…the point at which to reopen formal negotiations must be carefully judged.' If the employers were to rush into negotiations, it 'would effectively demonstrate to a newly-formed and relatively weak UCATT that only a modest show of strength on selected sites is all that is needed to get its way'. The result of that would be that 'the militant element would soon exploit this situation, and go on exploiting it'.[40]

In Birmingham a 4,000-strong march stopped 90 sites at the end of the third week, Friday 14 July. At a rally Pete Carter argued, 'If we are not careful we could lose this battle on the tactics of the selective strike… It is undermining the tremendous militancy shown here today. We must now extend the struggle. We need to stop all sites for a speedy settlement'.[41] At about this time workers in other centres were also getting more organised. The Manchester action committee met on Wednesday 12 July and agreed that a flying picket from the sites on strike should be used to enforce the overtime ban on working sites. The next day 60 building workers, supported by union officials, stopped five sites in an hour. Four more were stopped on the Friday, six on the Saturday and another on the Sunday, effectively ending overtime in the centre of Manchester. They then moved on to Openshaw.[42]

In the fourth week two large sites were organised in London. Officials from UCATT and the TGWU recruited 500 men at the Laing's Aylesbury Estate site, while at McInerney's Lambeth site 250 were recruited and six stewards elected.[43] Also, in London complaints were rising about the 'virtual press blackout' and a 1,000-strong meeting in Fulham town hall voted to picket Fleet Street newspapers. It is not clear whether this ever happened, but it was a real issue. The *New Statesman* later commented on the limited coverage in the main-stream press, 'For this relief, Mr Heath…should be enormously grate-ful,' especially given the events on the docks in July.[44]

By 20 July, while the NFBTE suggested only 160 sites involving 10,000 workers were stopped, 'many more jobs' were 'affected by over-time bans and "go-slow" tactics'. More significantly, an 'emergency letter' to member firms recognised that the dispute was 'the most se-rious the industry has experienced for 50 years', and that 'a new and potentially more serious form of attack' was developing:

> In addition to calling out individual sites of the large national con-tractors, in some areas the operatives have been making clear attempts to victimise old established local-based firms, even to the extent of stopping every one of the firms' jobs. *Such attempts to pick off individual firms one by one is precisely the reason for the formation of the NFBTE nearly 100 years ago.*[45] (added emphasis)

As a result, a special general meeting of the employers was called for 31 July to consider the raising of a levy. In the event this meeting agreed that the existing 'defence fund' should be drawn on until such time as a levy might be necessary.

An example of how the strike developed comes from the relatively quiet area of Norfolk. There was a slow start, with local employers spreading rumours that various sites had abandoned the overtime ban. The regional action committee called a mass meeting in Nor-wich and a shop stewards' committee was set up. Gradually, 23 large contracts were organised and shop stewards elected. In the second week, the regional action committee instructed the full time officials to withdraw the large University of East Anglia contract, but it took three attempts before the site was shut early in the third week. On 25 July, in the fifth week, four more sites were withdrawn, but the stew-ards' committee in Norwich was getting increasingly 'dissatisfied' with the official tactics and decided to halt all contracts in the city.[46]

A bricklayer in Bristol, another poorly unionised town, described what happened there:

> We were useless really—we came out on strike and we didn't know anything—we couldn't even mount an effective picket line at first. Blokes had never been on strike before and they would just wander off—but gradually the effect of being out on strike hit you and you

began to realise that the only way that you were going to get back to work with any money was to get everybody out. In Bristol we were one of the first areas to call for an all out stoppage and by then we knew that to achieve that you had to use a flying picket to get round all the sites.[47]

In Bristol a mass meeting of strikers called for a total stoppage, and on Monday 24 July 300 pickets closed seven sites. The TGWU (the dominant building union in the area and the one that organised the scaffolders who came out at the beginning of the strike) agreed to pay immediate strike pay to anyone joining it.

At about the same time the regional action committee in Birmingham also decided to close all sites. Six Bryant sites were called out on Tuesday 25 July, and other sites on the Wednesday and Thursday, with a view to shutting them all by the weekend, using mass pickets where necessary.[48] The selective strike strategy was therefore being increasingly challenged in practice by the activists. It was seen as not creating enough pressure on the employers while being demoralising for those strikers faced with most other sites still working. The activists were agreed that only by accelerating the dispute, and involving the maximum number of firms, would the employers collapse and resume negotiations that would lead to a worthwhile settlement. Lou Lewis recalled:

> There were action committees that were dominated by people on the [UCATT] regional councils. In some places they were quite militant, but the officials tried to control them. There was a clamouring from people who said 'we want our site to come out'. So then the leadership started to say 'we can't have any more strikes, we can't afford it, there would be no strike pay'.[49]

Meanwhile at the routine NJC on 19 July an ad hoc committee was established to start talks. On 28 July a possibly acceptable offer lay on the table. Craft rates were to rise immediately from £20 to £23, and then to £26 in May 1973. There would be a guaranteed bonus of £2 from November, rising to £3 in May 1973. Labourers' rates would be 85 percent of all these figures. A threshold clause would add 20p for both craftsmen and labourers for every 0.75 percent rise in the Retail Price Index above 8.5 percent from the start of the agreement.

When the full NJC met on Wednesday 2 August the union side indicated that the general structure of the offer was 'now satisfactory' but the immediate increase was not high enough. Further, the union side did not have the authority to settle. Informal talks led to the unions saying that the package would be acceptable if the operation of the guaranteed bonus was brought forward to August. The employers would not improve their offer unless the unions got the authority to accept. Representatives from UCATT, FTAT and NUGMW were able to do this (and did so) by 4 August but the TGWU, though amenable to the offer, wanted longer to consult its members, and the NJC was adjourned until 8 August.[50]

This delay was crucial. When news came out that the UCATT executive had decided to accept the employers' offer and would agree to it on Tuesday 8 August there was a strong reaction. To start with, most regional representatives of UCATT, meeting in London on Thursday 3 August, opposed the executive's decision. On Friday 4 August the London action committee, which had decided earlier to organise a half-day strike and demonstration for 9 August, made a rapid change of plan and brought it forward a day to Tuesday 8 August. Leaflets had already been printed and had to be altered. 25,000 leaflets were issued above the signatures of London UCATT and TGWU regional secretaries Len Eaton and Bob Johnson respectively. This left only Friday afternoon and Monday to work for a large turnout on the Tuesday. Independently a mass meeting of 600 in Bristol voted to reject the offer and agreed to send coaches to the London demonstration, as did meetings in Cambridge and Stevenage.[51]

On Saturday mass meetings in Leeds of the two main unions were totally against the proposed settlement, and the UCATT meeting demanded the resignation of the national executive if it accepted the offer. A mass meeting in Liverpool condemned the offer and proposed to escalate the action to an all-out strike. On Monday the UCATT north west regional committee also unanimously rejected its offer. Those sites represented on a lobby of this committee agreed to stay out, and by the afternoon all sites in central Manchester were stopped. It was agreed to continue the 'snowballing' until the whole Manchester area was out.[52] The TGWU trade group national committee, made up of regional lay members, rejected the employers' offer on the Monday despite a recommendation to accept by the national officials. This put added pressure on the UCATT executive.[53]

There were three major demonstrations on the Tuesday. In Glasgow 3,000 marched to the local employers' offices and decided on an immediate all-out strike, with every site to be picketed from Wednesday morning. There were 3,000-4,000 marchers in Birmingham with delegations from Bristol, Cardiff, Wolverhampton and the Isle of Man. Some 120 sites were already stopped in Birmingham. In London 5,000 marched from Hyde Park to the employers' offices. There were sizeable contingents present from Yorkshire (especially Leeds, Bradford, Rotherham and York), Bristol and Norwich, as well as smaller ones from around the country. Jack Henry, secretary of the London action committee, reported from a deputation to the employers that the latter had received a message from UCATT: 'They have stated that the agreement proposed by employers will not be ratified by UCATT and will not be signed by them'.[54] On the Tuesday morning the UCATT executive had reversed its earlier vote.

The employers believed that the TGWU, which had only three of the 12 votes on the operatives' side of the NJC, was 'more sensitive to the views of its members'. It also had 'the additional motivation, in its opposition to the settlement, of wishing in its own future interests to weaken the already weak UCATT'. The employers also recognised that the Building Workers' Charter 'and other extremist groups' were able 'to persuade most if not all the regional organisations of UCATT to oppose it as well'.[55] Smith later tried to rationalise UCATT's about-turn. He refuted the employers' claim that the union had 'backed down' on the wages deal, arguing that the ad hoc committee was only 'recommendatory'. The NJC meeting 'was never held to ratify the agreement because it was evident by the reaction of our members that the offer was just not good enough, despite our assessments'.[56]

All-out strike

Two days after UCATT's about-turn it was reported that it wanted 'large numbers of men to stay at work so that they can contribute to the fund set up to give strike pay to those men taking part in the stoppages'.[57] But on the Friday, 11 August, at a national meeting of UCATT regional officials held in Birmingham, a majority favoured an all-out stoppage. The *Times* commented, 'The militants have first captured key sites, then regional officials, and finally forced the moderate union leadership into an unprecedentedly tough bargaining position.' Lou Lewis was quoted as saying that 'we have solved the problem of a sell-out. It is now the employers against the rest of us'.[58]

Yet the 'moderates' on the UCATT executive still only wanted an escalation of the selective strike strategy, and the four unions agreed 'the most rapid intensification', but concentrating on employers with 60-200 workers. Smith said that the unions would entertain company agreements and firms signing them would 'get off the hook'.[59]

In reality there was to be no repeat of the Bryant agreement in Birmingham that had been negotiated earlier in the year. Few of the large employers were prepared to break ranks with the national policy of the NFBTE, although some 90 firms did at some point reach agreement with the unions.[60] A comparison with the engineering dispute is instructive. The Engineering Employers' Federation handed out over £2 million to strike-hit firms, and the local association set up local committees to advise and direct their affiliated companies (see Chapter 4). The building employers' federation now displayed a similar solidarity.

From this point on, however, the course of events was in tune with a resolution passed at the London demonstration: '...to escalate the strike to all-out without strike pay, and every region represented to carry through this policy immediately'.[61] Across the country action committees now followed the strategy pioneered in Birmingham and Bristol of stopping every organised site, and then deploying mass pickets to persuade unorganised sites to come out too. Lou Lewis recalled what happened in London:

> The London regional action committee convened a big meeting in the Conway Hall [on 10 August]... I was on the World's End site [in Chelsea] at the time. I laid out the Joint Sites Committee strategy, all-out with no strike pay. And from that moment on the leadership lost any grip of it, because strike pay had been the only weapon they had... I was the co-ordinator in London. We had a map with six grids on it, and teams in each grid to close the jobs down and others to make sure they stayed closed. It was like a military operation.[62]

As he explained at the time:

> The men already on strike would be the initial force to go out into each area and stop other jobs... We want every striker active, a strike centre which can send 50 or 100 pickets to a site if need be, the maximum number of cars available. We need an army of building workers.

This meeting also agreed 'to halt all sources of supply to the building industry'—cement, bricks, timber and so on.[63] Similar developments

were happening elsewhere. For example, the regional action committee in Birmingham was reported on 18 August to be organising 'a 200-
strong mobile picket to make an onslaught on building supply depots and
manufacturers'. Pete Carter described what had already been achieved:

> After a ten-day, 24-hour-a-day picket at Douglas Rapid Metal in
> Aldridge, who produce light structures and pre-cast concrete parts
> used all over the country, the firm conceded defeat and closed the
> plant. We have also shut down two of the Douglas ready-mixed con-
> crete batching plants, one at a place near Burton and another at Great
> Barr, Birmingham.
>
> The plan next week is to retain pickets on building sites already
> stopped, where there is a need, and draw more forces into an attack on
> the material supply end of the industry.[64]

Cement companies were targeted to cut off supplies to working sites,
successfully shutting down the Associated Portland Cement works at
Cauldon near Leek, north Staffordshire, for example. Twenty-six
pickets left Birmingham in the evening of 23 August and arrived
there at midnight, and kept out of sight until 4am, when they were
joined by 30 more from Stoke-on-Trent. By 5am there were 80 police
present. When the drivers came out with their lorries and tankers
fully loaded a special squad of police started laying into the pickets.
The drivers got through, but when they returned empty they held a
meeting where they agreed to stop further deliveries and a 24-hour
picket was then organised from Stoke.[65]

Elsewhere pickets were arrested outside Birmingham's Blue Circle
cement factory. Other major targets included the Tunnel Cement and
Rugby Portland plants and depots in Birmingham.[66] The workers 'knew
from their day-by-day experience that by preventing…the delivery of
materials, it was comparatively easy to bring to a standstill any major
contract'. One example was ready-mix concrete, used in walling and
flooring.[67] But, of course, with only about one third of the industry's
workforce unionised, stopping the workers at the huge number of separate building sites themselves was the overwhelming priority. Sometimes the pickets had to stay outside a site, such as one at Basildon in
Essex, where, after a week of being forced to cross picket lines, 24
workers were flown in and out of the site by helicopter.[68]

In Liverpool the secretary and treasurer of the local Charter group
were on the regional action committee, whose chair was also a Charter

supporter. All three sat on the Merseyside shop stewards' committee, a recognised committee in UCATT.[69] By 15 August there was a total stoppage in the city, with an estimated 35,000 building workers out across the Merseyside region. Seven thousand building workers marched in support of the claim through the streets of Liverpool, while 10,000 were present at a rally. One official spoke of '*this great revolt* of building workers now spreading throughout the country' (added emphasis).[70] A West of Scotland UCATT shop stewards' meeting on 13 August saw 277 vote for an all-out strike, and only 12 support the executive committee members who were arguing for selective strikes, and a ban on bonus and overtime working elsewhere. In the biggest demonstration of building workers ever seen in Scotland, on 18 August, more than 15,000 in Glasgow called for an all-out strike to win the full claim. A UCATT full-time executive member was heckled into silence for several minutes after declaring 'the question of an all-out strike is just not on'. This was met by shouts of, 'You are not on,' and steady chants of, 'All out—all out'.[71]

Even many towns that previously had little experience of trade unionism in the industry were also brought to a standstill. A coachload of strikers from Norwich had travelled to the demonstration outside the employers' offices in London on 8 August: 'This was the first time that many of us had come into contact with the more aware members from other parts of the country.' The strike then spread to Great Yarmouth and Lowestoft, 'where "subbies" [sub-contractors] were found to be working on the Labour Party Headquarters roof'. Yarmouth was stopped in two days and Lowestoft in a week, though here three were arrested for obstruction. A march was held on the sea front at Yarmouth, and holidaymakers (including building workers from elsewhere) joined a large rally. All stopped sites were kept out until the settlement.[72]

With nearly 1,000 strikers marching, Stoke-on-Trent saw one of its largest ever demonstrations on 10 August. On the same day, after a mass meeting in Preston, workers marched around the town, bringing out 22 sites. At the weekend nearly 2,500 attended a meeting at Connah's Quay in North Wales and voted for a total stoppage.[73] In Ipswich 70 workers 'boarded a specially chartered double decker bus for a tour of local building sites' and brought another 100 workers out. By 15 August the strike in Yorkshire was 'escalating so fast that strike leaders in Leeds cannot keep pace with the news of new sites coming out'. Two days later it was reported that there were 'approximately 45 Southampton sites out, and it is escalating fast'.[74]

In Stoke-on-Trent Tommy Walker, a CP member and the local Building Workers' Charter contact, explained his method of working:

> I carried three little notebooks on me. One contained the jobs that needed stopping, the second carried a day to day report of jobs stopped, and the third contained the names and addresses of all stewards being elected. I also presented each steward with a notebook so that he could get the names of his men and put them on a rota for pickets. Also I wrote my own name and address with phone number so that I could be contacted if need be. The system has worked very well, as now we have an army of 300 or 400 lads waiting for any action the employers may want.[75]

The TV and film actor Ricky Tomlinson, then a UCATT shop steward in North Wales, recalled:

> We joined the strike in full force... I think we put the rest of the country to shame because we had a 99 percent success rate. No one worked—people wouldn't even come out and paint their front doors, people wouldn't clear their blocked drains. We had it all boxed off, and we done it the right way. We were sent to picket here, picket there, and do the business. But when this was going on, the leadership of the trade union movement, UCATT and the T&G, became very panicky, because we'd actually take the reins from them, we were actually calling the shots.[76]

With the escalation of the strike to involve much wider numbers than previously, UCATT suspended payment of strike benefit. This further encouraged those who were drawn into activity to demand a short route to victory, and the flying picket fitted the need to stop all building sites irrespective of whether they were unionised or not. Thousands more sites were now brought to a standstill.

There were some amusing incidents. Thus, in Lancashire:

> A convener steward...on picket duty...suggested to his colleagues that they march down the road and gain the support of the workers on a site two miles away... [A police] Superintendent...drove up...asking him 'What's this all about?'... The police Superintendent decided that the law needed to accompany the marchers... On arrival...the stewards informed the [site] agent that there was a dispute... The police Superintendent...became impatient and...joined the stewards who

were...presenting the union's case to management. On approaching the stewards and management the Superintendent directed his remarks to the stewards and said 'When are you going?' In the confusion the agent...thought the law was asking *him*... He immediately pan-icked...and said, 'Yes, we are going, the site is now closed.' This valu-able information was quickly conveyed to the men on site who immediately joined the demonstrators and proceeded to march calmly back up the road, singing 'We shall overcome'.[77] (original emphasis)

The employers launched a propaganda campaign, insisting that the strike was being run by militants. On 9 August, the day after the failed settlement, the NFBTE president was reported as suggesting that 'militants were moving from site to site inciting workers into strike action...[and] these militants have called strikes official when they have not been'.[78] An NFBTE bulletin later claimed, 'In hired buses and convoys of private cars, gangs of militants went from site to site and called men out with no authority from the unions and in com-plete disregard of the official strike policy'.[79] The employers were ap-palled that pickets, particularly in Yorkshire, 'approached operatives even at bus stations and company pick-up points and warned them not to go to work'.[80]

The *Times* tended to agree and reported in late August that UCATT's selective strike campaign had been 'wholly overtaken by militant action', and that the union was 'now busily declaring more and more official strikes to keep pace with the sites being unofficially pulled out by the militants'.[81] During the course of the dispute, all-out stoppages were eventually achieved in a number of major centres, such as central London, Bristol, Birmingham, Manchester, Liverpool, Hull, Stoke-on-Trent, Leicester, Coventry, Wolverhampton, Glas-gow, Edinburgh, Aberdeen and Dundee, and in towns such as Hartle-pool, Huddersfield, Swindon, Norwich, Ipswich, Southend, Stevenage and York.[82] On 22 August UCATT provided the following regional breakdown of strikers and sites affected:[83]

Regional breakdown of stopped sites and numbers of strikers		
	Sites	Strikers
Scotland	2,200	50,000
Northern counties	250	14,000
Yorkshire	500	16,000
North west	2,650	60,000
Midlands	500	12,000
Eastern countries	320	10,200
London	400	30,000
Southern counties	400	4,500
South west	250	10,000
South Wales	70	3,000

The unions claimed that at its peak the strike involved 270,000 workers out at some 9,000 sites.[84] Under such circumstances the UCATT journal could easily rebuff the employers' propaganda that 'the militants are running this dispute', arguing that 'in actual fact it is the vast majority of building workers who are no longer prepared to tolerate difficulties over wages, labour-only and fringe benefits'. The general secretary even went into print to the effect that 'I'm more than impressed by the organisational ability that is obviously contained within our union, and which has the opportunity of expressing itself in the campaign.' He then spoilt it by adopting the tone of a school report: 'The competence that has been shown by people in the localities has been very cheering indeed'.[85]

The role of the Communist Party

The CP should have been admirably placed to give leadership to the strike. The leaders of UCATT had completely misjudged the mood of their own members. In addition, building was one industry where there was a viable rank-and-file organisation controlled by CP members. The *Building Workers' Charter* had appeared regularly, was backed up by some hundreds of militants, and was able to hold impressive national conferences. The CP was also able to substantially increase its membership during the course of the strike. For example, in Birmingham, in the run-up to, and during the first week of, the strike the CP recruited no less than 50 new building workers.[86] Moreover, there seemed little reason for the CP to hold back from criticising the leadership of the main union, UCATT.

In the 1960s the full-time executive of the ASW had connived with the London building employers to victimise stewards, mostly CP members. In 1970 the executive pushed through a rule change which abolished elections for the post of district secretaries and brought in a new regional structure with appointed officials, thereby removing from office the London district secretary of the union, Jack Rusca, a CP member.[87]

All this meant that, just as in the right-wing-led electrical workers' EETPU union, there was more of a need for CP building worker members to build rank and file organisation on a militant basis if they were to defend their base in the union. But some CP members were opposed to the Charter initiative and were more interested in obtaining official posts within the unions or establishing close relationships with existing left-wing full-time officials. There was a conflict between these two tendencies.[88] The latter was closer to official CP industrial policy as a whole and, despite the individual efforts of many building worker militants, it was to increasingly determine Charter policies after the strike.

But even during the 13 weeks of the biggest building workers' strike ever in Britain not one issue of the *Charter* newspaper was produced. In the issue that came out at the end of the strike the editorial apologised that this had been 'a weakness' and explained it as follows. '...this paper is written and produced by building workers—the same ones who were up to their necks in the day-to-day activities of the strike, organising, picketing, etc'.[89] There was also no attempt to convene a national meeting of Charter supporters. As Lou Lewis recalled, 'In the strike the Charter went to sleep. The key ones of us were so involved in running the dispute. There were a couple of meetings during the strike to discuss tactics—when they came down to London for the national demo—but there was no formal meeting as such'.[90]

But the failure to provide nationally coordinated leadership during the strike is primarily to be explained by the fact that the CP as a political party put no effort whatsoever, organisationally or politically, into assisting their building worker members to build the Charter group. Such a militant rank-and-file movement that organised independently of the union leadership was viewed with considerable suspicion. In fact the CP's own paper, the *Morning Star*, even invited the right-wing UCATT leader Smith to write a half-page article on the strike, literally days after he had attempted to foist a settlement which was massively rejected by the rank and file.[91]

The issue of local agreements demonstrated the contradiction at the heart of the CP. While CP members in Birmingham, and later in London, Liverpool and elsewhere, took the lead in escalating the strike, in some important places they were much more conservative. For example, in Scotland there were CP full-time UCATT officials whose reactions were closer to the national union leadership than to rank and file militants. Thus when two big firms in Aberdeen and Dundee, Camerons and Betts, offered local settlements that fell short of the union's claim, CP militants in areas like Birmingham insisted such deals would weaken the strike's national momentum and leverage, and leave weaker areas even more isolated. But the Scottish officials recommended acceptance.

This tactic was also championed enthusiastically by the *Morning Star*, whose front page headline on 26 August was 'Builders Notch Up Strike Victories', with an article underneath stating that 'some 20,000 of the strikers are to return because employers have conceded the claim'. As well as exaggerating the employers' concessions, the *Morning Star* did not report that the previous day 4,000 building workers in Edinburgh had voted down the recommendation of their CP full-time union organiser to accept the model Scottish agreements.[92] The Building Workers' Charter group also failed publicly to oppose such local agreements, although privately the leading militants were against them.[93]

The settlement

On Tuesday 12 September 12,000 building workers marched through Liverpool demanding no settlement except on the basis of the full claim. Two days later Mick Costello of the *Morning Star* wrote that 'press speculation about an end to the dispute today is groundless'. Smith, the UCATT general secretary, had agreed in advance to meet members of a lobby after talks with the employers.[94] In the event, a settlement was reached at 10pm that night with an agreement of a return to work the following Monday.[95] Smith 'said that the deal had been ratified at the negotiations. UCATT had no plans to put the deal before its members.' When Smith then met a delegation from the lobby, Norman Booth, chair of the Sheffield strike committee, walked out in disgust halfway through.[96] Writing in the *Morning Star* a fortnight after the deal, Lou Lewis complained that while the union leadership 'had been guilty' of not consulting members in the past, it had given 'assurances during the dispute that it would never again arrive at a settlement without consultation'.[97]

The deal was the largest single pay rise ever won in the industry. Craftsmen got an immediate 30 percent rise on the basic rate to £26 per week. After that, the rest of the deal was disappointing. From June 1973 the basic was to be raised to £27 plus a guaranteed bonus of £2.60. The cost-of-living adjustment proposed earlier was to kick in from October 1973, and a final rise to £29 basic plus £3 guaranteed bonus operated from June 1974. Labourers got proportionate increases. In each of the two years there would be an extra day's holiday. No new deal could start before November 1974.[98]

The *Economist* complained that 'while the Prime Minister was talking about wage restraint to the leaders of industry and the unions…the building employers agreed to raise their already hyperinflationary offer'.[99] But many militants believed that much more could have been won. As Lou Lewis of the CP argued:

> It is the general opinion of those I've talked to in the industry—and this goes for the average lad who doesn't take an active part in union affairs—that they felt another couple of weeks and they could have wrested that much more from the employers that would have made a settlement look reasonable.[100]

John Fontaine, an IS building worker at the time, believed:

> Had the strike continued another three weeks, then it is quite certain the full demands would have been met and a victory won that would have translated the slogan 'kill the lump' into reality.[101]

There was a mixed response at mass meetings. Although it was reluctantly accepted in Bristol, over 4,000 workers voted by a substantial majority to reject the deal in Glasgow. In Dundee 2,000 did the same, and in Birmingham 100 strikers occupied the local NFBTE offices in protest.[102] In Liverpool a 20,000-strong rally also rejected official union proposals for acceptance, and workers remained out on strike for another week, hoping to force extra concessions, before returning to work isolated nationally. A number of other towns also stayed out that extra week.

Aftermath

One immediate consequence of the strike was victimisation of activists. Sometimes this was resisted. In London the large World's End site in Chelsea had returned to work on 18 September, but found that the brickwork sub-contractor was refusing to pay the new national rate, and that the woodwork company had sacked all its employees due to their activity in the strike. A meeting voted to stay out. The dismissals were seen as a ruse to keep Lou Lewis off the site. The site strike committee later joined forces with another from Lovells at Guilford Street in London, which was out over the lump and the victimisation of two TGWU activists, one of whom was Peter Kavanagh (the former crane-top protester). The 'joint action was a major component' in victory at World's End (where the strike ended on 17 November), and 'was certainly responsible for forcing the T&GWU to maintain the "official strike" label on the Lovells dispute'.[103]

Another result of the unions having abandoned the strike was that a few months after the strike Pete Carter could report that 'we are once again riddled with' the lump in Birmingham, and that 'most other areas can claim the same experience'. More immediately there was a serious assault by hired thugs on Mike Shilvock, a Bryant shop steward and chair of the Birmingham action committee, at his home on the evening of Tuesday 19 September.[104]

Finally, one longer-term consequence of the strike was the changing official record. Very soon after the strike had finished the UCATT journal admitted that 'the Operatives' Side unanimously recommended' a deal in early August, which 'building workers at that stage in the strike were not prepared to accept'. As a result UCATT and the TGWU 'acknowledged the strength of membership feeling and escalated the strike campaign'. The UCATT journal also conceded that 'at this stage the Local and Regional Strike Committees came fully into their own', and that 'rank and file construction workers won for themselves a considerable measure of success'.[105] But only a few years later the official history of UCATT, published in 1979 and written by Les Wood, who had been assistant general secretary in 1972, obscured the role of the rank and file in escalating the strike. Thus 'with no sign of a tangible offer forthcoming, the strike rapidly escalated from being one of a selective nature to a full-scale industrial dispute', 'the strike proved more successful than originally anticipated because, once started, a snowball effect became apparent and this culminated in an industry wide stoppage', and 'with no positive offer forthcoming, the area of the dispute was extended to cover all forms of building'.[106]

In the second half of August the NFBTE had sent out letters to member companies to prepare dossiers on flying pickets, claiming that 'the moderate elements…are being forced into intemperate action by travelling groups of militants which move from site to site'.[107] On 8 September the NFBTE director-general wrote to member firms on the following lines:

> We are maintaining as strongly as we can to the Press and the other media that if it were not for the militant action being taken by a relatively small number of activists this strike would not have got off the ground on anything like the scale it has. *At present we don't want to make too much of this for fear of deterring men who want to go back to work from doing so by circulating scare stories of heavy-arm tactics.* Nevertheless we are compiling an 'intimidation dossier' which is daily getting fatter, and I would ask any member who has concrete evidence of such intimidatory tactics by pickets and others to let us have chapter and verse. It is anticipated that the material…which we gather will be passed to the Government with a view to trying to stop similar kinds of pressure being exerted in the future.[108] (added emphasis)

The NFBTE dossier, compiled from press reports and private communications, listed about 100 incidents or sets of incidents, all but one occurring from 7 August to 18 September. About 40 percent of these were from Yorkshire (plus a few from neighbouring Teesside and Lincolnshire). Another 30 percent were from the Midlands (particularly Coventry and Birmingham), North Wales and Shropshire, and Lancashire. The rest were scattered around the country. The bulk of the reports were of alleged threats and intimidation rather than damage to property or car tyres. However, it did include a long account of events at Shrewsbury.[109]

During the strike on 6 and 7 September, following a call for assistance from workers in the Oswestry area, the Chester and North Wales action committee organised a flying picket of some 250 building workers, who were transported in six coaches and a number of cars, to descend on lump labour sites in Shrewsbury. Two weeks before John Price, one of the lump sub-contractors on the Severn Meadows site, had proudly announced that he and other employers in the town had set up an anti-picketing squad. The *Shropshire Star* approvingly reported this development beneath the headline 'Freelance Builders To Defy Pickets': 'Mr Price who is based at Abbey Forgate does not think that any confrontation will come to violence', but his force 'will fight the pickets if necessary'.[110] At the first building site visited by the pickets they were confronted by Terence Parry, son of the man whose company had the contract for the job, who was armed with a 12-bore shotgun. Subsequently in court, Parry claimed that he had held the gun across his chest and had only threatened to use it, although other witnesses stated that he had pointed the gun at the pickets. Either way, he had been disarmed by the pickets, with the gun rendered harmless and handed in to the police. The pickets then moved to other sites where contractors were also expecting them.

They also went to a major site, named Brookside, in nearby Telford New Town, a huge lump contract being carried out by Sir Alfred McAlpine, one of the largest employers in the industry. Here there was disagreement between the pickets, site management and some strikebreakers, site equipment was damaged and fights took place. Tomlinson, one of the picket organisers, recalled:

> McAlpine and all the others had amassed all the 'subbies' [subcontractors] from all over the country and they had got them onto this one big site. It was like a fortress. We went in...we spoke to the lads. There was a little bit of a scuffle here and there, but I'm serious there was nothing intentional. And at the end of the day the lads actually went off the site. They weren't very pleased because they were on good money, but then nobody likes being out of work. But they done as they were asked, and they went.[111]

The alleged violence and intimidation in the strike was claimed to have been 'well organised, well directed and well financed'.[112] The NFBTE dossier was sent to both the government and the police, and provided the basis for legal action against the pickets. Robert Carr, now Home Secretary, was sent an advance copy and wholeheartedly agreed with its contents. In the House of Commons on 11 October, less than three weeks after the end of the strike, he said:

> There is nothing wrong with the law, the real problem was enforcement. *Following disturbing evidence of intimidation from many areas during the national building strike, I intend once again to draw the attention of Chief Constables to the provisions of the law and discuss with them what further action they might take to defeat such violence and intimidation in industrial*

disputes. The law as it stands makes it absolutely clear that obstruction and intimidation are illegal. It makes it clear that the right to picket is not a licence to intimidate. *It makes it clear that sheer numbers attending can of itself constitute intimidation.*[113] (added emphasis)

The hysterical views of Sir Robert Mark, Metropolitan Police commissioner, were perhaps not untypical of senior police officers: 'To some of us, the Shrewsbury pickets had committed the worst of all crimes, worse even than murder, the attempt to achieve an industrial and political objective by criminal violence, the very conduct, in fact, which helped to bring the National Socialist German Workers' Party [Nazis] to power in 1933'.[114]

Yet the *Financial Times* was moved to seriously question the contents of the employers' dossier: 'This document is itself flawed since it suggests the existence of a sinister plot without being able to substantiate the allegations. Many of the incidents that have been listed seem to be little more than the ordinary spontaneous angry behaviour that might be expected on a building site at any time (and especially during an industrial dispute)...the publication reads more like a politically motivated pamphlet than a serious study'.[115]

But early in November detectives from the West Mercia Constabulary began a full scale investigation into the Shrewsbury and Telford incidents, and in February 1973 the police swooped on the homes of many former pickets and charged them with numerous criminal offences. Tomlinson recalled, 'The police told of mass destruction, of violence. Apparently we had bands of armed pickets shouting "Kill, Kill, Kill". We were supposedly hell-bent on wiping out the entire scab labour force'.[116]

Eleven men were tried and acquitted at Mold Crown Court in July 1973 on charges of intimidation under Section 7 of the Conspiracy and Protection of Property Act 1875. Even if they had been found guilty, the maximum sentence was only three months. Twenty four were tried at Shrewsbury, six being given the extra charges of unlawful assembly, affray and conspiracy to intimidate. Conspiracy carried a maximum life sentence.[117] In the event, McKinsie Jones was imprisoned for nine months, and Tomlinson and CP member Des Warren for two and three years respectively.[118] The national leadership of both UCATT and the TGWU were ambivalent in their attitude to the vigorous unofficial national protest campaign that was mounted against the trials and for the release of the three pickets once their sentences had begun.

UCATT eventually went on the record:

> We have argued all along that we, in common with any other union, will support our members carrying out a specific decision, even if that decision involves acts deemed to be unlawful…but we have also argued that neither UCATT nor any other trade union should or could support its members committing acts which are obviously of a criminal nature and which are contrary to the union's instructions.
>
> In this situation, we have consistently argued that we have no power under union rule to grant legal aid to the Shrewsbury pickets who were charged with committing such acts, nor could we be seen to be condoning the use of these techniques to further industrial ends, however legitimate these ends may be.[119]

The prosecutions were widely seen as a deliberate and vindictive attempt to curtail the successful use of the flying picket. But in the late summer and early autumn of 1972 the building workers' strike victory represented another hammer blow to the wages and industrial relations policies of the government.

Chapter 7

Militancy and politics in 1972

The year 1972 was characterised by magnificent working class struggles. This was no sudden nationwide convulsion with a movement quickly rising to a crescendo then rapidly disappearing. Instead from early January, with the start of the miners' strike, to late September, when the last building workers went back to work, there was an almost continuous period of major disputes. For over eight months[1] there was the smell of workers' struggle in the air, punctuated by the sweet taste of victory.

As in all extraordinary periods of class struggle, the whole of society was affected. The very public success of some of the big disputes helped to inspire protests that year by other groups. In May a school students' strike in London led to the formation of the National Union of School Students.[2] Preservation of the Rights of Prisoners (PROP) was established, and a series of sit-downs in May and June culminated in a prison strike in August.[3] On 1 October rent strikes were launched in over 80 towns and cities.[4] There were also strikes over the Housing Finance Act in Liverpool and Dundee in October, and over state pensions at Scunthorpe in November.[5] At the end of October 500 Asian workers at Mansfield Hosiery Mills in Loughborough went on strike for a large pay rise *and* an end to discrimination in job opportunities in the factory. As Paul Foot wrote, 'Trade unionism in the sweat-shop mills of the East Midlands will never be the same again'.[6]

This concluding chapter draws together the main features of workers' struggle during 1972, particularly noting the militant tactics, the level of solidarity action and the widespread defiance of the law. Some comparisons are also made with earlier disputes. The shifting boundaries between official and unofficial action are examined, as is the resistance of both left-wing and right-wing union leaders to strikes being used for political ends. Finally, the ambivalent role of Communist

Party (CP) members in the events of 1972 is assessed—successfully leading the opposition to right-wing union leaders on several occasions, while slavishly supporting the established left-wing leadership in the AUEW even when this course of action led to defeat.

Tactics

Looking back, the audacity and militancy of the tactics used in 1972 is breathtaking. The miners' strike on its own set new benchmarks in industrial action, and the year would be memorable just for this. One commentator remarked, 'The miners taught the working class an old…[lesson]: that victory can only go to those who fight, and that aggressive action, far from frightening off support, can attract and hold it'.[7] Ken Coates and Tony Topham of the Institute for Workers' Control saw the miners' strike as 'the most important trade-union victory of modern times'.[8] From a very different viewpoint, a writer on the journal *Management Today* believed that of all recent disputes it 'was unquestionably the most bitterly contested. The determination, not to say ferocity, of the pickets will be remembered for a long time yet. Their tactic of preventing coal moving not just out of the collieries but into the power stations was novel, intelligent and very largely successful'.[9]

Picketing

Picketing in 1972 was on a scale not seen since the 1920s. Most previous post-war strikes had been over so quickly that it was often not necessary. Where it did take place there were relatively few instances of mass picketing and probably even fewer of secondary picketing. So who could have predicted the almost military-style organisation of picketing established and sustained across large parts of the country, in the otherwise very different mining and building strikes? Traditions of secondary picketing in Yorkshire had been extended to some other mining areas in the 1969 and 1970 unofficial strikes. But the almost unprecedented step of picketing power stations raised it to an altogether higher plane, requiring some coordination from the centre. The scale of the achievement is illustrated by the fact that there were twice as many power stations to picket in 1972 as in 1984.[10] In the building strike each action committee worked out its own strategy. Groups of pickets in both strikes learned quickly from their own experience and from the successes of others. Long ago Frederick Engels wrote that strikes were 'the military school of the workingmen'.[11] This was clearly the case in 1972.

With the National Union of Mineworkers (NUM) members on official strike there was no need to defensively picket their own work-places. The miners had to ensure that coal was not moved out of col-lieries, and this was secured early on by agreements with rail and transport unions. Instead such picketing of collieries that took place (which built up after the first couple of weeks) was offensive, aimed at stopping deputies from providing safety cover. The deputies were under instructions to do the work and only mass pickets could physi-cally stop them. The other group whom miners tried to stop working (again not initially) was National Coal Board (NCB) administrative and clerical staff in another union—again mass pickets were used.

But much of the miners' picketing was not of NCB premises, and the scale of secondary picketing was extraordinary. Initially aimed at stopping the general movement of coal and coke, it was extended rapidly in practice—particularly to cover materials needed to make serviceable and ignite the coal in power stations, and to stop the movement of oil into oil-fired power stations. This required a large number of separate picket lines to stop port, rail and transport work-ers from moving loads. Much of this picketing occurred within the coalfield areas, given the proximity of many ports and power stations to them. But a significant amount required miners travelling out of the coalfields and staying away from home for days at a time, which required substantial logistical support from trade unionist and so-cialist supporters.

Edward Heath's recent reflections confirm the shock that the strike was to give the Conservative government: 'What we did not antici-pate was the spasm of militancy from a union which had been rela-tively quiet for so long, and the tactics which it was willing to adopt. The use of "flying pickets"...took us unawares'.[12] Margaret Thatcher also recalled that in cabinet meetings before the strike:

> It is extraordinary how little attention we gave to 'endurance'—the period of time we could keep the power stations and the economy run-ning with limited or no coal supplies—and how easily Cabinet was fobbed off by assurances that coal stocks were high, without considering whether those stocks were in the right locations to be useable, i.e. ac-tually at the power stations. The possibility of effective mass picketing

which would prevent oil and coal getting to power stations, was simply not on the agenda.[13]

This is not just old politicians exaggerating events in their memoirs. At the time industry secretary John Davies told parliament, 'I would perhaps freely admit that the Government did not fully realise the degree to which picketing could restrain the capacity of the electricity industry to maintain supplies'.[14] Home Secretary Reginald Maudling conceded:

> ...the effect of picketing upon the power industry was greater than had originally been forecast. A great deal of the coal in the possession of the Central Electricity Generating Board has been immobilised by picketing, and there has been a substantial effect on the supplies of other essential materials, such as oil, for example, and other chemicals. This is a wider form of picketing than has been met in the case of previous disputes.[15]

Towards the end of the strike the effectiveness of the miners' picketing even led one Labour MP, Charles Pannell, to respond as follows to Davies's 'astonishment' that the miners picketed power stations: 'Did he think they would stand at the top of coal mines as they did in 1926? What use would that be?'[16] The shock of such extensive flying picketing was compounded by the number of mass pickets that occurred during the strike, of which Saltley and Longannet were only the most spectacular.

By contrast building workers, while they did eventually picket to stop the movement of cement and other building materials, were mainly concerned to close down a huge number of often relatively small construction sites, and to win more workers (both union and non-union) to the strike. This required very mobile (flying) pickets, also occasionally in large numbers (mass pickets). For London dockers, picketing was a necessary adjunct to the national unofficial policy of blacking particular transport companies. Picket lines were away from the docks, at container bases, and only occasionally were very large. Mass pickets were in evidence during the later official dockers' strike over the Jones-Aldington Report, particularly by Hull dockers attempting to stop work at the non-scheme Neap House Wharf near Scunthorpe.

The connection between the picketing in these disputes was commented upon at the time. For example, before the builders' strike had escalated, the *Economist* argued that 'the rewarding of the miners' violent picketing…led directly to the picketing of the container depots this summer… [The] spectacular rewarding of this will make it easier to arrange tougher picketing in…[future] strikes'.[17] At the end of the building workers' strike a correspondent on the *Times* noted that it had been 'the third major industrial dispute this year whose course was directed largely by the concerted action of pickets', that the 'flying pickets had considerable success', and that while some had been prosecuted, 'the pickets had generally stopped a site and moved on before police arrived at the scene'.[18]

Safety cover (in the mines)

The miners' strike was also remarkable for widespread unofficial decisions to call out safety men and then use mass pickets (often several hundred strong) to prevent pit deputies from carrying out their work. This action was particularly successful but was overshadowed by events at the power stations. Towards the end of the strike the *Economist* claimed that Midlands miners 'had believed that the damage to underground equipment would prove to be their biggest bargaining counter'—in fact, they were 'frankly amazed at the havoc they appear to have caused [by picketing]. None of them expected the strike to bite so deeply'.[19]

Before 1972 the stopping of safety work, especially pumping to stop pits from flooding, had been a little used but potentially very potent weapon in disputes. Its relative success in 1972 has to be considered against the background of the most spectacular attempts and failures of this tactic by miners earlier in the 20th century. While this issue is specific to mining, there are equivalents in some other industrial sectors but, more generally, it is another example of a daring tactic.

At the start of the very long Cambrian combine unofficial strike in South Wales in 1910, the strikers were unable to persuade the safety men (then in a different union) to come out and used mass picketing against them. Their initial success prompted Home Secretary Winston Churchill to import police, which led to the so-called Tonypandy riots.[20] Where miners were able to bring out the safety men officially, as in a Yorkshire strike in 1919, naval units were introduced to do their work.[21]

The biggest previous withdrawal of safety work was undoubtedly in the 1921 national miners' lockout. Official Miners' Federation of Great Britain (MFGB) policy was to bring out the safety men, especially as they had been served with notices along with other mineworkers. Mass pickets were used to prevent any others from performing this work. The employers and government made great efforts to get this action withdrawn, only succeeding after nine days when the miners' partners in the Triple Alliance persuaded them to allow managerial staff through on the promise of further negotiations with the government. As the socialist historian G D H Cole argued, this 'eliminate[d] the chief factor which would have necessitated a speedy settlement of the dispute'. The MFGB executive then rejected later calls to stop safety work. This capitulation was to rebound on the miners in the 1926 lockout. Radical measures agreed by the MFGB at the beginning of October 1926 (five months into the dispute) included calling out the safety men, but this had little impact then. Because many of their members' jobs had been taken by outside labour in 1921, the colliery enginemen's unions had left the MFGB in 1922.[22]

Despite the NUM's official policy to provide safety cover in 1972, there occurred the most sustained and effective withdrawal of it of any miners' strike in the 20th century. In terms of the strike's outcome, which was decided by starving the power stations of coal, oil and essential chemicals, it perhaps made little difference, but those involved were not to know that at the time.

Sit-ins

Another particularly militant tactic in 1972 was the sit-in or occupation. After the summer of 1971 the UCS 'work-in' popularised the idea of workers taking over factories throughout Britain, though they were usually sit-ins rather than work-ins. In 1972 the sit-in was used both as a defensive and an offensive tactic. The most obvious defensive use was as a means to try to protect jobs in the short term by physically stopping plant closure and the removal of machinery. There were several examples of this throughout 1972. The year started with the Allis Chalmers work-in, quickly followed by the Fisher-Bendix occupation. The most public was probably that of Briant Colour Printing in south London, where a work-in started on 21 June: 'It published a newspaper for the UCS stewards, thousands of posters for the dockers during the NIRC actions…and a whole volume of other trade union work.' Workers at the British Leyland subsidiary Thornycroft in Basingstoke undertook a 'three-month siege, which provoked two one-day solidarity stoppages from the whole British Leyland combine', resulting in about two thirds of the jobs being saved.[23]

The sit-in tactic, however, had rarely been used in Britain offensively. Perhaps the biggest use of it before had been in the little known series of 'stay-down' strikes in about a dozen South Wales collieries over a ten-day period in October 1935 to eradicate company unionism.[24] Even at the beginning of the Manchester engineering dispute in March 1972 it was also initially used defensively, this time as a counter to management's suspension or threats of suspension of workers taking limited industrial action. But the simplicity of the tactic caught on, and when the executive of the Amalgamated Union of Engineering Workers (AUEW) legitimised its use it became the dominant form of action rather than the strike in that dispute.

There are several reasons why the Greater Manchester engineering sit-ins achieved only limited publicity at the time and have been almost totally forgotten since. Almost all of them were sit-ins where management (and often white-collar staff) was allowed into the factory. In only a few was there a total occupation, with management locked out, and this was generally only for the latter part of the dispute. As they took the form of 'internal picketing' and there was no attempt by the local union leadership to link them up, they did not light a beacon to the rest of the working class. Therefore they cannot be compared with the occupation of the factories in Italy where up to half a million workers took over their workplaces for most of the month of September 1920. Here, production continued under workers' control while materials lasted. The even larger occupation movement in France in May and June 1936 eventually involved some 2 million workers.[25] Yet, on a very small scale, British workers showed that seizing their factories was not that difficult, and that their employers tended to be unable to do anything about it.

Solidarity action

A second distinctive feature of 1972 was the extent of solidarity action. This took several forms. The most common was the respecting of miners' picket lines by rail and transport workers. While this had official approval from the railway unions NUR and ASLEF, and the Transport and General Workers Union (TGWU) it still had to be translated into practice—particularly by lorry drivers who might be threatened with disciplinary action or even dismissal by their employers, and more generally when the pickets stopped non-coal products. Home Secretary Maudling recognised its significance:

> The reason why it [picketing] has been so effective—*this is a matter which possibly has escaped the notice of the newspapers*—is that the other unions have given instructions to their members not to cross the picket lines.[26] (added emphasis)

This level of solidarity with the miners was in great contrast to the big disputes of 1921 and 1926. In the former, following Black Friday (15 April 1921) when the rail and transport unions pulled out of a proposed strike in support of the miners, there was an attempted embargo on the movement of coal. With a big increase in imported coal, 'sporadic local refusals' to handle it led on 22 April 1921 to the executives of the NUR and the Transport Workers' Federation putting an embargo on such 'tainted' imported coal and any British coal destined for other than domestic use. However, some transport unions did not enforce this ban, and employers also dismissed or suspended many of the workers operating it. For example, the suspension of dockers led to a month-long total strike by the Scottish Union of Dock Labourers on the Clyde, but they were replaced by non-union labour. On the railways local NUR officials had the difficult task of deciding which coal was to be blacked and which not. Many members were reluctant to obey merely local instructions, and 300 were dismissed for carrying out the embargo. While there were sporadic stoppages, such as at Bristol docks and Greenwich power station, it was very difficult to make the embargo effective under such conditions and the unions lifted it at the end of May, while the miners fought on alone for another month.[27]

Soon after the collapse of the 1926 General Strike in support of the miners, the MFGB approached the transport unions for an embargo on coal. They were turned down. ASLEF and the NUR replied jointly that 'we have carried out our obligations' by joining the General Strike and were then facing problems getting members re-employed.[28] Ernest Bevin, TGWU general secretary at the time, invoked the experience of 1921 'when men came out…and never got back'—'to pick out small sections of men and tell them to carry the weight of the embargo means leaving them on the stones or putting the docks out in support'.[29]

In both 1921 and 1926 attempts at embargo came after the abandonment of sympathy strike action, which encouraged the employers in their hard line. By contrast, the transport workers' refusal to cross picket lines in 1972 did not follow any earlier capitulation. Local union organisation was much stronger than in the early 1920s, and the transport employers were generally reluctant to risk escalating the action by disciplining workers for respecting picket lines. There was also widespread blacking during the 1972 strike. Workers, especially in power stations and ports, often refused to handle goods or materials that could prolong the strike.

The most public form of solidarity was undoubtedly strike action. The most dramatic examples were those around Saltley and Pentonville. The former also involved a successful mass picket, for which it is best known, but as a solidarity strike for workers from a completely different industry it was very unusual. Its scale, although challenged in press reports, was probably larger than any other sympathy action since 1926. It was soon eclipsed, however, by the strikes around the country in support of the imprisoned dockers in July. These strikes were, as with the events at Saltley on 10 February, not 'spontaneous'. They did not arise from 'normal' trade union activity but had to be organised. Socialists were critical in working for them.

Trade unions organise workers according to their occupation, industry or employer. While today many very large unions (created by mergers) straddle old divisions between workers, this does not make them any more likely to promote solidarity. Trade union activity in Britain tends to follow the collective bargaining contours established by managers and by associations of employers, and thus divides groups of workers from each other whatever their union affiliation. The solidarity strikes of 1972 cut across such boundaries. They were argued for and organised by activists who had a class, rather than just a trade union, perspective.

Defiance of the law

The scale of open defiance of the law by trade unionists was another hallmark of 1972. They came up against some of the repressive agencies of the state—police, courts and prisons. Lenin long ago captured the essence of the state with his phrase 'special bodies of armed men, prisons, etc'. It would generally be accepted that it also consists of police, the judiciary, senior civil servants and government ministers. Governments come and go, but the capitalist state remains as long as capitalism survives.

Marxists argue that the state is not neutral, balancing between classes as social democrats believe, but that it represents the interest of the dominant class in society. Lenin further elaborated:

> The state is a product and a manifestation of the *irreconcilability* of class antagonisms...According to Marx, the state is an organ of class *rule*, an organ for the *oppression* of one class by another; it is the creation of 'order', which legalises and perpetuates this oppression by moderating the conflict between classes.[30] (original emphasis)

It is in periods of heightened struggle, such as in 1972, that the class nature of the state is more clearly laid bare. The police and judiciary do not act in some abstract legal vacuum. They have discretion and will retreat in the face of superior force only to counter-attack when they sense a weakness. While formally independent in the administration of 'justice', they do not generally ignore the consequences of their actions. Neither are they somehow immune from contact with other state agencies.

The most obvious example from 1972 concerns picketing. It is debatable to what extent mass pickets were lawful, even in 1972. Some picketing involved confrontations with large numbers of police, as at Saltley and Longannet in the miners' strike, and at Neap House Wharf during the dockers' official strike. Many other mass pickets heavily outnumbered the police, who were unable to escort people or vehicles through. This issue was raised in the House of Commons several times. Maudling, the minister responsible for policing, was reluctant to admit the government's weakness.

Thus on 9 February he stated that 'the job of the police...is to ensure that peaceful picketing, which is legal, is allowed and that intimidation and unlawful picketing are prevented'.[31] On 14 February he elaborated: 'It is difficult to know...when the right of people to persuade others not to go into a factory becomes intimidation. It is a difficult line to draw in law, and the drawing of the line must be left to chief officers of police'.[32]

After the miners' pickets had been withdrawn, but before their strike had ended, Maudling was still reluctant to attack them publicly. So on 24 February, in reply to questioning on the events at Saltley, he meekly commented:

I understand that there is a decision by the courts which holds that the mere numbers involved can turn lawful picketing into intimidation. This is a fact of the law, and in practice the law has to be administered by chief officers of police.[33]

The government's impotence in the face of the miners' stranglehold of the power stations had forced its chief spokesperson for law and order to continually hide behind the police. During the 1984-85 miners' strike—the same result occurred but for the opposite reason: the government's funding of the police's numerical superiority over the pickets allowed it to pretend that control of picket lines was purely a police matter. The view that large numbers of pickets can constitute intimidation arose again in the wake of the building strike, but this time the state agencies responsible for deciding on criminal prosecutions waited for the general militancy to subside before they acted.

The neutrality of the courts was called into question several times during the year, with political considerations blatantly affecting the administration of justice. On three occasions in the dockers' dispute the National Industrial Relations Court (NIRC) ordered unofficial leaders to explain their action—in May Walter Cunningham from Hull; in June Bernie Steer, Vic Turner and Alan Williams from London; and in July Steer, Turner, Tony Merrick, Con Clancy and Derek Watkins. In each case the dockers did not go, and in each case they continued their 'unlawful' activities. The court decided to ignore Cunningham as it had hooked a TGWU official. The decision to arrest the three dockers at Chobham Farm in June was dropped, using a legal manoeuvre involving an obscure state functionary (the Official Solicitor), for fear of the developing strike movement in their defence. The eventual arrest of the Pentonville Five saw them refuse to purge their contempt. Their release came in the wake of a developing unofficial and official movement in their support. This required further contortions by the courts to justify this open defiance of the NIRC.

The Scottish miners' actions around the arrests at Longannet in the penultimate week of their strike prompted perhaps even more blatant political intervention to speed up the legal process to release the pickets. When the clamour of 1972 had died down, the state machine took its revenge for its earlier impotence. The trial of the Shrewsbury pickets for conspiracy was a vindictive act, and the long prison sentences meted out were intended as a lesson for those contemplating militant action in the future.

One of the most important functions of the capitalist state is to provide a legal justification for, and means of enforcing, the private ownership of the means of production. But 'property rights' were challenged in 1972 when the Manchester engineers and other groups of workers either sat-in their factories, denying the owners and managers access to machinery and materials, or fully occupied them, barring any entry at all. The ownership of the means of production under capitalism confers 'rights' over workers, which are enforced by the full panoply of law. One consequence is that as workers are generally not allowed in factories and other workplaces, except when they are working, they usually leave them when they go on strike. Those sitting-in or occupying were trespassing on their employers' property and were therefore liable to court orders against them. In Manchester, however, only one small employer risked using an injunction against its factory's occupiers. The judge in this case speculated on the impracticability of removing large numbers.

In the building industry the individual crane-top protests at the end of May by Peter Kavanagh in London, and by Alan Prior and John Mahon in Birmingham, which were part of the build-up to the national strike, were also trespass. Here injunctions were eventually obeyed but not before substantial publicity had been gained for their protests against employer blacklists. Those miners who decided to withhold or limit safety cover, and often even to physically stop pit deputies from providing it, were also contesting the sanctity of employers' property. So was the NUM's use of permits to allow priority loads of fuel to be moved, sometimes with pickets accompanying vehicles to ensure the correct destination. This was a feature whose significance was perhaps not fully realised at the time. It suggests comparisons with strikers' use of the permit system for motor transport during the General Strike.[34]

Alongside open defiance of the law was the high incidence of 'political' strikes (part of a more general phenomenon in the 1969-74 period). During 1972 these strikes were mainly against the operation of the Industrial Relations Act—against the proposed arrests of dockers picketing Chobham Farm, the much bigger ones to free the Pentonville Five, and then the stoppages in December over the fines on the AUEW in the Goad case.[35] The call by the Trades Union Congress (TUC) for a one-day strike in July 1972, even though it was not needed, directly challenged the use of the act—even if union leaders were not prepared to openly admit it.

Official union leadership and the role of the TUC

Most of the big disputes covered in this book were run mainly from below by rank-and-file activists. The miners' strike was official but was characterised by mass involvement, with some activities going well beyond official guidelines. The building workers' strike was official, but the early strategy of limited selective strikes was superseded when rank-and-file members escalated the action into an attempted all-out strike. And the dockers' activities were totally unofficial, except for the national strike from late July to mid-August which came after the release of the dockers from Pentonville. In the Manchester engineering dispute it was the workers who started action before the local official deadline and then decided to sit in the factories, forcing national official support even though they were acting outside the national unions' agreed strategy. Even in the relatively quiet railway dispute unofficial action preceded the official work to rule and overtime ban, and then, after the first court intervention, it was several days before it was called off.

Many union activists hold lay official positions or sit on union committees, thus causing some confusion as to what is official and what is unofficial policy or action. In 1972 the mass participation in the miners' strike and eventually in the building workers' strike blurred the distinction. Sometimes national and area full-time officials were pulled along by rank-and-file initiatives, though they sometimes tried to take credit for any successes (as NUM president Joe Gormley did in his autobiography).[36] Elsewhere in the miners' strike the national, and often the area, union leaderships were clearly against the decision by miners in large numbers of collieries to provide no, or very limited, safety cover. But they were unable to enforce their policy or to use sanctions against members, such was the popularity of the tactic. The national leadership had to emphasise time and again the need for peaceful picketing, but the license to picket involved members on the ground making their own judgements as to what would make picket lines effective.

In the building strike the rank-and-file activists forced the unions to back away from a settlement in early August. Through their local action committees they took control of the strike, pulling most officials along behind them. The scattered nature of the industry required high levels of involvement and determination on the part of the pickets. This could not have been organised just by the officials, even if they had wanted to adopt such a militant policy. The action inspired by unofficial leaders in the docks was consistently disowned by the official TGWU leadership, but this had little effect given the support of dockers (in both the TGWU and the small NASD). The unofficial campaign was a prelude to the official national strike and strengthened the officials' negotiating position. Even TGWU general secretary Jack Jones argued that 'though the action in the docks...was unofficial, it was for the right purpose'.[37]

In every case apart from the dockers' blacking campaign the official nature of the disputes gave union leaders control over their ending. On the railways, and in engineering and building, national officials agreed a settlement and terminated the disputes without consultation. In mining, a majority on the executive called off the pickets, ending any chance that the ballot would reject the proposed settlement. While Hugh Scanlon was the only union leader to systematically defy the Industrial Relations Act, he used the Manchester engineers as a pawn in his game of chess with the employers and other union leaders.

Not only did union leaders exercise their authority within their own unions, they also exercised it collectively through the TUC, especially in the monthly meetings of the General Council. In the campaign against the Industrial Relations Act the TUC leadership and most national union leaders were reluctant to move beyond verbal opposition for fear of coming into conflict with the law. The early operation of the act saw one gradual concession after another, orchestrated by the TUC General Council majority. The dockers' unofficial action against containerisation became entangled with the act, but the traditions of unofficial activity in the docks were strong enough to resist the TGWU's (especially Jones's) attempts to get their action called off. The Court of Appeal judgment, leaving the way open for imprisonment of shop stewards, could not have been predicted. But the dockers' determination that theirs was an industrial struggle (which had to be won) and not a political one (in which case the blandishments of the TGWU and TUC leaders may have worked to defuse the situation) led to the jailings. The dockers' independence from the TGWU was critical to the fight against the Industrial Relations Act and, especially, the release of the five from Pentonville.

While receiving significant support from the official movement, the miners were never subservient to the TUC and were able to dictate their own fate. Gormley, the NUM president, was disappointed in the limited TUC response at the beginning of the miners' strike, but this was critical in the union's success. An editorial in the *Times* at the end of the strike suggested, 'If other unions or the TUC had given overt assistance to the NUM, it would politically have weakened the strike. There would have appeared to be a repetition of 1926'.[38] It has also since been suggested that the miners' 'understanding of their own history…resulted in the TUC being excluded from all negotiations'.[39]

Despite the politicisation of industrial relations by the Conservative government, the official trade union leadership continued to maintain the traditional divorce between economic and political activity, thereby reinforcing the process by which workers' struggles were confined within strict limits. Thus the idea that the unions might attempt to utilise industrial militancy for political ends to challenge the government was completely rejected, as it was in the General Strike of 1926. Gormley of the NUM remarked, 'As regards bringing the government down, I have always made it plain that I thought that was a very dangerous attitude. A strike, if it was necessary, should always be on industrial, and never on political grounds'.[40]

Frank Chapple of the electricians' union, despite the media's hounding of the power workers in December 1970, was totally hostile to any suggestion that the same group of workers should exploit their unique situation in early February 1972. He too saw the political threat that would be caused just by an overtime ban in the power stations at a time when the miners were also picketing them. Even Jones and Scanlon, the left-wing leaders of the two largest unions in the country, denied the political significance of the proposed one-day official stoppage for the release of the Pentonville Five.

Fearful of bringing down the government, left and right TUC leaders were happy to accept Heath's invitation to tripartite talks on economic strategy and incomes policy, even though by doing so they bolstered the government's position and gave ideological strength to its pay restraint objectives. These talks started on 18 July and were broken off by Heath on 2 November, four days before a wage freeze was instituted. Once they had begun talks on a voluntary wages policy the TUC leaders gave the impression that wage controls were acceptable, which paved the way for Heath to finally impose statutory controls. Jones and Scanlon were a part of the six-man TUC team and were as responsible as their right-wing counterparts for disarming the movement. As Douglas Hurd noted:

> Ministers knew clearly the drawbacks and dangers of the new [statutory incomes] policy... When we knew there was no agreement we began to think sadly of contingency plans against immediate industrial trouble. Nothing happened. The policy was respected. For a year there was industrial peace and the wage explosion was averted... It does show that an imposed statutory policy can be temporarily effective. I doubt if this would have been achieved if it had not been for the apparently abortive talks beforehand.[41]

There was some resistance to the five-month wage freeze. The workers' victories of 1972 helped to inspire the unlikely groups of hospital ancillary workers and gas workers into holding selective strikes, and there was the first ever civil service one-day national strike. Teachers in London held a series of stoppages over their 'London weighting allowance', while ASLEF train drivers acted unilaterally in calling one-day strikes and a ban on Sunday working.[42] But the incomes policy held until the miners challenged Stage 3 in the winter of 1973-74. The Conservatives panicked, instituted a three-day week long before the 1974 miners' strike, then called a general election and lost their parliamentary majority.

Almost all trade union leaders had placed their faith in a Labour government to solve their problems. The TUC-Labour Party Liaison Committee had agreed a programme for the next Labour government, which included the repeal of the Industrial Relations Act and of statutory incomes policy. Both of these were duly delivered after the Conservatives' defeat in the February 1974 general election. Labour kept the act on the statute book until it had enacted a replacement. In the meantime there had been a national strike of AUEW members following sequestration of its assets in April 1974 when it refused to pay damages to a small employer, Con-Mech. This was resolved by 'an anonymous donor—a reliable source...suggested...that it was the Newspaper Proprietors' Association'.[43]

Stage 3 of the Conservative incomes policy was also allowed to remain until July 1974, when it expired. But an inflationary spiral had been triggered by the shock of the massive rise in oil prices in October

1973 immediately following the Yom Kippur Arab-Israeli war. By July 1975 the Retail Price Index was running at an annual rate of 26.9 percent. Many companies were raising prices every three months. Labour, having suffered massive unpopularity over its own statutory incomes policy in the late 1960s and having fought the February 1974 election on a pledge to abolish that of the Conservatives, was reluctant to act. It needed the support of the TUC for a voluntary policy and this was forthcoming in the Social Contract.

According to one union general secretary, following a meeting of TUC leaders with the government, 'Scanlon said, "I have looked into the abyss", and what he'd seen frightened him to death'.[44] Jones justified his position at the September 1975 TUC:

> In recent months there has been a fantastic level of wage claims, which would have meant 30, 40, 50 or 60 per cent in some firms. Arising out of fear for the future, yes, but they did affect prices and they have affected jobs...the union I lead and myself personally have never supported the idea that trade unionism is a license for any group to look after themselves and to hell with the rest...Not a free for all but a fair for all—that is our policy...we cannot afford the luxury of destroying the Labour Government and handing power to Mrs Thatcher.[45]

Jones and Scanlon were the two most important union leaders of their generation. Not only did they lead the two largest and most powerful unions in the country, but their left-wing credentials also gave them an authority denied to their right-wing contemporaries on the TUC General Council. The result of their support for the government meant that 'the network of activists who had resisted *In Place of Strife* and the Tory attacks of 1970-74 were torn apart'.[46]

The Communist Party and the revolutionary left

The Communist Party (CP), with a claimed membership of about 29,000 in 1972, had for many years provided the political cement binding together militants within different industries and unions, and played an important role in building shop-floor union organisation. Such an achievement has largely been ignored by academic historians, or distorted by the mythology of official party history and the demonology of the CP's right wing opponents.[47] As we have seen, individual CP members and close sympathisers played a leading role in most of the big disputes in 1972, for example, Jock Kane and Mick McGahey among the miners, John Tocher of the Manchester engineers, Bernie Steer and Vic Turner of the London dockers, and Lou Lewis and Pete Carter in the building industry.

The broad opposition to the Industrial Relations Act owed much to the earlier work of the CP-controlled Liaison Committee for the Defence of Trade Unions (LCDTU) in opposing *In Place of Strife* and the Industrial Relations Bill. Once the bill became an act and the terrain changed from general protest against the government to intervening in specific disputes, the LCDTU was hamstrung. Organising support for workers defying the law risked bringing it into conflict with union leaders whose friendship the CP was anxious to cultivate. John McIlroy and Alan Campbell have commented of the LCDTU that:

> Unlike the shop stewards' movement [of the First World War] or the early Minority Movement [of the mid-1920s], it did not privilege the rank-and-file or emphasize the desirability of autonomy *per se*; independent organization was a means necessary to exert pressure on the apparatus, not as a substitute for it. Its sponsors embraced more limited objectives and a more optimistic view of 'the bureaucracy' and existing union organization than did their predecessors.[48]

The LCDTU was composed of delegates from sponsoring organisations which had been canvassed by its CP chairman, Kevin Halpin, and secretary, Jim Hiles. But committee meetings were never publicised and invitations were issued directly to sponsoring bodies, which were usually shop stewards' bodies that were under CP influence. Discussion at LCDTU conferences was largely on the basis of 'declarations' drawn up by the committee with no amendments permitted so as to ensure that the line presented by the CP was not successfully challenged from the floor. Its mission was 'to activate the official machinery of the unions and TUC, not to replace it',[49] and on the Industrial Relations Bill it had been fairly successful. This position was consistent with the CP's own line that 'rank-and-file action was the forward moment in the mobilization of the official machinery, not an alternative to it'.[50]

Yet the events of 1972 exemplified the flaw in the CP's industrial strategy. Its implantation in the AUEW's official structure, and its support for the union's leader Scanlon, demobilised its membership and supporters in that year's engineering dispute. CP officials and leading stewards in Manchester engineering started a militant district-wide campaign. But their own traditions of working made it difficult for them to trust the union membership by instituting regular mass meetings and finding ways of linking together the sit-ins. They then reluctantly but loyally accepted the national AUEW's decision to drop the demand for a shorter working week, which led to most sit-ins folding and proved a turning point in the national fortunes of the Broad Left.

In three of the other disputes covered in this book the role of CP members was oppositional to the incumbent union leadership to varying degrees. In the miners' dispute the left within the NUM had pushed for a national strike and was responsible for the tactics adopted. While Gormley publicly announced to the press that picket lines would be put where needed, it was the left-wing members on the executive, with the CP at their core, who had the courage to push for what was then the unprecedentedly militant tactic of wide scale *secondary* picketing, particularly beyond the coalfields. This gave rank-and-file activists (including CP members) an official platform on which to build, even if they went way beyond the official line on safety cover. Again, it was the left-wing executive members who formed the centre of opposition to a number of possible compromises late in the strike. When the court of inquiry was announced, they refused to stop the strike, and they also refused to call off the pickets. When the Wilberforce inquiry reported, they rejected its proposals and then the extra offers from the NCB. They squeezed as much as they could before the centre group on the executive took fright and joined the right in agreeing to the final concessions in Downing Street. Even then the left did not want the pickets called off while the ballot was held, but they were also defeated on this.

In the dockers' case individual CP members were a significant part of the unofficial leadership which acted, for most of the year, independently of the TGWU officials. In the building dispute CP members were again an important component of the local leadership of the activists who wrested the initiative away from the national officials by dramatically extending the official strike in practice. But the CP as a political party did not see such actions as providing an alternative to the disastrous national policy pursued in engineering. This had already been highlighted by the *Morning Star*'s failure to criticise UCATT leader George Smith. In the years after 1972 the CP's emphasis on getting left officials elected took precedence over sustaining rank-and-file activity in the mines and the building industry (in both of which it was already a significant current). In the London docks the autonomy of the activists soon drove most away from the CP line.[51]

Yet independence from individual unions, and from the TUC, had been critical in putting workers in a much stronger bargaining position at key moments in 1972. This contrasted strongly with the CP's slogan in 1926: 'All Power to the General Council'. Such a policy disarmed opponents of the TUC's bureaucratic control of the General Strike and made it difficult to resist the TUC's inevitable capitulation to the government.[52] In 1974, with the Broad Left's increasing influence within the NUM, the second miners' victorious strike was passive compared to 1972. It led John Monks, the current TUC general secretary, to argue that 'the 1974 miners' strike did not rely on mass picketing but on TUC-supported guidelines of six pickets and agreements between the NUM and unions in transport and energy. These features did not create the same potent symbols as the 1972 strike'.[53]

The CP generally dismissed the small revolutionary socialist groups as 'ultra-left'. But they did present, in different ways, a revolutionary alternative to its policies. The Socialist Labour League (later the Workers Revolutionary Party) had a significant base at the British Leyland assembly plant in Cowley and in the actors' union, Equity, but elsewhere it was known for its 'catastrophism'—'capitalism had entered permanent crisis, a pre-revolutionary situation lay around the corner'. The International Marxist Group had only 400 members in 1972 and was overwhelmingly student-based.[54] Its weekly newspaper, *Red Mole*, had extensive coverage of the major disputes but its base was extremely weak.

The International Socialists (IS) had managed to make contact with significant numbers of workers during the wages revolt of 1969-70. Tony Cliff's book, *The Employers' Offensive: Productivity Deals and How to Fight Them*, was sold to thousands of shop stewards and union branch secretaries in 1970, and gave the group some credibility. It was part of the transformation of IS, during the early 1970s, from a predominantly student organisation to one with significant manual and white-collar worker membership. The group's growth was reflected at an industrial conference held in Manchester in January

1972, at the height of the miners' strike, when more than 700 delegates attended, twice as many as at the previous conference in 1970.[55] The print run of the IS weekly paper, *Socialist Worker*, rose to 27,000 in February 1972.[56] During the Pentonville dispute the group's printshop was given over to producing the national port shop stewards' committee's propaganda.

But, as Chris Harman has argued, 'so long as workers were winning, activists saw little reason to join a small revolutionary organisation'.[57] Thus, despite the CP's self-imposed limitations, IS (and the other Trotskyist groups) was not sufficiently rooted, large or credible enough to influence the direction of industrial and political militancy in 1972, though it did help to 'oil the wheels'.[58]

Conclusion

Bob Light, a London docker in 1972, has recently asked:

> Why is it there are no badges, no mugs? Why is it that Pentonville is the forgotten epic? It is precisely because it doesn't suit the rotten, stinking politics of all the reformists who control the labour movement in the country. The lessons of Pentonville are essentially revolutionary.[59]

His questions mirror the paradox noted in the introduction to the book. Victories tend not to be celebrated in the British labour movement. They are dangerous, while defeats are safe. It has even been suggested that 'labourism is a tradition of losing, not winning'.[60] This is because, as was discussed in the first chapter and has been illustrated in the rest of the book, union leaders, whether left or right, draw back from pressing too hard any temporary advantage over employers. They will continue to do this, especially during periods of heightened class struggle.

It may be argued that the events of 1972 were unique, and that the subsequent redundancy of most miners and dockers means that the tactics deployed then are of little use in the future. But this would miss the point for a number of reasons. First, it was far from inevitable that any of the groups of workers that feature in this book would fight in 1972. For ten years until the late 1960s the miners were a demoralised group facing continual job loss and some wage reductions. The dockers also could do little to stop their jobs disappearing. Building workers were increasingly disorganised due to the growing influence of the 'lump'. Railway workers were generally quiescent. Yet all of these groups were able to take action in ways that astonished most commentators.

Second, there are many groups of workers who have since demonstrated their willingness and ability to fight back against rampant employers in the wake of the mass unemployment unleashed during the 1979-83 Thatcher government and the devastating defeat inflicted on the miners in 1985. These include rail and postal workers and contract electricians, as well as schoolteachers, hospital workers, local government and bank employees.

Third, all sorts of workers have been written off as unorganisable at different points over the last 150 years. These have included dockers, lorry drivers and refuse collectors, all of whom became extremely well organised at certain points. In the 1930s few car workers were in unions—in the 1960s and 1970s they epitomised shop-floor power. Bank workers were split for most of the 20th century by the employers' policy of establishing staff associations. Examples are legion of weak groups getting organised and finding sanctions that gave them some leverage over their employers.

In many ways our account of 1972 is a guidebook of militant working class struggle. In particular it shows the unevenness of workers' action even within the same dispute and how the activists tried to solve the practical problems that they faced. But it is not a 'how to' book. Its lessons have to be applied creatively in changing circumstances. History does not repeat itself exactly, but the tactics available to workers on strike have not altered greatly. The current laws make some strike tactics more problematic than in 1972, but when workers are confident enough then laws are defied and employers are often impotent, as this book has shown. Workers have always had to deal with some form of legal sanction against themselves and their unions.

The year 1972 provides wonderful examples of the importance of solidarity action in helping to win certain strikes, how workers have been prepared to defy the law (sometimes in large numbers), and that they can act independently of their own unions' official disavowal. It demonstrates that 'pure and simple' trade unionism was not behind the building of organisation capable of sustaining the most significant industrial action that developed that year. Organised left-wing activists (particularly individual, and small groups of, CP members in that period) were central to the unofficial movements that preceded and led several of the big disputes. For deep-rooted political reasons, connected with the degeneration of the Russian Revolution, the British CP for most of its existence has subordinated workers' rank-and-file activity to its pursuit of position and influence within full-time union officialdom. Yet militant rank-and-file action, working with union officials when they supported it or independent of them when they did not, was a necessary ingredient of the startling victories of 1972. Although the CP in Britain has collapsed organisationally, its reformist ideas—that fundamental political and social change comes through winning elections, in parliament and in the unions—have not.

This book shows that another tradition—that of workers being prepared to operate independently of their union officials when necessary—was still alive in the movement and could be devastatingly effective. The successors to the generation of 1972 must learn from, and hopefully will surpass, that 'glorious summer'.

Notes

Introduction

1. 'Now is the winter of our discontent Made glorious summer...'. At least one writer has cited the full quotation from Shakespeare, but without the particular use we have made of it: Crouch, 1982, p229, n1.
2. *Guardian*, 6 September 1997.
3. Goodman, 1975, pp68-69.
4. 'Introduction', in Harrison, 1978, p1.
5. By way of comparison, all but three of the 14 major strike movements in the period 1910-14 were only district- or region-wide. Following the rise of national wage bargaining during the First World War, there were 'four industry-wide stoppages in shipbuilding...three in coalmining, two each in cotton and in railways, and one each in building, docks, engineering, foundries, printing, and wool' between 1919-1926, excluding the General Strike: Clegg, 1985, pp26, 550.
6. For details on all of these, see Harman, 1988.
7. For example, in a speech to Labour's hundredth party conference: *Guardian*, 29 September 1999.

Chapter 1

1. Barnett, 1973, p3.
2. Figures for Great Britain only, in Bain and Price, 1980, Table 2.2, pp39-40.
3. Turner, Clack and Roberts, 1967, p340.
4. Townsend, 1979, p641.
5. Bain and Price, 1980, Table 2.2, pp39-40.
6. Bain and Price, 1983, chapter 1.
7. Lyddon, 1996, pp186-211.
8. McCarthy and Parker, 1968, p15; Donovan Report, 1968, para 701.
9. Cliff and Barker, 1966, pp105, 104, 135.
10. G Goodman, 'Outline of Events', in *Contemporary Record* 2:1, 1988, p36.
11. Jenkins, 1970, pp12, 15.
12. Donovan Report, 1968, paras 70-71. During this period, government statistics on strikes significantly underestimated the actual number as many were too short or small to reach the minimum criteria for inclusion and many others were not notified. The only attempt to estimate the under-recording (for manufacturing industry in the two-year period 1976-77) suggested that only about a quarter of all stoppages were actually included. See Brown, 1981, pp98-100.

13 Donovan Report, 1968, paras 412-413, 415.
14 Donovan Report, 1968, paras 57-58, 311.
15 Flanders, 1970, p169.
16 Donovan Report, 1968, paras 65-68.
17 Donovan Report, 1968, paras 103-107.
18 Donovan Report, 1968, para 110.
19 *Economist*, 4 September 1965, p896.
20 Donovan Report, 1968, paras 163-171.
21 Allen, 1966, pp88-93.
22 Hyman, 1973, p102.
23 Kelly, 1991, p53.
24 Seifert, 1987, pp94-103; Burke, 1971, pp43-122.
25 Hyman, 1973, p142.
26 Roche, 1970, p162; Hyman, 1973, p143.
27 Friedman and Meredeen, 1980, chapters 3 and 4. On p297 they quote the *Daily Mirror*, 2 July 1968: 'The 8^1/$_2$ million women workers should raise their teacups today in a toast to the petticoat strikers at Fords, for they have taken a big step forward in the battle for equal pay.'
28 Sewill, 1975, p48.
29 Jones, 1973, pp126-127.
30 'Chronicle', *British Journal of Industrial Relations* 9:1 (1971), pp101-102; *Department of Employment Gazette*, May 1971, p438.
31 Fryer and Williams, 1993, pp91-92.
32 Wigham, 1976, p166.
33 Wigham, 1976, p167.
34 Wigham, 1976, p167; Heath, 1998, p336.
35 'Chronicle', *British Journal of Industrial Relations* 9:1 (1971), pp100-101
36 Barker, 1972, p36.
37 Heath, 1998, pp332-333.
38 Barker, 1972, pp37, 41-42.
39 Chapple, 1984, p121.
40 Barker, 1972, p39.
41 Hurd, 1979, p101.
42 Clinton, 1984, p558.
43 Speaking in the House of Commons, 22 February 1971, cited in Holmes, 1982, p59.
44 *Times*, 18 February 1971, cited in Clinton, 1984, p563.
45 Clinton, 1984, p572.
46 Clinton, 1984, p568.
47 Barnett, 1973, p7.
48 D Winchester, 'Public Sector Pay: The Past Year's Lessons', *Industrial Relations Review and Report* 13, August 1971, pp7, 9.
49 Taylor, 1993, pp177-181.
50 The term 'black' or 'blacking' used in this context means the refusal to work or handle particular goods. It derives from the term 'blackleg', which was invented to describe coal miners who scabbed during strikes as they could be identified by their black legs.

51 *Fair Deal at Work*, 1968, pp8, 30, 31, 41.

52 *Fair Deal at Work*, 1968, p39.

53 *Fair Deal at Work*, 1968, pp18-27.

54 Jenkins, 1970, pp24, 30, 33-34.

55 *In Place of Strife*, 1969, paras 60, 62, 93-96, 97-98, 109, 116.

56 Jenkins, 1970, p136; the quote is from McIlroy and Campbell, 1999, p11.

57 McIlroy and Campbell, 1999, pp8-11; Gennard and Bain, 1995, p387.

58 Jenkins, 1970, pp132, 137-138.

59 Jenkins, 1970, chapter 8.

60 Barnes and Reid, 1980, p137.

61 Moran, 1977, p88.

62 TV interview, 26 May 1976, quoted in Holmes, 1982, p20.

63 Interview with Hugh Scanlon.

64 Moran, 1977, p88. In a 1980 interview with Anthony Seldon, Carr recalled, 'It was one thing I had never expected the trade unions to do. Had they come to negotiate I am sure we could have made a number of changes which would have made the legislation more acceptable to them': reproduced in *Contemporary Record* 2:1, 1988, p46. During the years in opposition, Sewill, as the Director of the Conservative Research Department, 'asked Ted Heath several times…what would happen if the unions didn't accept it and he said that he and Robert Carr had had confidential discussions, and they had been assured that all was well': *Contemporary Record* 2:1, 1988, pp38-39.

65 TUC, 'General Council's Report to a Special Congress on the Industrial Relations Bill', 18 March 1971, para 27.

66 McIlroy and Campbell, 1999, p14.

67 McIlroy and Campbell, 1999, p15.

68 Holmes, 1982, p21; Gennard and Bain, 1995, p389.

69 Quoted in Moran, 1977, p115.

70 McIlroy and Campbell, 1999, pp14-15; Jefferys, 1975, p11.

71 Holmes, 1982, p22. Quote from Trades Union Congress, 1972a, p1.

72 *AUEW Journal*, March 1971, p111.

73 Mortimer, 1994, p245; Gennard and Bain, 1995, p295.

74 Moran, 1977, pp97, 99, 100.

75 Moran, 1977, p100.

76 Moran, 1977, p98.

77 Quoted in Moran, 1977, pp103-105.

78 Moran, 1977, pp125-128.

79 Moran, 1977, pp127-128.

80 Moran, 1977, p135.

81 Moran, 1977, p135.

82 *Times*, 28 October 1971, quoted in Holmes, 1982, p23. Carr later admitted, 'I never expected the trade unions would oppose the bill on the question of registration… And from their narrow short-term point of view it was a damnably effective tactic': Whitehead, 1985, p73.

83 The NUGMW and NALGO were the third and fourth largest unions at the time respectively.

84 Weekes, Mellish, Dickens and Lloyd, 1975, p259.

85 Quoted in Glyn and Harrison, 1980, p68.
86 Heath, 1998, pp340-341.
87 Thompson and Hart, 1972, pp15, 49.
88 Thompson and Hart, 1972, pp16, 51-53.
89 Foster and Woolfson, 1986, p16.
90 Thompson and Hart, 1972, p90.
91 Coates, 1973, p25.
92 Marks, 1974, p12.
93 *Socialist Worker*, 15 January 1972.
94 Marks, 1974, p14.
95 Figures adapted from Gennard, 1977, pp100-101.
96 This was translated as 'Teoriia i praktika angliiskago tred-iunionizma' (The theory and practice of English trade unionism) in two volumes, St Petersburg, 1900-1901: Hammond, 1974, pp80, 149. Also see Ulam, 1969, p175.
97 Webb and Webb, 1894, pp454, 431.
98 Webb and Webb, 1894, p456.
99 Mills, 1948, p9.
100 Following the capitulation of the TUC leaders in calling off the 1926 General Strike, leaving the miners to fight alone, there were few large-scale strikes until the end of the 1960s. In fact apart from a flurry of five major textile industry strikes during 1929-32 there were no national disputes of note until the shipbuilding and engineering strikes of 1957 (for which, see Chapter 4). Subsequent to these the London bus strike of 1958 and the 1966 seafarers' strike were the two most politically significant, large disputes before the 1969-74 strike wave. For references on these and other big disputes see Lyddon, 1998, especially pp117-130.
101 Hyman, 1973, p108.
102 The AEF was the immediate predecessor of the AUEW.
103 Beynon, 1973, chapter 10.
104 Mathews, 1972.
105 Walton and McKersie, 1965, especially chapters 8-9.
106 For example, J Torode, 'The Terrible Twins', *New Statesman*, 1 October 1971, pp428, 430.
107 Cliff and Gluckstein, 1986, chapter 6.
108 Cliff and Gluckstein, 1986, pp124-125, 128; also see Darlington, 1998, pp111-122.
109 Communist Party, 1968, p6.
110 Birchall, 1972, p32.
111 McIlroy, 1999, p236.
112 Barker, 1973, p47.
113 Harman, 1988, p237.
114 *Comment*, November 1971.

Chapter 2

1 Handy, 1981, p8.
2 The number of days lost was about five times that in the 1984-85 strike.

3   Durcan, McCarthy and Redman, 1983, Chapter 8.
4   Church and Outram, 1998, p221.
5   Handy, 1981, p48.
6   Hughes and Moore, 1972, pp74-77.
7   Taylor, 1984, p88.
8   Ashworth, 1986, p305.
9   Allen, 1981, pp118-119, 124-135, 141, 166-168; Minkin, 1980, p252.
10 Allen, 1981, pp137-139.
11 Taylor, 1984, p204.
12 Scargill had joined the Young Communist League at the age of 15 and became a member of its national executive committee, but left about six years later to join the Labour Party. Nonetheless, he shared many Communist Party ideas about work in the unions. See Routledge, 1993, pp43-47; Scargill, 1975, pp3-33.
13 Allen, 1981, pp139-140. See also Crick, 1985, pp39-41.
14 Scargill, 1975, pp9-10.
15 Interview with Frank Cave.
16 Oldham and others, 1970, pp129-136; Allen, 1981, p156.
17 Allen, 1981, p158.
18 Allen, 1981, p159.
19 Allen, 1981, pp162-166.
20 Allen, 1981, pp174-175; Taylor, 1984, p214.
21 Interview with Derek Ezra.
22 Quoted in Hall, 1981, p174.
23 Gormley, 1982, p89.
24 Allen, 1981, pp177-179.
25 Gormley, 1982, pp90-94.
26 Allen, 1981, p180.
27 Diary entry for 17 March 1972 in King, 1975, p186.
28 Quoted in Hall, 1981, p175.
29 Quoted in Allen, 1981, p207.
30 *Times*, 8, 11 January 1972.
31 This policy was communicated in circular AS 300/71 and stated that 'pumpsmen, winding enginemen, fan attendants and telephone operators (where necessary)...be allowed to work during the strike, together with those required for the safe operation of machinery, apparatus and equipment associated with pumping, winding and ventilation': reported in NUM circular AS 65/72, 'Strike Action', 10 February 1972, TUC file.
32 *Labour Research*, April 1972, p67.
33 *Times*, 10 January 1972; *Financial Times*, 11 January 1972.
34 *Times*, 11, 12 January 1972; *Financial Times*, 13 January 1972.
35 *Financial Times*, 17 January, 1 February 1972; *Times*, 24, 28 January, 21 February 1972.
36 Reported at TUC General Council, 26 January 1972.
37 *Times*, 25 January 1972.
38 McCormick, 1979, pp205, 223.
39 *Guardian*, 28, 29 January 1972; *Financial Times*, 29 January 1972.
40 Griffin, 1989, pp156-157.

41   Francis and Smith, 1980, pp470-473.
42   *Financial Times*, 1 February 1972; *Guardian*, 2 February 1972; *Times*, 1, 2, 4 February 1972; McCormick, 1979, p223.
43   *Guardian*, 8 February 1972; *Financial Times*, 8 February 1972; Hall, 1981, p184; Taylor, 1984, pp226-227, gives more examples of the bitterness displayed by pickets in Yorkshire in early February.
44   *Times*, 28 January 1972.
45   *Guardian*, 10 February 1972.
46   NUM circular AS 65/72, 10 February 1972, TUC file; McCormick, 1979, p223.
47   *Economist*, 5 February 1972, p71.
48   Gormley, 1982, pp95, 97.
49   *Times*, 13, 15 January 1972.
50   Francis and Smith, 1980, p471.
51   *Financial Times*, 13, 17 January 1972; *Guardian*, 17 January 1972.
52   *Guardian*, 25 January 1972.
53   Pitt, 1979, p140.
54   *Times*, 21, 22 January 1972; *Guardian*, 24 January 1972; Hall, 1981, p183; Allen, 1981, p195.
55   Quoted in *Hansard*, vol 832, 2 March 1972, col 728.
56   *Hansard*, vol 829, 24 January 1972, col 972.
57   *Guardian*, 24 January, 7 February 1972.
58   Francis and Smith, 1980, p472; *Times*, 1 February 1972.
59   *Guardian*, 28, 29 January 1972.
60   *Times*, 25 January 1972.
61   *Morning Star*, 22 January 1972.
62   Taylor, 1980, p362.
63   Taylor, 1984, pp220, 222.
64   *Morning Star*, 12 January 1972; *Times*, 13 January 1972; *Guardian*, 13 January 1972; Hall, 1981, p177; Taylor, 1984, pp219-220; Crick, 1985, pp53-54.
65   Taylor, 1984, p220.
66   Allen, 1981, p191.
67   *Morning Star*, 12 January 1972; *Financial Times*, 13 January 1972; Allen, 1981, p191.
68   Bagwell, 1982, p244; NUR circular, TUC file; *Financial Times*, 7 January 1972; *Times*, 8 January 1972; *Guardian*, 10 January 1972.
69   TUC Finance and General Purposes Committee (F&GPC), 10 January 1972; TUC annual report, 1972, pp97-98.
70   *Financial Times*, 11 January 1972.
71   *Morning Star*, 11 January 1972.
72   *Times*, *Financial Times*, 11 January 1972. Daly later suggested that it was CP member Jock Kane from Yorkshire who had suggested using flying pickets: Whitehead, 1985, p74.
73   *Times*, 21 February 1972.
74   NUM press statement, 11 January 1972, in TUC file.
75   NUM circular AS 17/72, 'Peaceful Picketing', reproduced in Allen, 1981, p201. The union also apparently announced that there should be 24-hour picketing, and the *Guardian*, 12 January 1972, commented, 'If the NUM carries

off this operation it could be a huge success.'

76   NUM circular, 'Instructions to Pickets', 12 January 1972; NUM area circular 19/72, 'NUM Pickets—Power Stations', 12 January 1972, reproduced in Allen, 1981, pp202-203.
77   Griffin, 1989, pp147-149.
78   Interview, cited in Griffin, 1989, p161.
79   Pitt, 1979, pp142-144.
80   *Morning Star*, 12 January 1972.
81   NUM area circular 22/72, 'Non-Colliery Picketing', 13 January 1972, reproduced in Allen, 1981, p204.
82   Pitt, 1979, pp126-133; quote from p132.
83   Pitt, 1979, p150.
84   Pitt, 1979, pp151-152.
85   Allen, 1981, p194; Pitt, 1979, p153; NUM area circular 35/72, 'Instructions to Pickets', 21 January 1972, reproduced in Allen, 1981, p206.
86   *Financial Times*, 17 January 1972.
87   Pitt, 1979, pp161-162.
88   Pitt, 1979, pp145-148, quotation from p148.
89   C Adam, 'The Other Price of Coal', *New Society*, 4 February 1972, p132.
90   Taylor, 1984, p222.
91   Allen, 1981, p192; Taylor, 1980, pp363-364; Scargill, 1975, pp11-12. According to Routledge, 1993, p67, Scargill's 'version has now entered the official myth'.
92   *Times*, 25, 26, 27 January 1972; Taylor, 1980, p365; Taylor, 1984, p223.
93   Geary, 1986, p94
94   Geary, 1986, p100.
95   Geary, 1986, p93.
96   *Financial Times*, 14 February 1972.
97   Allen, 1981, p189.
98   Allen, 1981, p200; 'The Miners' Strike', *Labour Research*, April 1972, pp74-75; *Hansard*, vol 832, 2 March 1972, col 727; Barnett, 1973, p10, uses the 40,000 figure.
99   Allen, 1981, p214, though this figure does not appear in the edited evidence in Hughes and Moore, 1972; *Times*, 2 February 1972; E P Thompson, 'A Special Case', *New Society*, 24 February 1972, p403, also cites 60,000. The lower figure tallies with NUM executive member Dai Francis's 'tens of thousands': *Morning Star*, 5 February 1972. Allowing for rotas operating across and within days, it could well be consistent with the 9,000 figure in early February cited by two Labour MPs, Alex Eadie (also on the NUM executive) and Eric Varley (from Chesterfield), the latter claiming 'about 9,000 miners per day…on constant picket duty' on '1,000 picket lines': *Hansard*, vol 830, 8 February 1972, cols 1196 (Eadie), 1209 (Varley). Taylor, 1980, p263, suggested 11,000 on 'continuous picket duty every day' by 5 February. Hall, 1981, p191, repeats this figure.
100 Interview with Frank Cave.
101 Allen, 1981, p200.
102 During the 1984-85 national miners' strike 11,291 people were arrested, of whom 8,932 were charged. Most of the offences were for breach of the peace,

obstructing the police and obstructing the highway, but there were also charges of unlawful assembly, riot, affray, arson, grievous bodily harm and murder: Wallington, 1985, p150.

103 *Times*, 2, 5, 15 February 1972.

104 *Times*, 24 January 1972.

105 *Financial Times*, 31 January 1972.

106 *Financial Times*, 29 January 1972.

107 *Economist*, 5 February 1972, pp71-72.

108 *Economist*, 26 February 1972, p71.

109 *Morning Star*, 24 January 1972.

110 *Socialist Worker*, 22 January 1972.

111 *Morning Star*, 24 January 1972.

112 *Morning Star*, 11, 12, 13 January 1972

113 Pitt, 1979, p154; *Morning Star*, 27 January 1972.

114 *Financial Times*, 16, 17 February 1972; *Times*, 17 February 1972.

115 *Times*, 2 August 1972.

116 Barnett, 1973, p11.

117 *Morning Star*, 26 January 1972; *Financial Times*, 2 February 1972.

118 *Morning Star*, 20, 27 January 1972.

119 *Morning Star*, 28 January; 7, 16 February 1972.

120 *Morning Star*, 4 February 1972.

121 Taylor, 1980, p364; Pitt, 1979, p177.

122 *Morning Star*, 25 February 1972.

123 J Gormley, 'The Miners' Strike', *TASS Journal*, May 1972.

124 *Times*, 18, 19, 27 November, 10, 17 December 1971.

125 *Times*, 15 January 1972.

126 *Times*, 10 January 1972; Pitt, 1979, p151.

127 Pitt, 1979, p152; *Times*, 21 January 1972.

128 Pitt, 1979, pp157-158; *Times*, 28 January 1972.

129 *Times*, 3 February 1972.

130 *Economist*, 5 February 1972, p72.

131 *Times*, 7 February 1972.

132 *Times*, 8, 9 February 1972.

133 Chapple, 1984, p126.

134 *Financial Times*, 9 February 1972.

135 *Financial Times*, 4 February 1972; *Times*, 9 February 1972.

136 'The Miners' Strike', *Labour Research*, April 1972, p73.

137 Barnes and Reid, 1980, p153. The gas workers settled on 24 January, backdated to 16 January, and the water workers settled on 27 January, backdated to 6 December 1971: *Times*, 25, 28 January 1972; *Industrial Relations Review and Report* 25, February 1972.

138 J Torode, 'Miners: A "Special Case"?', *New Statesman*, 11 February 1972, p173.

139 *Times*, 9 February 1972.

140 Barnes and Reid, 1980, p153.

141 *Hansard*, vol 830, 8 February 1972, col 1152; *Hansard* 10 February 1972, cols 1560-1562.

142 Entry for 16 February 1972 in King, 1975, p180.

143 Gormley, 1982, pp107-108.
144 Gormley, 1982, pp108-109; *Hansard*, vol 830, 11 February 1972, cols 1727-1728.
145 *Morning Star*, 4 February 1972.
146 Hall, 1981, p188; Allen, 1981, pp197-198.
147 *Birmingham Evening Mail*, 3 February 1972.
148 Griffin, 1989, p150.
149 Corfield, 1982, pp150-152.
150 *Morning Star*, 10 February 1982, reproduced in Watters, 1992, p67.
151 Scargill, 1975, p14.
152 Frank Watters, a former Scottish miner, was sent by the CP to the Yorkshire coalfield in 1953 in order to help to organise a broad-based left wing to oppose the local right-wing NUM leadership. In the process he worked alongside Scargill and other young militants. Between 1967 and 1974 Watters was full-time CP secretary in Birmingham. See *Bulletin of the Society for the Study of Labour History* 43 (1981), pp54-67, and Watters, 1992.
153 *Morning Star*, 7 February 1972. Strictly speaking it should not have been open for trading on a Sunday.
154 Geary, 1986, p74; Hall, 1981, pp189-190.
155 *Birmingham Evening Mail*, 7 February 1972.
156 *Times*, 8 February 1972.
157 *Socialist Worker*, 12 February 1972.
158 Interview with Frank Watters; see also Watters, 1992.
159 Interview with Frank Watters.
160 Account of Scargill's speech given by Frank Watters in the *Morning Star*, 10 February 1982, reproduced in Watters, 1992, p66.
161 Interview with Frank Watters; Watters, 1992, p63.
162 Interview with Mick Rice.
163 *Times*, 10 February 1972.
164 Scargill, 1975, p18.
165 *Financial Times*, *Morning Star*, 11 February 1972; Clutterbuck, 1978, pp69, 296 n2.
166 Cliff, 1985, pp45-46.
167 Quoted in Charlton, 1973, p11.
168 Scargill, 1975, p19.
169 Scargill, 1975, p19.
170 Maudling, 1978, pp160-161.
171 *Times*, 11 February 1972.
172 *Hansard*, vol 830, 10 February 1972, cols 1565-1574; quote from col 1573.
173 *Morning Star*, 11 February 1972.
174 *Morning Star*, 11 February 1972; *Times*, 12 February 1972.
175 Both quoted in Crick, 1985, p61.
176 Geary, 1986, p77, Table 7.
177 *Keesing's Contemporary Archives*, p25186.
178 *Hansard*, vol 830, 11 February 1972, cols 1736-1737.
179 *Keesing's Contemporary Archives*, p25186.
180 NUM circular AS 67/72, 14 February 1972, TUC file.

181 *Morning Star*, 16 February 1972.
182 Gormley, 1982, p109.
183 *Hansard*, vol 831, 14 February 1972, cols 155, 156, 157.
184 *Financial Times*, 16 February 1972.
185 Allen, 1981, p199.
186 *Morning Star*, 15, 16 February 1972; *Times*, 18 February 1972; quotations from Wallington, 1972, p221.
187 *Times*, *Financial Times*, 17 February 1972.
188 Wallington, 1972, pp220-222; *Financial Times*, 18 February 1972; *Guardian*, *Morning Star*, 19 February 1972.
189 Heath, 1998, p351.
190 Wilberforce Report, 1972, para 8.
191 Barnett, 1973, p11.
192 *Hansard*, vol 830, 17 February 1972, cols 623-624.
193 *Hansard*, House of Lords, vol 328, 17 February 1972, col 327.
194 'Striking Victory', *Spectator*, 19 February 1972, p267.
195 Wilberforce Report, 1972, paras 36-39.
196 Wilberforce Report, 1972, para 40.
197 J Torode, 'The Lessons of Wilberforce', *New Statesman*, 25 February 1972, p228.
198 *Hansard*, vol 831, 21 February 1972, col 902.
199 J Torode, 'The Lessons of Wilberforce', *New Statesman*, 25 February 1972, p228.
200 Wilberforce Report, 1972, para 43.
201 J Torode, 'The Lessons of Wilberforce', *New Statesman*, 25 February 1972, p228.
202 Interview with Robert Carr; Hurd, 1979, p102.
203 'Coalmining Industry Dispute', TUC F&GPC, 21 February 1972.
204 TUC F&GPC, 15 February 1972.
205 Heath, 1998, p352.
206 Gormley, 1982, p112; Barnes and Reid, 1980, pp153-154.
207 Pitt, 1979, p197.
208 Campbell, 1994, p418; quotation from Allen, 1981, p217.
209 *Hansard*, vol 831, 21 February 1972, col 899; Hughes and Moore, 1972, pp149-150; *Labour Research*, April 1972, p74.
210 Pitt, 1979, pp198-199.
211 Gormley, 1982, p115.
212 Campbell, 1994, p419.
213 Thatcher, 1995, p218.
214 *Times*, 19 February 1972; *Hansard*, vol 831, 21 February 1972, col 899; *Hansard*, vol 832, 29 February 1972, written answers, cols 83-84; interview with Campbell Adamson; Heath, 1998, p352; Pitt, 1979, p198; Gormley, 1982, p116.
215 Pitt, 1979, p199; Gormley, 1982, p117.
216 *Times*, 19 February 1972; Pitt, 1979, p199.
217 According to Campbell Adamson, who saw him at 1am on 19 February: entry for 24 March 1972 in King, 1975, p187.

218 *Daily Express*, 19 February 1972, quoted in *Labour Research*, April 1972, p74.
219 *Financial Times*, 19 February 1972, Campbell, 1994, p419. Nicholas Ridley's answer to a parliamentary question suggested the post-Wilberforce additions increased the cost by £5 million in the first year: Hansard, vol 832, 29 February 1972, written answers, col 84.
220 *Economist*, 26 February 1972, p67.
221 *Times*, 22 February 1972.
222 E P Thompson, 'A Special Case', *New Society*, 24 February 1972, p404.
223 *Morning Star*, 19 February 1972.
224 *Guardian*, 19 February 1972.
225 *Morning Star*, 19 February 1972.
226 Allen, 1981, p219.
227 Pitt, 1979, pp200-203.
228 Hughes and Moore, 1972, pp150-151; *Financial Times*, 24, 28 February, 1 March 1972.
229 *Financial Times*, 28 February 1972.
230 Hills, 1973, p261.
231 *Guardian*, 8 January 1972.
232 Thatcher, 1995, p216.
233 *Hansard*, vol 830, 31 January 1972, col 194; 2 February 1972, col 596.
234 *Hansard*, vol 830, 8 February 1972, col 1180.
235 *Economist*, 19 February 1972, p67.
236 *Guardian*, 1 May 1972.
237 *Financial Times*, 21 February 1972; Hills, 1973, p261.
238 Interview with Douglas Hurd.
239 'Mr Heath's Duty', *Spectator*, 26 February 1972, p308.
240 Taylor, 1980, p367.
241 Hughes and Moore, 1972, pp9-10.

Chapter 3

1   Bagwell, 1982, p245.
2   Marsh, 1978, p171.
3   Bagwell, 1982, p92; *Economist*, 13 May 1972, p14.
4   Bagwell, 1982, p246; TUC F&GPC, 18 April 1972.
5   Wallace, 1996, pp323, 383.
6   Bagwell, 1982, p246; *Guardian*, 25 February 1972.
7   Ferris, 1972, pp91-92.
8   *Guardian*, 21 February 1972.
9   *Economist*, 26 February 1972, p72; 1 April 1972, p61.
10 J Torode, 'The Rail Workers' Case', *New Statesman*, 31 March 1972, p418.
11 *Guardian*, 13 April 1972.
12 *Financial Times*, 12 April 1972.
13 *Financial Times*, 14 April 1972; *Guardian*, 13 April 1972; *Economist*, 15 April 1972, pp14-15.
14 Clegg, 1970, p338; Allen, 1966, pp27-29.
15 McLeod, 1970, pp79-81; Bagwell, 1982, pp188-190; quote on p189.

16   Clegg, 1970, p259.
17   British Railways Board, 1966, para 32 and appendix 4.
18   Interview in *Red Mole*, 5 June 1972.
19   Ritson, 1972, pp170-178.
20   *Financial Times*, 23 February, 6 March 1972.
21   *Financial Times*, 4, 23 March 1972; *Guardian*, 10 March, 4 April 1972; Bagwell, 1982, pp248-250.
22   *Times*, 14 April 1972.
23   *Financial Times*, 11 April 1972; *Times*, 13, 14, 15 April 1972.
24   *Times*, 11 April 1972.
25   *Financial Times*, 13 April 1972.
26   *Guardian*, 6 April 1972.
27   Bagwell, 1982, pp247-250.
28   *Economist*, 22 April 1972, p85.
29   Entry for 14 April 1972 in King, 1975, p196.
30   Barnes and Reid, 1980, p160.
31   Bagwell, 1982, pp250-251; *Times*, 17 April 1972.
32   Marsh, 1978, p175.
33   J Torode, 'In Place of Strikes?', *New Statesman*, 21 April 1972, p616.
34   Wallace, 1996, pp383-384.
35   Bagwell, 1982, pp264-265, claims that it was the first occasion, but *Transport Salaried Staffs Journal*, February 1972, suggests that that was the official strike by 250 at Southampton docks from 3 to 31 January 1972.
36   *Guardian*, 8 April 1972.
37   Bagwell, 1982, pp252-253.
38   TUC General Council meeting with Secretary of State for Employment, 17 April 1972.
39   Bagwell, 1982, p253.
40   TUC F&GPC, 18 April 1972.
41   *Times*, 18, 19, 20 April 1972.
42   *Guardian*, 19 April 1972.
43   *Financial Times*, 12 April 1972.
44   *Guardian*, 18 April 1972.
45   Bagwell, 1982, p254; *Economist*, 29 April 1972, p16; Donovan Report, 1968, para 428.
46   TUC F&GPC, 19 April 1972.
47   *Financial Times*, *Guardian*, 19 April 1972.
48   TUC F&GPC, 19 April 1972; *Socialist Worker*, 6 May 1972.
49   Conference speech in *Transport Salaried Staffs Journal*, June 1972. *Sunday Times*, 23 April 1972, confirms, 'At 12.45 on Wednesday a messenger arrived at the...[NIRC] bearing a buff envelope in which was contained Macmillan's application for a cooling-off period.'
50   Bagwell, 1982, p255.
51   *Economist*, 22 April 1972, p85.
52   Bagwell, 1982, p256; Wallace, 1996, p386.
53   *Guardian*, 20 April 1972.
54   *Guardian*, 21 April 1972.

55 TUC General Council, 26 April 1972.

56 *Guardian*, 21 April 1972.

57 Ferris, 1972, pp94-95.

58 *Financial Times*, 21 April 1972.

59 Barnes and Reid, 1980, p160.

60 Bagwell, 1982, pp256-257.

61 *Times*, 22 April 1972.

62 *Financial Times*, 22 April 1972.

63 *Financial Times*, 24 April 1972; *Times*, 25 April 1972.

64 Wallace, 1996, p386.

65 Bagwell, 1982, p257.

66 *Times*, *Financial Times*, 25 April 1972.

67 *Financial Times*, 26 April 1972; Bagwell, 1982, p257.

68 *Guardian*, *Times*, 22 April 1972.

69 *Guardian*, 24 April 1972.

70 TUC F&GPC, 24 April 1972; *Financial Times*, 25 April 1972.

71 *Financial Times*, 27 April 1972; TUC General Council, 26 April 1972.

72 *Locomotive Journal*, June 1972.

73 TUC F&GPC, 1 May 1972; TUC General Council, 4 May 1972.

74 Hills, 1973, p266.

75 P Paterson, 'Counting on Mr Neal', *New Statesman*, 26 May 1972, p698.

76 Barnes and Reid, 1980, pp160-161.

77 Bagwell, 1982, p258; *Guardian*, 8, 10 May 1972.

78 Lewis, 1973, p76.

79 *Financial Times*, 10 May 1972; P Paterson, 'Counting on Mr Neal', *New Statesman*, 26 May 1972, p698; A Watkins, 'No Medals for Maurice', *New Statesman*, 9 June 1972, p774.

80 Bagwell, 1982, p259; *Guardian*, 1 May 1972.

81 Marsh, 1978, pp172-173.

82 *Financial Times*, *Guardian*, 13 May 1972.

83 *Guardian*, 12 May 1972; Bagwell, 1982, pp259-261; *Financial Times*, 15 May 1972.

84 *Times*, 15 May 1972.

85 *Financial Times*, 15, 16 May 1972; *Times*, *Morning Star*, 16 May 1972.

86 Ferris, 1972, p96.

87 *Financial Times*, 17 May 1972.

88 *Morning Star*, 17 May 1972.

89 Ferris, 1972, p96.

90 P Paterson, 'Howe Now?', *New Statesman*, 2 June 1972, p735; *Economist*, 20 May 1972, p106.

91 Bruce-Gardyne, 1974, p85.

92 *Economist*, 3 June 1972, pp15-16.

93 Bagwell, 1982, p263; Wallace, 1996, p390.

94 TUC, 1972b, para 80.

95 Interview in *Red Mole*, 5 June 1972.

96 *Labour Research*, July 1972, p156.

97 *Hansard*, vol 838, 6 June 1972, written answers, cols 51-52.

98   *Guardian*, 1 June 1972, *Labour Research*, July 1972, p156, *Transport Salaried Staffs Journal*, June 1972, and Lewis, 1973, p86, all suggest that non-unionists were counted; Wallace, 1996, p391, gives the formulation presented.
99   A Watkins, 'No Medals for Maurice', *New Statesman*, 9 June 1972, p774. Apparently, the cabinet 'expected, at worst, a sixty/forty vote in favour': Barnett, 1973, p12.
100 *Guardian*, 1 June 1972.
101 Howe, 1994, p63.
102 Davies and Freedland, 1993, p315.
103 Whitehead, 1985, p77.
104 Bagwell, 1982, p265.
105 *Economist*, 13 May 1972, p94.
106 Bagwell, 1982, p266.
107 Barnes and Reid, 1980, p161.
108 Sewill, 1975, p50.
109 Bagwell, 1982, pp266-267; Holmes, 1982, p26.
110 Sewill, 1975, p50.
111 *Hansard*, vol 836, 11 May 1972, col 1575.
112 Marsh, 1978, p174.
113 P Paterson, 'And Now, the Strike-to-Rule', *New Statesman*, 16 June 1972, p813.
114 Moran, 1977, p139.
115 *Hansard*, vol 838, 6 June 1972, col 234.

Chapter 4

1   *Times*, 1 March 1972.
2   Wigham, 1973, p272.
3   Wigham, 1973, p277.
4   Wigham, 1973, pp82-83, 268-270.
5   Wigham, 1973, p307; Marsh, 1965, pp2-3.
6   This was known as the Amalgamated Engineering Union (AEU) from 1920 to 1967, then the Amalgamated Union of Engineering and Foundry Workers (AEF) from 1968 to 1971. It became the AUEW in 1971 with four sections—engineering, foundry, construction engineering and TASS (technical and supervisory section).
7   Undy, 1979, p24.
8   Frow and Frow, 1982, p440.
9   Minkin, 1980, p178.
10 Roberts, 1994, p105. The 'Pope' was Carron and the AEU headquarters was in Peckham Road, south London. Roberts was the first treasurer of the Anti Nazi League in 1978 and became a Labour MP in 1979.
11 Edelstein and Warner, 1975, pp283-285.
12 Interview with Tocher, *Socialist Review* 5 (1978), p36.
13 Cited in Armstrong, , 1978, pp18-19.
14 Undy, 1979, pp27, 30.

15   Undy, Ellis, McCarthy and Halmos, 1981, pp107-109, 111-112.
16   Wigham, 1973, p232.
17   *AUEW Journal*, June 1971, p249; October 1971, p448.
18   D McGarvey, Boilermakers' Society Delegate Conference, private session proceedings, 31 May 1972, p7.
19   *IDS Report* 112, May 1971, p31.
20   Wigham, 1973, pp260, 267.
21   Wigham, 1973, pp239-240.
22   *Guardian*, 28 March 1972.
23   'Summertalk', BBC TV, 21 July 1972, quoted in Ferris, 1972, p57.
24   Wigham, 1973, pp168, 215, 231-232.
25   Marsh, 1965, p151.
26   *Times*, 17 November 1971.
27   President's address, recalled 1971 AUEW National Committee, 10 January 1972, p8.
28   Wigham, 1973, pp239-240.
29   *Times*, 16 December 1971.
30   Clegg and Adams, 1957, pp102-106; Fishman, 1999, pp253-257.
31   Clegg and Adams, 1957, pp107-108; Fishman, 1999, p265, n66.
32   Smith, 1969, pp152-158; Wigham, 1973, pp231, 229.
33   President's address, recalled 1971 AUEW National Committee, 10 January 1972, pp9-10.
34   *Financial Times*, 27 April 1972.
35   Report of CSEU-EEF Joint Working Party, 27 November 1970, *AUEW Journal*, January 1971, p18.
36   Proceedings at a special conference between EEF and CSEU, 15 September 1971, London.
37   Clegg, 1979, p66.
38   EEF summer 1971 economic report, 'Wage Inflation and Employment', quoted in *Industrial Relations Review and Report* 36, July 1972, p3.
39   *Times*, 10 December 1971.
40   *IDS Report* 112, May 1971, p30.
41   Wigham, 1973, pp258-259.
42   *Times*, 7 January 1972.
43   President's address, recalled 1971 AUEW National Committee, 10 January 1972, pp10-11.
44   *Times*, 11 January 1972.
45   *AUEW Journal*, February 1972, pp64-65.
46   *Financial Times*, 14 January 1972.
47   *Economist*, 1 April 1972, p67.
48   *Times*, 18 January 1972.
49   *IDS Report* 129, February 1972, p7; *IDS Report* 131, February 1972, p6; CSEU EC minutes, 10 February 1972; *Financial Times*, 11 February 1972.
50   CSEU circular 72/36, cited in CSEU EC minutes, 9 March 1972.
51   *Financial Times*, 26 February 1972; *Times*, 1 March 1972.
52   'President's Address', Report of AUEW (E) Youth Conference, 16 March 1972, p15.

53 *Times*, 11 March 1972.
54 *Times*, 20 January 1972.
55 *Financial Times*, 31 January 1972.
56 *Morning Star*, 14, 26, 28 February 1972; *Times*, *Financial Times*, 28 February 1972.
57 *Financial Times*, 11 March 1972; *Morning Star*, 8 March 1972.
58 *Financial Times*, 26 February 1972; *Times*, 1 March 1972.
59 Interview with Hugh Scanlon.
60 *Times*, 10 December 1971.
61 Manchester AUEW DC minutes, 6 January 1972; *AUEW Journal*, February 1972, p71.
62 Manchester AUEW DC minutes, 18, 27 January, 1 February, 7 March 1972.
63 *Times*, 9 February 1972.
64 *Guardian*, *Times*, 25 February 1972; *Morning Star*, 26 February 1972; Manchester AUEW DC minutes, 29 February 1972; interview with Tocher, *Socialist Review* 5 (1978), p38.
65 *Times*, 11 March 1972.
66 Wigham, 1973, pp221-222, 305; Marsh, 1965, pp238-239.
67 *Guardian*, 11 March 1972.
68 *Financial Times*, 11 March 1972.
69 *Financial Times*, *Times*, 14 March 1972. The *Financial Times* says 800 were present; the *Morning Star*, 14 March 1972, gives 'nearly 1,000'. Elsewhere Tocher reports 'over 900': *AUEW Journal*, May 1972, p224; CSEU annual report 1972, p377.
70 *Morning Star*, 14 March 1972.
71 Chadwick, 1973, p115.
72 *Guardian*, 17 March 1972.
73 *Morning Star*, 17 March 1972; Chadwick, 1973, p115; *Guardian*, 21 March 1972. Chadwick, 1973, p117, suggests, across the whole area, a total of 7,000 workers operating sanctions by 24 March.
74 *Times*, 20 March 1972.
75 *Times*, 21 March 1972; the quote is from Chadwick, 1973, p115.
76 *Guardian*, 23 March 1972; *Financial Times*, 18 March 1972.
77 *Morning Star*, 24 March 1972.
78 *Greater Manchester Engineer* no 1, 26 March 1972.
79 Chadwick, 1973, p117.
80 *Guardian*, 25 March 1972, reported nine such agreements to date.
81 J Forrester, 'The Story of the Manchester Sit-In', *TASS Journal*, August 1972, p9.
82 Chadwick, 1973, pp116-117; *Times*, *Guardian*, 21 March 1972.
83 Ferris, 1972, p59.
84 *Guardian*, 25 March 1972, quoted in J Fenton, 'The Manchester Sit-Ins', *New Statesman*, 28 April 1972, p550.
85 *Guardian*, 24 March 1972. The *Morning Star*, 29 March 1972, reported, 'One employer has insisted on a non-publicity clause in order to escape the wrath of the employers' association.'
86 *Times*, 28 March 1972; Chadwick, 1973, p120.

87   *Times*, 1 April 1972; Chadwick, 1973, p121.

88   *Financial Times*, 27 March 1972; Chadwick, 1973, p116.

89   *Times*, 29 March 1972; *Morning Star*, 29, 30 March 1972; *Financial Times*, 5 April 1972.

90   *Morning Star*, *Times*, *Guardian*, 28 March 1972.

91   *Morning Star*, 29 March 1972.

92   *Morning Star*, 29 March 1972.

93   *Greater Manchester Engineer* no 2, 29 March 1972.

94   *Morning Star*, 29 March 1972.

95   *Greater Manchester Engineer* no 2, 29 March 1972.

96   *Financial Times*, 29 March 1972; *Guardian*, 30 March 1972.

97   *Greater Manchester Engineer* no 1, 26 March 1972; *Greater Manchester Engineer* no 2, 29 March 1972.

98   *Voice of the Engineers* 1, April 1972, broadsheet of the Gorton and Openshaw Joint Shop Stewards' Liaison Committee.

99   Chadwick, 1973, p121.

100 *Morning Star*, 28 March 1972.

101 *Guardian*, *Financial Times*, 7 April 1972; *Economist*, 15 April 1972, p74; also see *IDS Report* 134, April 1972, p5.

102 *Guardian*, 25 March 1972, in which Scraggs quote also given.

103 *Times*, 4 April 1972; Chadwick, 1973, p121.

104 T Bishop, 'When Workers Take Control', *Personnel Management*, March 1973, p26.

105 For lists, see *Economist*, 22 April 1972, p82; J Gretton, 'To Sit or Not to Sit', *New Society*, 15 June 1972, p566; Tuckman, 1985, p146.

106 *Financial Times*, *Times*, 5 April 1972.

107 *Times*, 4 April 1972.

108 *Financial Times*, 11, 12 April 1972; *Times*, 13 April 1972.

109 *Guardian*, 13, 14 April 1972; CSEU EC minutes, 13 April, 11 May 1972.

110 *Guardian*, 14 April 1972; Manchester AUEW DC minutes, 25 April 1972. Chadwick, 1973, p122, suggests 900 stewards turned up, many having 'to stand outside at an overflow meeting'.

111 *Greater Manchester Engineer* no 5, 18 April 1972.

112 J Fenton, 'The Manchester Sit-Ins', *New Statesman*, 28 April 1972, p550.

113 *Greater Manchester Engineer* no 5, 18 April 1972.

114 *Greater Manchester Engineer* stewards' meeting special, 13 April 1972.

115 *Greater Manchester Engineer* no 2, 29 March 1972.

116 *Morning Star*, 10 April 1972, which reported that two more companies had been expelled from the employers' association—Muschamps and Nettle Accessories.

117 *Greater Manchester Engineer* stewards' meeting special, 13 April 1972.

118 *Times*, 17 April 1972.

119 President's Address, AUEW (Engineering Section) National Committee, 17 April 1972.

120 *Financial Times*, 27 April 1972.

121 *Guardian*, 27 April 1972.

122 *AUEW Journal*, June 1972, p264.

123   *Guardian*, 11 April 1972; *Times*, 11, 15, 19 April 1972; *Financial Times*, 18 April 1972.

124   *Times*, 21 March 1972.

125   *Times*, 5, 18 April, 2 May 1972.

126   *Guardian*, 5 June 1972; *Times*, 12, 16, 22 June 1972.

127   *AUEW Journal*, July 1972, p312

128   *Industrial Relations Review and Report* 36, July 1972, p4.

129   Lyddon, 1998, p120.

130   Undy, Ellis, McCarthy and Halmas, 1981, p295.

131   J Fenton, 'The Manchester Sit-Ins', *New Statesman*, 28 April 1972, p549.

132   Diary entry for 8 May 1972 in King, 1975, p201.

133   *Guardian*, 30 March 1972.

134   Chadwick, 1973, p113.

135   *Financial Times*, *Times*, 20 April 1972.

136   *Times*, *Guardian*, 26 May 1972.

137   Chadwick, 1973, pp119-120; Deason, 1975, p12.

138   Interview with Tocher, *Socialist Review* 5 (1978), p38.

139   CSEU EC minutes, 13 April 1972.

140   International Socialists, 1973a, p5.

141   Gollaglee, Boilermakers' Society Delegate Conference, private session proceedings, 31 May 1972, p10.

142   *Morning Star*, 5 April 1972; Manchester AUEW DC minutes, 4 April, 13 June 1972.

143   *AUEW Journal*, October 1972, p464.

144   *Greater Manchester Engineer* no 1, 26 March 1972; *Greater Manchester Engineer* no 5, 18 April 1972.

145   *Morning Star*, 19 April 1972.

146   *Times*, 21 April 1972; *Guardian*, 22 April 1972.

147   Tuckman, 1985, pp125-126.

148   *IDS Report* 135, May 1972, p5; *Guardian*, 19 April 1972; Manchester AUEW DC minutes, 18 April 1972.

149   *Guardian*, 18, 19 April 1972.

150   Manchester AUEW DC minutes, 21 April 1972.

151   Ferris, 1972, p64.

152   *Financial Times*, 25 April 1972; *Morning Star*, 25, 29 April 1972.

153   *Financial Times*, 22 April 1972; *Times*, 26 April 1972.

154   *Guardian*, 28 April 1972.

155   *Times*, 9 May 1972.

156   *Financial Times*, 10 May 1972.

157   'Abstract Report of Councils's Proceedings', *AUEW Journal*, June 1972, p264.

158   *Financial Times*, 11 May 1972.

159   *Financial Times*, 11, 13 May 1972; *Guardian* 11, 13, 16 May 1972.

160   Chadwick, 1973, p119.

161   James, 1984, p104.

162   *Guardian*, 13 May 1972.

163   Reported in Manchester AUEW DC minutes, 23 May 1972.

164   *Guardian*, *Financial Times*, 16 May 1972.

165 *Morning Star*, 16 May 1972.

166 Deason, 1975, p12, who suggests 300 were present, but four newspapers all say 600.

167 Interview with Tocher, *Socialist Review* 5 (1978), p38.

168 Interview with Hugh Scanlon.

169 Ferris, 1972, p62.

170 Manchester AUEW DC minutes, 16 May 1972.

171 *Financial Times*, 17, 20 May 1972.

172 *Financial Times*, 18 May 1972.

173 *Economist*, 20 May 1972, p106.

174 *Financial Times*, 18, 23 May 1972.

175 *Economist*, 3 June 1972, p81.

176 *Financial Times*, 18 May; *Guardian* 26 May, 1 June 1972.

177 Ferris, 1972, p61.

178 *Greater Manchester Engineer* no 5, 18 April 1972; *Greater Manchester Engineer* no 9, 7 June 1972.

179 *Guardian*, 20 July 1972; *Financial Times*, 12 August 1972.

180 Manchester AUEW DC minutes, 4, 17 July 1972.

181 *Morning Star*, 14 April 1972.

182 'Sit-Ins: The Experience', *International Socialism* 1:53 (1972), p10.

183 *Economist*, 1 April 1972, p67; 8 April 1972, p72.

184 *Morning Star*, 10 April 1972.

185 P Hildrew, 'Unions Pin Hopes on Sitting in', *Guardian*, 8 April 1972.

186 Chadwick, 1973, pp115-116.

187 P Hildrew, 'Unions Pin Hopes on Sitting in', *Guardian*, 8 April 1972.

188 Chadwick, 1973, p116.

189 *Greater Manchester Engineer* no 5, 18 April 1972.

190 *Greater Manchester Engineer* no 8, 16 May 1972.

191 *Greater Manchester Engineer* no 4, 12 April 1972.

192 *Guardian*, 5 June 1972.

193 *Morning Star*, 13 May 1972.

194 *Greater Manchester Engineer* no 2, 29 March 1972; *Greater Manchester Engineer* no 4, 12 April 1972.

195 *Greater Manchester Engineer* no 7, 1 May 1972. Chadwick, 1973, p122, went further and claimed that the strikers 'were keeping staff workers and management out of their factory by means of concrete blocks placed in the main entrances'.

196 *Greater Manchester Engineer* no 9, 7 June 1972.

197 Ferris, 1972, pp60-61; also see *Financial Times*, 18 May 1972 and J Gretton, 'To Sit or Not to Sit', *New Society*, 15 June 1972, p565.

198 *Greater Manchester Engineer* no 7, 1 May 1972.

199 *Guardian*, 26 May 1972; quote from Deason, 1975, p11.

200 Deason, 1975, p11.

201 R W Shakespeare, 'Engineering Strikes are Starting to Hurt', *Times*, 22 May 1972.

202 Quoted in *Morning Star*, 14 April 1972.

203 J Gretton, 'To Sit or Not to Sit', *New Society*, 15 June 1972, p565.

204 P Hildrew, 'Unions Pin Hopes on Sitting in', *Guardian*, 8 April 1972.
205 Chadwick, 1973, pp118, 122.
206 *Greater Manchester Engineer* no 7, 1 May 1972; *Greater Manchester Engineer* no 8, 16 May 1972.
207 Proceedings at Special Conferences between EEF and CSEU on 14, 15 and 18 August 1972.
208 *AUEW Journal*, September 1972, p407.
209 'Address of Bro J Conway, General Secretary, 1972 Final Appeal Court', *AUEW Journal*, November 1972, p492.
210 J Conway, 'Union Efficiency', *AUEW Journal*, July 1971, p285.
211 'Abstract Report of Council's Proceedings', *AUEW Journal*, November 1972, p508.
212 T Bishop, 'When Workers Take Control', *Personnel Management*, March 1973, p26.
213 *Times*, 15 August 1972.
214 P Routledge, 'Lessons from the Engineering Pay Deal', *Times*, 17 August 1972.
215 *Economist*, 19 August 1972, p65.
216 Wigham, 1973, p306.
217 Chadwick, 1973, p122.
218 Diary entry for 14 April 1972 in King, 1975, p195.
219 Interview with Tocher, *Socialist Review* 5 (1978), p38.
220 *Economist*, 19 August 1972, p65.
221 Undy, Ellis, McCarthy and Halmas, 1981, p296.
222 Lyddon, 1998, p121.
223 T Bishop, 'When Workers Take Control', *Personnel Management*, March 1973, p26.
224 Interview with Tocher, *Socialist Review* 5 (1978), p38.
225 Undy, 1979, p31.

Chapter 5

1   This chapter draws heavily on Lindop, 1998a, pp33-72; and Lindop, 1998b, pp65-100.
2   Fishman, 1999a, especially pp67-71.
3   Lavalette and Kennedy, 1996, p9; Wilson, 1972.
4   Turnbull, 1993, pp189-190.
5   Lindop, 1983, pp21-33.
6   Philips, 1996, pp107-130.
7   Turnbull, 1993, pp191-192; Durcan, McCarthy and Redman, 1983, Chapter 9.
8   Wilson, 1972, pp327-329.
9   Devlin Report, 1965.
10 See Lindop, forthcoming; and B Light, letter, 'To Break a Strike?', *Socialist Worker Review* 94 (1987), p34.
11 Jackson, 1975, p103ff; Turnbull, Woolfson and Kelly, 1993, p194.
12 Lindop, 1998a, pp43-46. For Liverpool see Hunter, 1994; for London see Dash, 1969. Both of these sources are coloured by the author's politics.
13 Topham, 1973, pp219-232.

14 Lindop, 1998a, pp49-52.
15 *Morning Star*, 12 December 1971.
16 *Morning Star*, 26 January 1972.
17 *Morning Star*, 8 March 1972; Lindop, 1998a, p55.
18 Lindop, 1998a, pp55-56.
19 *Morning Star*, 24 March 1972.
20 Jones, 1986, p247.
21 C R Seaton, Secretary NIRC, to J L Jones, TGWU, 13 April 1972, document attached to TUC F&GPC minutes, 24 April 1972.
22 *Socialist Worker*, 15 April 1972.
23 *Morning Star*, 21 April 1972.
24 *Guardian*, 22 April 1972.
25 Lindop, 1998a, pp58-60.
26 *Observer*, 2 April 1972.
27 Lindop, 1998a, p62.
28 TUC F&GPC, 24 April 1972.
29 TUC General Council, 26 April 1972.
30 TUC F&GPC, 26 April 1972.
31 Interview with Len Murray.
32 Jones, 1986, p249; Lindop, 1998a, pp64-65; *Financial Times*, 2 May 1972.
33 Interview with Jack Jones.
34 TUC F&GPC, 1 May 1972.
35 In the following week even the one big union controlled by the CP was not against compromise with the act. At the C A Parsons engineering works in Newcastle the fight against redundancies was intertwined with the defence of the closed shop against the use by the company of a 'yellow' union, UKAPE. The AUEW-TASS (draughtsmen's union) conference voted to defy an NIRC order to accept UKAPE. But the union's national leadership urged a compromise on the Parsons members. The chair of the office committee at the factory, Terry Rogers, an IS member, recommended rejection, but lost the vote at an office meeting: Harman, 1988, p249; *Socialist Worker*, 6, 20 May 1972.
36 TUC General Council, 4 May 1972.
37 *Guardian*, 2 May 1972.
38 *Labour Weekly*, 5 May 1972.
39 *Financial Times*, 13 May 1972.
40 Despite its exceptional procedures and membership, the NIRC was nevertheless a branch of the High Court and, as such, its judgments were subject to review by higher courts, the Court of Appeal and the House of Lords.
41 *Financial Times*, 18 May 1972.
42 *Morning Star*, 19, 23 May 1972.
43 TGWU letter to TUC, attached to TUC General Council minutes, 4 May 1972.
44 *Morning Star*, 4 May 1972.
45 *Morning Star*, 15 June 1972. See Lindop, 1998a, p67, n122, for records of Jones-Aldington Committee.
46 Interview with Vic Turner.

47 Lindop, 1998b, pp68-71. To collect evidence that could be used in court against the three dockers, the employers resorted to the use of private detectives (who passed themselves off as journalists), radio cars, secret photographers, hidden tape recorders and bugged telephones.
48 *Socialist Worker*, 17 June 1972.
49 *Morning Star*, 13 June 1972
50 Lindop, 1998b, pp68-69.
51 Whitehead, 1985, p78.
52 Heath, 1998, p406.
53 Howe, 1994, p64.
54 Tomison, 1972, pp243-244.
55 *Morning Star*, 12 June 1972.
56 *Morning Star*, 17 June 1972.
57 Lindop, 1998b, p70.
58 Lindop, 1998b, p71.
59 *Morning Star*, 17 June 1972; *Labour Research*, August 1972, p175.
60 'Note on the Churchman case by Sir Peter Pain', in G Lewis, 1997, Appendix 1, 'The Dockers' Cases of 1972', pp348-349; Denning, 1983, pp169-173.
61 *Sunday Times*, 18 June 1972; quoted in Thomson and Engelman, 1975, p101.
62 Whitehead, 1985, p79.
63 *Times*, 27 June 1972.
64 TUC F&GPC, 26 June 1972.
65 The lorry drivers' action was later backed by the London TGWU Road Transport Commercial trade group stewards' committee, whose chair was a CP member. This led to the ridiculous but not unusual situation where leading CP industrial members, inside the docks and lorry drivers' sections of the TGWU in this case, were publicly in dispute with each other. It reflected the CP's growing inability to coordinate its members' work. See Lindop, 1998b, pp78-79, for more detail on this incident.
66 Interview with Vic Turner.
67 *Socialist Worker*, 22 July 1972.
68 Lindop, 1998b, p79.
69 *Sunday Times*, 23 July 1972.
70 Eddie Prevost speaking at Marxism 97.
71 This figure consists of full time production, maintenance, distribution, editorial and clerical staff, plus regular 'casuals' in certain occupations: various tables in McGregor Report, 1976.
72 Interview with Bob Light.
73 Interview with Mike Hicks; interview with Mike Power.
74 Interview with Ross Pritchard; interview with Mike Britton. It should be noted the CP officially disapproved of the informal print workers' group that met in Fleet Street, but some key CP members, including Bill Freeman (junior) of SOGAT, ignored them and participated in its activities.
75 Cited in Cliff, 1979, p6.
76 Interview with John Mitchell.
77 Interview with Sean Geraghty.
78 Interview with Mike Britton.

79   Interview with Ross Pritchard.

80   Lindop, 1998b, p85.

81   McIlroy, 1999a, p239; interview with Mike Power. Nonetheless, it should be noted that when the London docks stewards wanted leaflets printed, they had to turn first to the IS and then to the Briant occupation rather than to the much bigger CP presses. The CP itself did not put out any leaflet calling for industrial action to release the dockers until at least three days after the jailings, by which time many sections of workers were already on strike: Harman, 1973, p24.

82   McIlroy and Campbell, 1999, p19.

83   McIlroy and Campbell, 1999, pp18-19.

84   Lindop, 1998b, pp86-87. There is also a very good breakdown of some of the specific workplaces involved in taking strike action in *Department of Employment Gazette*, September 1972; *Labour Research*, September 1972; *Morning Star*, 27 July 1972; *Socialist Worker*, 29 July 1972.

85   Bob Light, speaking at Marxism 97, University of London, July 1997.

86   Interview with Mike Hicks.

87   Lindop, 1998b, p90.

88   Lindop, 1998a, p72.

89   Interview with Vic Turner.

90   *Times*, 22 July 1972.

91   Fifty-one Labour MPs backed a motion in the House of Commons calling for the release of the five dockers without requiring them to purge their contempt. Not one supported a motion which Bernadette Devlin (Independent MP for Mid-Ulster) brought to the Commons from the solidarity demonstration on Tuesday 25 July which called on the TUC General Council to call a general strike to free the dockers: Lindop, 1998b, p91 n79.

92   *Observer*, 23 July 1972

93   TUC F&GPC, 24 July 1972.

94   'Report of Meeting Held at 10 Downing Street' at 7.30pm on July 24 1972 between the Finance and General Purposes Committee and the Prime Minister' attached to TUC General Council minutes, 26 July 1972.

95   Lindop, 1998b, pp94-95.

96   Dorfman, 1979, p62.

97   Lindop, 1998b, pp94-95.

98   Lewis, 1997, p347.

99   Dorfman, 1979, p63 and p162 n32.

100 TUC F&GPC, 21 August 1972; *Socialist Worker*, 5 August 1972.

101 J Griffith, 'Reflections on the Rule of Law', *New Statesman*, 24 November 1972, pp756, 758. The opposite ruling to Heaton was reached a few years later in the General Aviation case started under the Industrial Relations Act—but with a lot less fuss. See Clark and Wedderburn, 1983, p220, n7.

102 Vic Turner recalled the Official Solicitor visiting him in prison on the Monday morning: 'When the Official Solicitor came to see us we were shown into the governors drawing room and this bloke walked in, and he had come to see us to get our agreement to go to the Industrial Court that morning to plead on our behalf. We said, "No way, we don't recognise that court, we're certainly not

pleading to it." The five of us said, "No, you're not on." They used to ask us every day, did we want to purge our contempt, and we said "no"': interview with Vic Turner.

103 *Economist*, 29 July 1972, p57.

104 Griffith, 1977, p73. Another legal commentator, Michael Zander, wrote: 'Force of circumstances required the sacrifice of the rule of law at the risk of some lessening of respect for the courts': *Guardian*, 28 July 1972, cited in Dorfman, 1979, pp63-64.

105 J Griffith, 'Reflections on the Rule of Law', *New Statesman*, 24 November 1972, p759. Griffith also makes the point: 'We do not have to be too shocked by suggestions of government intervention. We know that when the Poplar borough councillors were in prison in 1921 in circumstances not dissimilar in that their imprisonment was also on account of contempt and wholly embarrassing to the government, the Minister of Health sent a personal message to the Lord Chancellor urging him to ask the judges to release the prisoners. So also when miners at Betteshanger Colliery were imprisoned in 1941, the Home Secretary under political pressure released them, and the court was advised by the Ministry of Labour not to seek to enforce the payment of fines unpaid by other miners.'

106 Interview with Jack Jones.

107 Martin, 1980, p323.

108 Even Cliff, 2000, p106, suggests this version of events. See Lindop, 1998b, and Lyddon, 1999, pp334-339, which also gives examples of the many inaccuracies of detail in most accounts of the Pentonville events.

109 TUC General Council, 26 July 1972. A note in brackets at the end of this section of the meeting states: 'At a later stage in the meeting Mr Jones informed the General Council that the House of Lords had overturned the Appeal Court decision on all counts and that the NIRC would be meeting at 3pm.' No time is given for this, but it is probable that the information was not released before a vote had taken place (see main text). Frank Chapple of the EETPU argued that if the Official Solicitor was taking action 'that meant the Government was backing down', while Reg Bottini of the Agricultural Workers argued that 'if the intervention of the Official Solicitor secured the quick release of the dockers, the motion before the Council was academic'.

110 P Paterson, '1926 and All That', *New Statesman*, 4 August 1972, p150.

111 Moran, 1977, p187, n111.

112 TUC General Council, 26 July 1972.

113 Interview with Jack Jones.

114 Interview with Len Murray.

115 For example, National Union of Railwaymen's leader Jimmy Thomas who said, on the day just before the General Strike: '...in a challenge to the Constitution, God help us, unless the government won': Cliff and Gluckstein, 1986, p181.

116 TUC General Council, 26 July 1972.

117 TUC circulars nos 206 and 208 (1971-72), 26 and 27 July 1972.

118 Interview with Sean Geraghty.

119 Interview with Ross Pritchard.

120 *Sun*, 28 July 1972, cited in Lindop, 1998b, p97.

121 Denning, 1983, p177.
122 Topham, 1973, p227; Geary, 1986, pp78-83.
123 Interview with Douglas Hurd.
124 P Paterson, 'Card-Vote Democracy', *New Statesman*, 1 September 1972, p277.
125 Jones, 1986, p253; *Morning Star*, 17 August 1972.
126 McIlroy and Campbell, 1997, pp49-50.

Chapter 6

1 *Financial Times*, 17 March 1972.
2 National Federation of Building Trades Employers (NFBTE) circular, 'Emergency: Read Carefully—Wage Negotiations', 26 May 1972.
3 Phelps Brown Report, 1968, paras 463-465.
4 National Board for Prices and Incomes, 1968, paras 22, 27.
5 Phelps Brown Report, 1968, paras 473-474.
6 Austrin, 1978, p250.
7 Undy, Ellis, McCarthy and Halmas, 1981, pp173-174.
8 Undy, Ellis, McCarthy and Halmas, 1981, p287.
9 Austrin, 1980, pp302-315.
10 Undy, Ellis, McCarthy and Halmas,1981, p175.
11 Austrin, 1980, p303.
12 Goulding, 1975, pp22-27.
13 Austrin, 1978, pp201-202.
14 Interview with Lou Lewis.
15 Cited in Austrin, 1978, p278.
16 Cameron Report, 1967, para 213.
17 *Building Workers' Charter* 1, 1970.
18 Austrin, 1978, p281.
19 Interview with Lou Lewis.
20 Austrin, 1978, pp274-282.
21 Austrin, 1978, p288.
22 *Morning Star*, 8, 17 and 26 February 1972; *Socialist Worker*, 8 April 1972. Two weeks later there was a dramatic new development in Birmingham when 40 'lump' workers on the Cubbits site on Wiggin Street walked out on strike against the lump. Their unprecedented action came as a result of the Bryant wage agreement, which made it more attractive to be a direct employee. When they picketed the gates 20 other direct workers joined them: *Morning Star*, 10 March 1972.
23 *Morning Star*, 9 February 1972.
24 Austrin, 1978, p290.
25 *Morning Star*, 25 April 1972.
26 *Morning Star*, 1 May 1972.
27 *Morning Star*, 2 May 1972.
28 *Morning Star*, 27, 31 May, 1 June 1972; *Socialist Worker*, 3 June 1972; *Financial Times*, 31 May 1972; *Guardian*, 1, 3 June 1972.
29 *Morning Star*, 6 June 1972.
30 Cited in Austrin, 1978, p293.

31   Austrin, 1978, p294.
32   *Financial Times*, 5, 11 May 1972; *Times*, 14 June 1972.
33   NFBTE Council, 'Wage Dispute', 17 August 1972.
34   Wood, 1979, p19.
35   *Morning Star*, 26 June 1972.
36   *Times*, 27 June 1972.
37   *Guardian*, 5 June 1972.
38   NFBTE, 'Wage Dispute: Emergency Letter no 2', 23 June 1972.
39   *Morning Star*, 27 June, 4 July 1972.
40   NFBTE circular, no date (about 7 July 1972).
41   *Morning Star*, 15 July 1972.
42   *Socialist Worker*, 22 July 1972; *Red Mole*, 24 July 1972.
43   *Morning Star*, 21 July.
44   *Socialist Worker*, 22 July 1972; K Sim, 'What Building Strike', *New Statesman*, 11 August 1972, pp188-189.
45   NFBTE, 'Wage Dispute: Emergency Letter no 3', 20 July 1972.
46   *Building Workers' Charter* vol 2 no 6, 1973.
47   Quoted in Austrin, 1978, pp299-300.
48   *Socialist Worker*, 29 July 1972.
49   Interview with Lou Lewis.
50   NFBTE Council, 'Wage Dispute', 17 August 1972.
51   *Morning Star*, 5 August 1972; *Building Workers' Charter* vol 2 no 5, 1972.
52   *Morning Star*, 7, 8 August 1972.
53   *Times*, 8 August 1972.
54   *Morning Star*, 9 August 1972. *Socialist Worker*, 12 August 1972, claimed 8,000 on the London demonstration.
55   NFBTE Council, 'Wage Dispute', 17 August 1972.
56   *Morning Star*, 18 August 1972.
57   *Times*, 10 August 1972.
58   *Times*, 12 August 1972.
59   *Times*, 15, 16 August 1972; *Morning Star*, 16 August 1972.
60   *Morning Star*, 6 September 1972.
61   *Building Workers' Charter* vol 2 no 5, 1972.
62   Interview with Lou Lewis.
63   *Morning Star*, 11 August 1972. Lewis later wrote that most London sites were 'being picketed by mobile picket squads each day and, if there is an attempt to re-open, a big picket at 7.00am next morning': *Building Workers' Charter* vol 2 no 5, 1972.
64   *Morning Star*, 18 August 1972.
65   *Building Workers' Charter* vol 2 no 5, 1972.
66   *Morning Star*, 25 August 1972; *Socialist Worker*, 2, 9 September 1972.
67   Wood, 1979, p20.
68   *Times*, 9 September 1972.
69   Austrin, 1978, p300.
70   *Morning Star*, 16 August 1972. Coordinating committees were set up in different localities in the Merseyside region. Those in central Liverpool, Birkenhead, Skelmersdale and Warrington met daily, the Kirkby committee

three times a week and St Helens weekly: *Building Workers' Charter* vol 2 no 5, 1972.

71 *Morning Star*, 14, 19 August 1972.

72 *Building Workers' Charter* vol 2 no 6, 1973.

73 *Morning Star*, 11, 14 August 1972.

74 *Morning Star*, 15, 16, 18 August 1972.

75 *Building Workers' Charter* vol 2 no 5, 1972.

76 Ricky Tomlinson, speaking at *Socialist Worker* May Day Rally, 1992. Tomlinson has appeared in films such as *Riff Raff* (1991) and *Raining Stones* (1993), as well as in the TV series *Brookside* and *The Royle Family*.

77 *UCATT Viewpoint*, September 1972.

78 *Times*, 1, 7, 8, 9, August 1972.

79 NFBTE, Industrial Relations Bulletin 5, September 1972.

80 NFBTE, 'Wage Dispute', 17 August 1972.

81 *Times*, 21, 22 August 1972.

82 *UCATT Viewpoint*, September 1972; Austrin, 1978, pp304, 309.

83 *Morning Star*, 23 August 1972.

84 *Financial Times*, 29 August 1972.

85 *UCATT Viewpoint*, September 1972.

86 *Morning Star*, 4 July 1972.

87 Harman, 1973, p24.

88 Goulding, 1975, p25.

89 *Building Workers' Charter* vol 2 no 5, 1972.

90 Interview with Lou Lewis.

91 *Morning Star*, 26 August 1972.

92 *Socialist Worker*, 2 September 1972.

93 Harman, 1973, pp24-25.

94 *Morning Star*, 13, 14 September 1972.

95 *Morning Star*, 28 September 1972.

96 *Morning Star*, 15 September 1972.

97 *Morning Star*, 28 September 1972.

98 *Building Workers' Charter* vol 2 no 5, 1972.

99 *Economist*, 16 September 1972, p79.

100 *Morning Star*, 28 September 1972.

101 *Socialist Worker*, 23 September 1972.

102 *Morning Star*, 16 September 1972

103 *Building Workers' Charter* vol 2 no 6, 1973.

104 *Building Workers' Charter* vol 2 no 6, 1973.

105 *UCATT Viewpoint*, November 1972.

106 Wood, 1979, pp16-17, 18, 19. By the time of this book, Wood was UCATT general secretary.

107 *Times*, 21 August 1972.

108 *NFBTE Newsletter*, 8 September 1972.

109 NFBTE, 'Violence and Intimidation: A Dossier of Examples of Personal Violence, Injury, Arson and Damage during the Building Strike 1972' (1972).

110 *Shropshire Star*, 21 August 1972, cited in International Socialists, 1973b, p8.

111 Ricky Tomlinson speaking at *Socialist Worker* May Day Rally, 1992.

112 NFBTE, 'Violence and Intimidation' (1972).
113 Cited in TUC F&GPC Report on 'Picketing', 23 October 1972.
114 Mark, 1978, p512. The analogy is stupid as the Nazis were pathological opponents of trade unionism among other things. See, for example, Gluckstein, 1999.
115 Cited in International Socialists, 1973b, p9. The *News of the World*, 22 October 1972, launched a three part series on 'strife-makers in society' with an attack on the 'dangerous subversives' in Britain's building industry, claiming the strike was the result of 'two years of meticulous planning by Communists and other extremists'.
116 Ricky Tomlinson speaking at *Socialist Worker* May Day Rally, 1992.
117 Wallington, 1975, pp70-74.
118 Arnison, 1974; Warren, 1982; Flynn, 1975. In his speech from the dock Tomlinson said: '…if you repeat a lie often enough it becomes accepted as truth. This I have discovered in this court and now know it to be true… [T]he constant use of the words "petrified", "terrified", "afraid", "frightened" and "scared to death" by witness after witness led even myself to think for a moment that I had done the things I have been accused of… How can anyone say this was just an ordinary trial when 1,000 police were on duty outside…? … The sentence passed on me…will not matter. My innocence has been proved time and time again by the building workers of Wrexham whom I led, and, indeed, by building workers from all over the land, who have sent messages of support… I look forward to the day when the real culprits, the McAlpine's, Wimpey's, Laing's and the Bovis and their political puppets, are in the dock facing charges of conspiracy and intimidating workers from doing what is their lawful right, picketing': *Socialist Worker*, 5 May 1974.
119 Union of Construction, Allied Trades and Technicians, 'UCATT and the Shrewsbury Trials' (no date).

Chapter 7

1 About the same length of time as that between the February and October 1917 revolutions in Russia.
2 *Morning Star*, 18 May, 3 June 1972.
3 Fitzgerald, 1977, chapter 5.
4 Kerr, 1973, pp8-10.
5 *Socialist Worker*, 7 October, 25 November, 2 December 1972; *Morning Star*, 3, 31 October, 23 November 1972.
6 *Socialist Worker*, 25 November 1972. Also see other issues in November and December, and 'Chronicle', *British Journal of Industrial Relations* 11:1 (1973), pp158-159.
7 Barnett, 1973, p40.
8 Coates and Topham, 1974, p9.
9 G Foster, 'Coal after Wilberforce', *Management Today*, November 1973, p75.
10 In March 1972 there were 183 power stations in England and Wales, of which 158 were coal-fired or oil-fired. In March 1984 there were 90, which included a

higher number of nuclear power stations: CEGB *Statistical Yearbook 1972*, p6; *The Electricity Council Annual Report, 1983-84*, p8.

11 Engels, 1962, p260.

12 Heath, 1998, p350.

13 Thatcher, 1995, p216.

14 *Hansard*, vol 830, 11 February 1972, col 1740.

15 *Hansard*, vol 831, 14 February 1972, col 38.

16 *Hansard*, vol 831, 14 February 1972, col 79. There was some picketing of other premises during the miners' lockout in 1926; see, for example, Carr, 1976, p346.

17 *Economist*, 5 August 1972, p13.

18 *Times*, 18 September 1972.

19 *Economist*, 19 February 1972, p68.

20 Clegg, 1985, p29.

21 Cole, 1923, pp107-111.

22 Cole, 1923, pp207, 225; Clegg, 1985, pp300, 416-417.

23 Coates, 1973, pp33-39; quotes from pp34, 38-39.

24 Francis and Smith, 1980, chapter 8, especially pp277-294; see Knowles, 1954, for a few other examples.

25 Spriano, 1975, especially chapter 4; Danos and Gibelin, 1986, especially chapters 6 and 8.

26 *Hansard*, vol 831, 14 February 1972, col 40.

27 Clegg, 1985, pp315-316; Coates and Topham, 1991, pp786-788; Bullock, 1960, pp182-183; Bagwell, 1963, pp464-465; Cole, 1923, pp222-228.

28 Arnot, 1953, p466.

29 Bullock, 1960, p352.

30 Lenin, 1974, pp392-393.

31 *Hansard*, vol 830, 9 February 1972, col 1341.

32 *Hansard*, vol 831, 14 February 1972, col 40.

33 *Hansard*, vol 831, 24 February 1972, col 1487.

34 Cliff and Gluckstein, 1986, pp213-221.

35 Moran, 1977, p144; *Morning Star*, 19, 20, 21 December 1972; *Socialist Worker*, 23 December 1972. See the chronology at the front of the book for some details on the Goad case.

36 Gormley, 1982, pp95-118.

37 TUC General Council, 4 May 1972.

38 *Times*, 21 February 1972.

39 Francis and Smith, 1980, p476.

40 Gormley, 1982, p 89.

41 Hurd, 1979, p105.

42 See 'Chronicle', *British Journal of Industrial Relations* 11:2 (1973), pp310-312.

43 Moran, 1977, pp145-146.

44 Quoted in Whitehead, 1985, p152.

45 TUC annual report, 1975, pp460-461.

46 Harman, 1988, p275.

47 Fishman, 1995, p337.

48 McIlroy and Campbell, 1999, p25.

49 McIlroy and Campbell, 1999, pp12-13, 24-25.
50 McIlroy, 1999a, p219.
51 McIlroy, 1999a, pp227, 237-241; Charlton, 1973, p14.
52 Cliff and Gluckstein, 1986, pp165, 230, 275.
53 Monks, 1992, p211.
54 McIlroy, 1999b, pp262-263, 266-270; p264 for quote.
55 *Socialist Worker*, 5 February 1972.
56 *Socialist Worker*, 26 February 1972.
57 Harman, 1988, p264.
58 This phrase is attributed by Ian Birchall to Granville Williams, then IS organiser in Birmingham; Harman, 1988, pp263-264. Nonetheless, IS did make some important gains. After the miners' strike IS organised a conference in Barnsley, which 56 NUM members attended, and launched the rank-and-file paper the *Collier*. A handful also joined IS. After the dockers' strike a *Socialist Worker* meeting was organised in east London attended by 300 and addressed by one of the Pentonville Five. With the *Dockworker* rank-and-file paper launched later in the year, half a dozen dockers were recruited and sales of *Socialist Worker* increased from about 20 to over 300 per week over the next two years: Shipley, 1976, p137; interview with Trevor Brown; interview with Bob Light.
59 Interview with Bob Light.
60 Barnett, 1973, p41.

Chronology

January

3   Work-in starts at Allis-Chalmers in Mold, Flintshire.

5   Workers occupy Fisher-Bendix factory in Kirkby, Merseyside, to prevent redundancies.

6   450 AUEW shop stewards in Manchester district agree overtime ban from 1 February.

9   National miners' strike begins. More than half the pits deprived of NUM safety cover against official instructions.

10   Only 46 of 289 pits have full safety cover.
Recalled AUEW NC agrees plant bargaining policy for national engineering pay claim.

12   NUM circular on picketing power stations in mining regions.

13   NUM executive agrees to picketing of power stations in non-mining regions.

14   Electricity supply unions give notice of overtime ban from 1 February over pay claim.

17   NUM white-collar section, COSA, joins miners' strike.
Over 200 Kent miners start picketing London power stations.

18   200 Barnsley miners arrive in East Anglia for picketing.
Allis-Chalmers work-in to end. Factory to stay open.

20   Unemployment figures rise above one million for the first time in 25 years.

21   600 picket Coal House in Doncaster.

24   Workers at some London power stations start unofficial overtime ban.
1,000 Barnsley miners now in East Anglia.

26   Unofficial national one-day dockers' strike in protest against

job cuts. 24-hour stoppage on Merseyside in support of miners, dockers and Fisher-Bendix occupation.

27   Electricity supply unions reject improved pay offer but delay overtime ban until midnight, 7 February.

Yorkshire miners stop deputies working in seven pits.

30   First voltage reductions.

'Bloody Sunday' British troops fire on crowd in Derry, Northern Ireland, killing 13 on the day.

400 Sheffield AUEW shop stewards meet over engineering pay claim.

31   250 pickets clash with 300 police at Clipstone colliery, Notts, resulting in 20 arrests.

February

2   50,000-strong demonstration in Dublin to protest at Bloody Sunday. British Embassy is burnt down.

3   Miner Fred Matthews is killed on picket line in Yorkshire. Picket of Saltley coke depot in Birmingham starts.

7   Electricity supply union negotiators split over new pay offer. Casting vote of Frank Chapple to accept offer and call off threatened overtime ban.

600 Birmingham building workers demonstrate outside court where Charter activist Pete Carter is facing charges.

8   Cabinet agrees to introduce state of emergency. In the afternoon the Secretary of State for Employment, Robert Carr, announces resumption of mining pay negotiations the next day. In the evening Arthur Scargill wins support from Birmingham East AUEW district committee for mass picket at Saltley.

9   State of emergency announced in parliament, effective from midnight.

No progress made in negotiations.

Emergency Birmingham East AUEW district shop stewards' meeting endorses call for solidarity action at Saltley. TGWU and NUVB district committees also agree to support the action.

Deputies stopped in 10 of the 21 pits in North Yorkshire.

10   40,000 Birmingham engineering and car workers take strike action. More than 10,000-strong mass picket forces the closure

of the Saltley coke depot at 10.43am. National pay negotiations collapse in morning. Employment secretary Carr convenes a court of inquiry.

Confederation of Shipbuilding and Engineering Unions executive agrees strategy for engineering pay claim.

11   NUM executive refuse to call off strike while court of inquiry sits. Areas allocated four-hour periods when power cuts are likely.

13   800 Sheffield engineering shop stewards give employers until 24 February to reply to claim.

14   Effective three-day week starts in industry. Estimated 800,000 laid off this day. Industry secretary John Davies announces that even with cuts there are only two weeks before electricity generation will be down to 20-25 percent of normal load. 2,000 miners' pickets clash with police outside Longannet power station in Scotland, with 13 pickets charged with 'mobbing and rioting' and detained in custody.

15   Wilberforce inquiry opens.

16   Lord Advocate flies to Scotland to speed up legal process for Longannet 13.

      1,000 building workers from 16 Bryant's sites in Birmingham demonstrate outside company offices.

17   Mass protests lead to Longannet 13 being released on bail.

18   Estimated 1.6 million laid off in industry. Wilberforce inquiry report available at 10am. NUM executive rejects it and squeezes extra concessions from NCB. NUM go to Downing Street in evening. NCB resume negotiations at 11.45pm.

19   Final settlement agreed at 1am. Pickets called off.

23   Miners' ballot starts.

24   700 engineering stewards from Greater Manchester agree to submit carbon-copy claims to employers on 1 March.

25   Miners' ballot result announced accepting settlement.

27   700 Sheffield and district engineering stewards agree to propose district-wide strike action to mass meeting two weeks later.

28   Miners return to work.

29   Sheffield AUEW officials told by national leaders to follow correct procedures.

March

9   Prime minister Edward Heath and other cabinet ministers meet TUC leaders at Downing Street for talks on the economy.

13   900-strong Manchester meeting of engineering shop stewards agrees to ban overtime and impose a work to rule from 27 March in support of claim.

16   First engineering sit-in in Greater Manchester.

20   Stockport engineers start sanctions one week early.
     Fisher-Bendix occupation proved successful as new company is formed.
     Deadline for haulage firms on Merseyside to sign unofficial dockers' document guaranteeing certain terms and conditions in their companies.

21   Budget to reflate economy, with big increase in public expenditure.
     AUEW executive gives official support to first sit-in.

22   Industry secretary Davies announces a U-turn on government spending plans, putting an extra £800 million into development areas, and setting up new industrial development boards.

23   Two more engineering sit-ins ahead of start of official sanctions in Greater Manchester.
     The National Industrial Relations Court (NIRC) instructs TGWU to stop its Liverpool docker members blacking Heaton Transport.

24   Suspension of the Stormont Parliament and imposition of direct rule in Northern Ireland announced.

27   Engineering workers in Greater Manchester start overtime ban and work to rule in support of claim. More sit-ins over following days

28   Government announces £35 million for UCS.

29   NIRC imposes £5,000 fine on the TGWU for failing to stop Liverpool dockers blacking Heaton Transport lorries.

30   Sit-ins now operating at 12 Greater Manchester factories. Police unable to serve writ for eviction of occupiers at Sharston Engineering.

31   Workers at Sharston Engineering leave factory.

April

8	Sit-ins now operating at 20 Greater Manchester factories.
10	Unofficial action starts on Southern and Eastern regions of British Rail.
11	AUEW executive gives official support to 10,000 members either sitting in or locked out in Greater Manchester.
12	NUGMW gives official support to its 1,500 members involved in Greater Manchester action.
13	First CSEU stewards' meeting in Manchester since industrial action began hears AUEW president Hugh Scanlon.
	NIRC sends letter to TGWU giving three weeks to pay fine or face sequestration on 4 May.
16	Unsuccessful last minute attempt at mediation in forthcoming railway dispute.
17	The three main railway unions impose official work to rule and overtime ban in support of their pay claim.
18	Sit-ins now operating at 27 Greater Manchester factories.
19	Employment secretary Maurice Macmillan applies to the NIRC, which imposes a 14-day cooling-off period on the railway unions. Unions do not defend themselves in court in line with TUC policy.
20	NIRC imposes a further fine of £50,000 on TGWU for failing to stop Liverpool dockers blacking container lorries.
	Railway unions decide to cooperate with NIRC order. They will call off work to rule, but suggest that members do not work overtime or rest days. Unofficial action continues.
	Press reports of Engineering Employers' Federation £1million subsidy to Greater Manchester firms.
21	Liverpool TGWU docks shop stewards agree to defy the NIRC and continue action.
24	London train driver suspended at 3am for not working normally. Rapid escalation of unofficial action. Management order rescinded under government pressure.
	Appeal by TGWU leader Jack Jones to lift blacking action is rejected by Liverpool docks shop stewards.
	The TUC Finance and General Purposes Committee (F&GPC) agrees to draw up document setting out circumstances 'in which unions should be permitted to defend themselves' in the NIRC.

Also agrees to support TGWU 'in its actions'.

25 At 6pm Macmillan confirms to the NIRC that all industrial action on railways has ceased and cooling-off period can start.

26 TUC General Council votes for F&GPC to reconsider support for TGWU. The TUC F&GPC then advises the TGWU to pay the fines imposed by the NIRC, because of threat to TUC. General secretary Vic Feather and other TUC leaders meet with government ministers.
AUEW NC votes narrowly to continue current plant bargaining campaign

27 London dockers vote in favour of blacking the Midland Cold Storage Company for refusing to employ registered dockers.

29 900 delegates attend third national Building Workers' Charter conference in Birmingham to plan campaign in support of their wage claim.

May

1 24-hour May Day strikes by Merseyside and Preston dockers. Southampton dockers on strike against TGWU fines. Unofficial national port stewards' committee extends blacking campaign to two transport firms in each port.
TGWU executive, on casting vote of chair, agrees to pay fines imposed by NIRC.
TUC F&GPC recommends that unions defend themselves at NIRC without TUC permission.
Building worker marches in London and Glasgow in support of pay claim.

3 TGWU pays NIRC fines.

4 TUC General Council agrees new policy on unions appearing before NIRC.
TGWU docks delegate conference gives 28 days notice of national strike action on the question of unregistered dock work (later postponed).

8 Railway cooling-off period expires.

9 Railway unions agree to resume sanctions on 12 May.
AUEW executive circular drops hours from minimum list of demands in current pay campaign.
Panalpina haulage firm blacked in Hull applies to NIRC.

11   Employment secretary Macmillan applies to the NIRC for compulsory ballot on railways pay offer. Unions have lawyers in court.

12   British Rail decide to shut down railway network from 10pm on Saturday 13 May to 6am on Monday 15 May.

NIRC president Sir John Donaldson gives TGWU 21 days notice to take action to stop Merseyside stewards continuing to black container lorries.

GEC-AEI Trafford Park stewards vote to drop hours demands from pay claim.

13   (Saturday) The NIRC orders a compulsory ballot on the railways and that industrial action must be called off.

14   (Sunday) Court of Appeal starts hearing railway unions' appeal.

15   NUR instructions to stop sanctions delayed until early evening. Most London stations disrupted. Many drivers take unofficial action.

Following an emergency CSEU district committee in Manchester, a 600-strong shop stewards meeting agrees to drop the hours component of their national claim. Many sit-ins fold up over next ten days.

16   Normal working on railways by end of day.

17   3,000 school students from the Inner London Education Authority take one-day strike action to protest at petty rules and conditions in schools.

A TGWU official appears before NIRC for first time. Hull docker Walter Cunningham ordered to attend NIRC over Panalpina blacking but refuses.

18   The NIRC orders Hull dockers to stop blacking Panalpina.

19   Court of Appeal upholds NIRC ruling that railway unions must ballot their members.

22   Mass meeting of Hull dockers votes to continue blacking two transport firms in container dispute,

Peter Kavanagh starts crane-top sit-in protest above London building site.

23   Some London railworkers walk off job to collect ballot papers not delivered to them.

25   Only six long-running sit-ins still operating in Manchester plus six new ones (over previous fortnight) in Ferranti factories.

30   Court of Appeal begins hearing TGWU appeal against the fines.

Alan Prior and John Mahon start crane-top sit-in 120 feet above Birmingham city centre.

31 Railway workers' ballot shows six to one majority in favour of resuming industrial action.

Peter Kavanagh ends crane-top protest.

June

2 Birmingham crane-top protest ends.

3 Five engineering sit-ins still running in Greater Manchester.

6 A mass picket of 1,000 dockers is mounted outside the Chobham Farm container depot in London.

9 Three railway unions agree to resume industrial action on 14 June.

10 Liaison Committee for Defence of Trade Unions (LCDTU) national conference, attended by 1,000 delegates, calls for strike action if any trade unionist is imprisoned by NIRC.

12 The NIRC orders injunction against shop stewards' committee and three named London dockers (Bernie Steer, Vic Turner and Alan Williams) to stop picketing Chobham Farm container depot and blacking firms using it.

13 Following the TGWU's appeal against the £55,000 fines, the Court of Appeal overrules the NIRC judgment. Individual shop stewards, not the union, now liable.

The railway unions accept improved pay offer and call off threatened industrial action only six hours before it is due to start.

14 NIRC threatens to arrest three London dockers' shop stewards unless, by 2pm on 16 June, they explain why they have disobeyed its order. Hundreds of dockers lobbying TGWU head offices protest at that day's docks delegate conference decision to postpone national strike action for six weeks to allow inquiry (Jones-Aldington committee).

16 In response to warrants issued for the arrest of three London shop stewards there is a national unofficial strike by about 35,000 dockers, with a mass picket outside Chobham Farm container base. Official Solicitor intervenes and appeal court sets aside the committal orders.

20 Heaton Transport appeals to the House of Lords to try to overturn Court of Appeal judgment.

23   The pound sterling is allowed to float.
26   National building workers' selective strike campaign commences.
      Half-day stoppages in many towns and cities in north west.

July

3   2,000-strong building worker demonstration in Birmingham.
4   The NIRC hears another blacking and picketing case, Midland
      Cold Storage.
      Talks between Prime Minister Edward Heath and the TUC
      General Council.
      6,000 prisoners in 22 jails involved in one-day strike in protest
      at prison conditions.
8   Seven dockers refuse to appear before the NIRC after writs
      issued to prevent them picketing the Midland Cold Storage
      depot.
11   Law Lords start hearing Heaton Transport appeal.
12   In Manchester flying picket of building worker strikers used to
      enforce overtime ban on working sites over next few days.
14   In Birmingham a 4,000-strong march stops 90 building sites.
18   The first of a series of tripartite talks between the government,
      TUC and CBI.
19   Law Lords finish hearing Heaton appeal.
21   Warrants issued for arrest of five London dockers for contempt
      of order to stop picketing Midland Cold Storage. Four (Steer,
      Con Clancy, Tony Merrick and Derek Watkins) arrested. Un-
      official national dockers' strike starts and mass picket outside
      Pentonville prison.
22   (Saturday) Fifth London docker (Turner) arrested while pick-
      eting Pentonville prison. Briant Colour print workers' occu-
      pation march joined by thousands of striking London dockers.
      National newspaper production (dailies and Sundays) on Fleet
      Street gradually brought to a standstill by printers following ap-
      peals for solidarity action by dockers.
24   AUEW executive calls on TUC to organise a one-day general
      strike on Monday 31 July. TUC F&GPC meets Heath, as un-
      official strike wave sweeps across the country.
      Building workers in Bristol start closing down sites after deci-
      sion for all-out strike on national claim.

25   Demonstration of 30,000 to Pentonville prison. Unofficial strikes spread.
        Building sites in Birmingham progressively stopped from today in line with regional action committee decision.

26   TUC General Council votes for one-day 'protest stoppages of work' on 31 July. Law Lords reverse Court of Appeal ruling that individual shop stewards are liable, thus reinstating the TGWU fine. The NIRC releases the five dockers from prison, even though they have not purged their contempt.

27   TGWU docks delegate conference calls official national strike over unregistered labour from 28 July.

28   Official national dock strike starts.
        National newspapers reappear.

August

2   Building industry NJC agrees to reconvene on 8 August to get union agreement to proposals to end strike.
        400 docker pickets shut Neap House Wharf near Scunthorpe.

3   Government announces state of emergency because of national dock strike.
        Most UCATT regional representatives meeting in London oppose executive decision to accept building employers' offer.

4   London building workers' action committee calls for half-day strike and demonstration on Tuesday 8 August. Mass meeting in Bristol rejects offer.
        Thousands of prisoners organise sit-ins and refuse to work in prisons in protest over conditions.

5   Mass meetings in Leeds and Liverpool reject building offer.

7   TGWU trade group committee rejects building offer and UCATT north west regional committee unanimously rejects building offer.
        Neap House Wharf working, not stopped by 350 docker pickets.

8   Thousands of building workers in London, Birmingham and Glasgow demonstrate to call for escalation of the strike.
        UCATT executive now votes to reject employers' offer.

9   700 docker pickets at Neap House Wharf face 500 police.

10   London regional action committee convenes big meeting and all-out strike with no strike pay agreed. Large building worker

demonstration in Stoke-on-Trent. Building workers march around Preston, bringing out sites.

11   At national meeting of UCATT regional officials majority favour all-out strike.

Last Manchester engineering sit-in, at Bason and Son of Stockport, finishes.

13   At West of Scotland UCATT stewards' meeting tiny minority support executive's selective strike strategy. Rest of meeting wants all-out strike.

14   900 docker pickets confront 800 police at Neap House Wharf.

15   Building union leaders agree 'most rapid intensification' but still want to be selective. From this date the local activists around the country are working for an all-out strike.

16   TGWU docks delegate conference votes in favour of further proposals from Jones-Aldington committee and call for a resumption of work by dockers. The unofficial national port shop stewards' committee recommends a continuation of the strike.

18   Mass meetings of dockers in London and Hull vote to go back to work.

Biggest building workers' demonstration ever in Scotland.

National agreement finalised in engineering.

24   Building workers from Birmingham and Stoke picket cement works near Leek

28   Further rooftop protests organised by prisoners across the country.

Building unions claim 270,000 strikers from 9,000 sites.

September

4   Annual TUC meeting in Brighton suspends 32 unions for remaining registered under the Industrial Relations Act.

5   Lobby of TUC conference called by the LCDTU to demand stiffer action against the Industrial Relations Act.

6-7   Flying mass pickets in Telford and Shrewsbury by North Wales building workers, which subsequently leads to conspiracy trial.

12   Large building workers' demonstration in Liverpool.

14   TUC leaders meet with government and CBI.

Building workers' union leaders agree a pay deal with the employers, with return to work on Monday 18 September.

15   In a number of areas meetings of building workers reject the deal signed by their union leaders.

18   Most building workers return to work, although there remain pockets of resistance in Birmingham, Liverpool, Manchester and elsewhere (many of which stay out for another week). World's End site in Chelsea comes out on strike again within hours (ends 17 November).

26   The government announces proposals for an incomes policy of limiting pay rises to £2, and 5 percent ceiling on price rises on which it hopes to secure agreement from the TUC.

October

1   Mass demonstration of tenants and trade unionists in London against the Housing Finance Act.

2   10,000 Liverpool dockers take one-day strike action against the Housing Finance Act, with a mass march of tenants and trade unionists through the city.

9   Further tripartite talks between government, TUC and CBI.

16   Tripartite talks.

25   TUC General Council gives go-ahead for negotiators to seek price and incomes deal with government and CBI.

26   Tripartite talks.

28   500 Asian workers strike over discrimination at Mansfield Hosiery Mills in Loughborough.

30   One-day strike against Housing Finance Act in Dundee involving 25,000 workers and tenants.
      Tripartite talks.

November

1   Tripartite talks.

2   Heath breaks off tripartite talks.

6   The government imposes a 90-day pay freeze (later extended to 1 April 1973).

8   The NIRC imposes a fine of £5,000 on AUEW for refusing to admit James Goad to membership at CAV, Sudbury, Suffolk.

10   AUEW executive agrees not to pay fine.

21   Commissioners appointed to enforce fine.

22   TUC national lobby of parliament to protest at low level of pensions, and 5,000 construction workers at British Steel Anchor site in Scunthorpe take one-day strike action on issue.

23   Half-day strike by 35,000 London teachers over blocking of increase in London weighting allowance.

27   Mansfield Hosiery Mills strikers return, but walk out again on same day.

28   Bank ordered to pay AUEW fine from union's account under the sequestration order made against the union in the Goad case.

29   Bank pays fine.

December

3   2,000 protestors march in Clay Cross, Derbyshire, to support local councillors' defiance of the Housing Finance Act.

5   Mansfield Hosiery Mills strike made official.

7   Mass meeting of 1,300 engineers at CAV Sudbury vote to refuse to work with James Goad, and he is sent home on full pay.

8   NIRC orders second fine, of £50,000, on AUEW.

11   CAV workers strike in protest at fines on AUEW.

12   AUEW executive calls on members to take 'appropriate steps to defend the policy of the union' as rank-and-file pressure for strike action mounts.
        National one-day strike and demonstrations by National Health Service ancillary workers against the freeze on their pay claim.

18   One-day strike by 55,000 engineers over fines imposed by the NIRC.

20   Further one-day strike by 160,000 engineers over the NIRC fine, supported by Liverpool dockers.

Inflation and unemployment monthly figures, 1969-1972

	Percentage change on retail prices in previous 12 months	Wholly unemployed (000s)	Temporarily stopped (000s)	Total unemployed (000s)
1969				
January	6.2	624.7	11.2	635.8
February	6.2	616.2	16.3	632.6
March	6.3	604.3	24.2	628.5
April	5.5	586.2	8.2	594.5
May	5.3	545.3	14.6	560.0
June	5.3	517.9	15.9	533.8
July	5.3	541.7	9.1	550.8
August	4.6	590.4	16.0	606.4
September	5.1	576.7	20.1	596.9
October	5.4	577.7	30.1	607.8
November	5.4	587.8	19.9	607.7
December	4.7	601.8	8.2	610.0
1970				
January	5.0	649.3	17.7	667.0
February	4.9	642.4	18.4	660.8
March	5.1	637.3	22.9	660.2
April	5.6	628.5	23.9	652.4
May	6.1	586.7	25.3	612.0
June	5.9	555.3	23.4	578.8
July	6.7	588.3	18.9	607.2
August	6.8	635.5	9.1	644.6
September	7.0	616.4	49.3	665.6
October	7.4	611.2	22.3	633.5
November	7.9	623.8	14.4	638.2
December	7.9	640.8	17.0	657.8

continued overleaf…

	Percentage change on retail prices in previous 12 months	Wholly unemployed (000s)	Temporarily stopped (000s)	Total unemployed (000s)
1971				
January	8.4	714.4	16.8	731.2
February	8.5	722.5	38.3	760.8
March	8.8	737.9	54.6	792.5
April	9.4	768.7	44.8	813.5
May	9.8	752.9	40.7	793.7
June	10.3	724.2	38.0	762.1
July	10.1	786.2	43.4	829.6
August	10.3	861.4	42.7	904.1
September	9.9	854.9	73.9	928.9
October	9.4	861.6	68.1	929.7
November	9.2	894.0	75.9	969.9
December	9.0	910.9	56.0	966.9
1972				
January	8.2	973.5	50.1	1,023.6
February	8.1	968.3	652.9*	1,621.2*
March	7.6	967.1	50.2	1,017.3
April	6.3	972.9	32.2	1,005.1
May	6.1	872.1	29.5	901.6
June	6.1	806.1	28.0	834.1
July	5.8	848.6	19.5	868.1
August	6.6	908.3	21.8	930.1
September	7.0	890.5	31.1	921.6
October	7.9	829.6	15.1	844.7
November	7.6	807.1	11.8	818.9
December	7.6	781.6	8.0	789.6

Note: Price increases for Great Britain only. Monthly unemployment figures for United Kingdom taken on one particular day each month.
* Inflated by layoffs caused by miners' strike (monthly unemployment count on 14 February 1972).
Source: Employment and Productivity Gazette (1970, 1972); Department of Employment Gazette (1973); Annual Abstract of Labour Statistics (1972, 1973).

Bibliography

Primary sources

From the Modern Records Centre, University of Warwick (with archive main reference)

TUC General Council minutes (MSS 292)
TUC Finance and General Purposes Committee minutes (MSS 292)
TUC circulars (MSS 292)
AUEW National Committee reports (MSS 259)
CSEU annual reports (MSS 259)
CSEU executive committee minutes (MSS 259)
NFBTE, miscellaneous papers on 1972 building strike (MSS 187)
NUM strike circulars, press statement (MSS 292)
ASLEF and NUR circulars on miners' strike (MSS 292)

From the Working Class Movement Library, Salford

AUEW Manchester district committee minutes
Building Workers' Charter

Union journals from various library collections

AUEW Journal
Locomotive Journal
TASS Journal
Transport Salaried Staffs Journal
UCATT Viewpoint

Authors' own or loaned to the authors

TUC annual reports
Boilermakers' Society delegate conference minutes (1972)

Proceedings at special conferences between EEF and CSEU (1971, 1972)

Report of AUEW (E) youth conference (1972)

Greater Manchester Engineer (1972)

Voice of the Engineers, broadsheet of the Gorton and Openshaw Joint Shop Stewards' Liaison Committee (1972)

UCATT, 'UCATT and the Shrewsbury Trials' (no date)

Official publications

Parliamentary Debates (Hansard) 5th series (House of Commons unless otherwise specified)

Committee of Inquiry into Certain Matters Concerning the Port Transport Industry (Devlin), *Final Report*, Cmnd 2734 (1965)

British Railways Board, *Minutes of Evidence* 14, Royal Commission on Trade Unions and Employers' Associations (1966)

Court of Inquiry into Trade Disputes at the Barbican and Horseferry Road Construction Sites in London (Cameron), *Report*, Cmnd 3396 (1967)

Royal Commission on Trade Unions and Employers' Associations (Donovan), *Report*, Cmnd 3623 (1968)

Committee of Inquiry into Certain Matters Concerning Labour in Building and Civil Engineering (Phelps Brown), *Report*, Cmnd 3714 (1968)

National Board for Prices and Incomes, Report 92, *Pay and Conditions in the Building Industry*, Cmnd 3837 (1968)

In Place of Strife: A Policy for Industrial Relations, Cmnd 3888 (1969)

Court of Inquiry into a Dispute between the National Coal Board and the National Union of Mineworkers (Wilberforce), *Report*, Cmnd 4903 (1972)

British Labour Statistics Year Book (1972, 1973)

CEGB Statistical Yearbook 1972

Royal Commission on the Press (McGregor), *Industrial Relations in the National Newspaper Industry: A Report by the Advisory, Conciliation and Arbitration Service*, Cmnd 6680 (1976)

The Electricity Council Annual Report, 1983-84

Oral sources

Interview with John Tocher, 'The Desire for Change', *Socialist Review* 5 (1978), pp36-38

'An Interview with Frank Watters', *Bulletin of the Society for the Study of Labour History* 43 (1981), pp54-67

'Symposium: The Trade Unions and the Fall of the Heath Government', *Contemporary Record* 2:1 (1988)

Ricky Tomlinson, speaking at *Socialist Worker* May Day Rally, Alexandra Palace, London, 1992

Bob Light, speaking at Marxism 97, University of London, July 1997

Eddie Prevost, speaking at Marxism 97, University of London, July 1997

List of interviewees, position in 1972, and date of interview

Campbell Adamson, CBI director general, 7 April 1998

Mike Britton, NATSOPA 'Imperial chair' *Sunday Times* joint chapels, chair Fleet Street Broad Left group, 12 May 1998

Trevor Brown, NUM Houghton Main, Yorkshire, IS member, 12 August 1998

Robert Carr, Secretary of State for Employment (until March), then Leader of the House, 10 June 1998

Frank Cave, NUM branch delegate Brodsworth, Yorkshire area executive member, 13 September 1998

Derek Ezra, chairman National Coal Board, 22 April 1998

Sean Geraghty, chair EETPU London Press branch, 6 May 1998

Mike Hicks, SOGAT casual on *Daily Express*, Fleet Street CP branch secretary, CP executive member, 12 May 1998

Douglas Hurd, political secretary to Edward Heath, 29 April 1998

Jack Jones, TGWU general secretary, 1 July 1998

Lou Lewis, UCATT shop steward, CP executive member, 29 April 1998

Bob Light, Royal Group, London docker, TGWU, IS member, 9 February 1999

John Mitchell, SOGAT FoC *Daily* and *Sunday Express*, 6 May 1998

Len Murray, TUC assistant general secretary, 23 April 1998

Mike Power, FoC at *Kentish Times*, NGA London regional council member, CP member, 9 June 1998

Ross Pritchard, NGA printer at Frederick Printing Company, editor of *Printworker*, IS member, 10 June 1998

Mick Rice, Birmingham East AUEW district committee member, IS member, 19 August 1998

Hugh Scanlon, AUEW president, 6 August 1998

Vic Turner, TGWU, chair of the Royal Docks shop stewards' committee, chair of the port of London joint shop stewards' committee, chair of the national port shop stewards' committee, 23 April 1998

Frank Watters, Birmingham CP district organiser, 8 May 1998

Newspapers and contemporary journals

Birmingham Evening Mail
British Journal of Industrial Relations
Comment
Department of Employment Gazette
Economist
Employment and Productivity Gazette
Financial Times
Guardian
IDS Report
Industrial Relations Review and Report
International Socialism
Keesing's Contemporary Archives
Labour Research
Labour Weekly
Management Today
Morning Star
New Society
New Statesman
Observer
Personnel Management
Red Mole
Socialist Review
Socialist Worker
Socialist Worker Review

Spectator
Sunday Times
Times

Secondary sources

(books published in London unless otherwise indicated)

Allen, V L (1966), *Militant Trade Unionism: A Re-analysis of Industrial Action in an Inflationary Situation* (Merlin Press)

Allen, V L (1981), *The Militancy of British Miners* (Moor Press, Shipley)

Arnison, J (1974), *The Shrewsbury Three: Strikes, Pickets and 'Conspiracy'* (Lawrence & Wishart)

Arnot, R P (1953), *The Miners: Years of Struggle—A History of the Miners Federation of Great Britain (from 1910 onwards)* (Allen & Unwin)

Ashworth, W (1986), *The History of the British Coal Industry, vol 5: 1946-1982—The Nationalized Industry* (Oxford University Press, Oxford)

Austrin, T (1980), 'The "Lump" in the UK Construction Industry', in T Nichols (ed), *Capital and Labour* (Fontana)

Bagwell, P S (1963), *The Railwaymen: The History of the National Union of Railwaymen* (Allen & Unwin)

Bagwell, P S (1982), *The Railwaymen, vol 2: The Beeching Era and After* (Allen & Unwin)

Bain, G S and R Price (1980), *Profiles of Union Growth: A Comparative Statistical Portrait of Eight Countries* (Blackwell, Oxford)

Bain, G S and R Price (1983), 'Union Growth: Dimensions, Determinants, and Destiny', in G S Bain (ed), *Industrial Relations in Britain* (Blackwell, Oxford)

Barker, C (1972), *The Power Game* (Pluto Press)

Barker, C (1973, first published 1967), 'The British Labour Movement: Aspects of Current Experience', *International Socialism* 1:61

Barnes, D and E Reid (1980), *Governments and Trade Unions: The British Experience, 1964-79* (Heinemann)

Barnett, A (1973), 'Class Struggle and the Heath Government', *New Left Review* 77

Beynon, H (1973), *Working for Ford* (Penguin, Harmondsworth)

Birchall, I (1972), 'The British Communist Party: 1945-64', *International Socialism* 1:50

Brown, W (ed) (1981), *The Changing Contours of British Industrial Relations: A Survey of Manufacturing Industry* (Blackwell, Oxford)

Bruce-Gardyne, J (1974), *Whatever Happened to the Quiet Revolution? The Story of a Brave Experiment in Government* (Charles Knight)

Bullock, A (1960), *The Life and Times of Ernest Bevin, vol 1: Trade Union Leader* (Heinemann)

Burke, V (1971), *Teachers in Turmoil* (Penguin, Harmondsworth)

Campbell, J (1994), *Edward Heath: A Biography* (Pimlico)

Carr, B (1976), 'From the Yorkshire Coalfield', in J Skelley (ed), *The General Strike, 1926* (Lawrence & Wishart)

Chadwick, G (1973), 'The Manchester Engineering Sit-Ins, 1972', in M Barratt Brown and K Coates (eds), *Trade Union Register 3* (Spokesman, Nottingham)

Chapple, F (1984), *Sparks Fly! A Trade Union Life* (Michael Joseph)

Charlton, J (1973), 'The Miners: The Triumph of 1972 and the Way Ahead', *International Socialism* 1:57

Church, R and Q Outram (1998), *Strikes and Solidarity: Coalfield Conflict in Britain, 1889-1966* (Cambridge University Press, Cambridge)

Clark, J and Lord Wedderburn (1983), 'Modern Labour Law: Problems, Functions and Policies', in Lord Wedderburn, R Lewis and J Clark (eds), *Labour Law and Industrial Relations: Building on Kahn-Freund* (Clarendon Press, Oxford)

Clegg, H A (1970), *The System of Industrial Relations in Great Britain* (Blackwell, Oxford)

Clegg, H A (1979), *The Changing System of Industrial Relations in Great Britain* (Blackwell, Oxford)

Clegg, H A (1985), *A History of British Trade Unions since 1889, vol 2: 1911-1933* (Clarendon Press, Oxford)

Clegg, H A and R Adams (1957), *The Employers' Challenge: A Study of the National Shipbuilding and Engineering Disputes of 1957* (Blackwell, Oxford)

Cliff, T (1970), *The Employers' Offensive: Productivity Deals and How to Fight Them* (Pluto Press)

Cliff, T (1979), 'The Balance of Class Forces in Recent Years', *International Socialism* 2:6

Cliff, T (1985), 'Patterns of Mass Strike', *International Socialism* 2:29

Cliff, T (2000), *A World to Win: Life of a Revolutionary* (Bookmarks)

Cliff, T and C Barker (1966), *Incomes Policy, Legislation and Shop Stewards* (London Industrial Shop Stewards Defence Committee)

Cliff, T and D Gluckstein (1986), *Marxism and Trade Union Struggle: The General Strike of 1926* (Bookmarks)

Clinton, A (1984), *Post Office Workers: A Trade Union and Social History* (Allen & Unwin)

Clutterbuck, R (1978), *Britain in Agony: The Growth of Political Violence* (Faber and Faber)

Coates, K (1973), 'Introductory Review: Converting the Unions to Socialism' in M Barratt Brown and K Coates (eds), *Trade Union Register 3* (Spokesman, Nottingham)

Coates, K and T Topham (1974), *The New Unionism: The Case for Workers' Control* (Penguin, Harmondsworth)

Coates, K and T Topham (1991), *The History of the Transport and General Workers' Union, vol 1: The Making of the Transport and General Workers' Union—The Emergence of the Labour Movement* (Blackwell, Oxford)

Cole, G D H (1923), *Labour in the Coal-Mining Industry* (Clarendon Press, Oxford)

Communist Party (1968), *The British Road to Socialism: Programme of the Communist Party* (Communist Party, 3rd revised edition)

Conservative Political Centre (1968), *Fair Deal at Work: The Conservative Approach to Modern Industrial Relations* (Conservative Political Centre)

Corfield, T (1982), *The Rule of Law: A Study in Trade Union Organisation and Method* (R Brierley Publications, Birmingham)

Crick, M (1985), *Scargill and the Miners* (Penguin, Harmondsworth)

Crouch, C (1982), *The Politics of Industrial Relations* (Fontana)

Danos, J and M Gibelin (1986), *June '36: Class Struggle and the Popular Front in France* (Pluto Press)

Darlington, R (1998), *The Political Trajectory of J T Murphy* (Liverpool University Press, Liverpool)

Dash, J (1969), *Good Morning Brothers!* (Lawrence & Wishart)

Davies, P and M Freedland (1993), *Labour Legislation and Public Policy: A Contemporary History* (Clarendon Press, Oxford)

Deason, J (1975), 'The Broad Left in the AUEW', *International Socialism* 1:79

Denning, Lord (1983), *The Closing Chapter* (Butterworths)

Dorfman, G A (1979), *Government versus Trade Unionism in British Politics since 1968* (Macmillan)

Durcan, J W, W E J McCarthy and G P Redman (1983), *Strikes in Post-War Britain: A Study of Stoppages of Work due to Industrial Disputes, 1946-73* (Allen & Unwin)

Edelstein, J D and M Warner (1975), *Comparative Union Democracy: Organisation and Opposition in British and American Unions* (Allen & Unwin)

Engels, F (1962), 'The Condition of the Working Class in England' (1845), in K Marx and F Engels, *On Britain* (Foreign Languages Publishing House, Moscow)

Ferris, P (1972), *The New Militants: Crisis in the Trade Unions* (Penguin, Harmondsworth)

Fishman, N (1995), *The British Communist Party and the Trade Unions 1933-1945* (Scolar Press, Aldershot)

Fishman N, (1999), ' "A Vital Element in British Industrial Relations": A Reassessment of Order 1305, 1940-51', *Historical Studies in Industrial Relations* 8

Fishman, N (1999), ' "The Most Serious Crisis since 1926": The Engineering and Shipbuilding Strikes of 1957', in A Campbell, N Fishman and J McIlroy (eds), *British Trade Unions and Industrial Politics, vol 1: The Post-War Compromise, 1945-64* (Ashgate, Aldershot)

Fitzgerald, M (1977), *Prisoners in Revolt* (Penguin, Harmondsworth)

Flanders, A (1970; first published 1967), 'Collective Bargaining: Prescription for Change', in A Flanders, *Management and Unions: The Theory and Reform of Industrial Relations* (Faber and Faber)

Flynn, L (1975), *Workers Against the Law: The Truth about the Shrewsbury Trials* (Socialist Worker)

Foster, J and C Woolfson (1986), *The Politics of the UCS Work-In: Class Alliances and the Right to Work* (Lawrence & Wishart)

Francis, H and D Smith (1980), *The Fed: A History of the South Wales Miners in the Twentieth Century* (Lawrence & Wishart)

Friedman H and S Meredeen (1980), *The Dynamics of Industrial Conflict: Lessons from Ford* (Croom Helm)

Frow, E and R Frow (1982), *Engineering Struggles: Episodes in the Story of the Shop Stewards' Movement* (Working Class Movement

Library, Manchester)

Fryer, R and S Williams (1993), *A Century of Service: An Illustrated History of the National Union of Public Employees, 1889-1993* (Lawrence & Wishart)

Geary, R (1986), *Policing Industrial Disputes: 1893 to 1985* (Methuen)

Gennard, J (1977), *Financing Strikers* (Macmillan)

Gennard, J and P Bain (1995), *A History of the Society of Graphical and Allied Trades* (Routledge)

Gluckstein, D (1999), *The Nazis, Capitalism and the Working Class* (Bookmarks)

Glyn, A and J Harrison (1980), *The British Economic Disaster* (Pluto Press)

Goodman, J (1975), 'Great Britain: Toward the Social Contract', in S Barkin (ed), *Worker Militancy and Its Consequences, 1965-75: New Directions in Western Industrial Relations* (Praeger, New York)

Gormley, J (1982), *Battered Cherub* (Hamish Hamilton)

Goulding, A (1975), 'The Building Industry: Background to a Rank-and-File Movement', *International Socialism* 1:75

Griffin, C (1989), *The Leicestershire Miners, vol 3: 1945-1988* (NUM Leicester Area, Coalville)

Griffiths, J (1977), *The Politics of the Judiciary* (Manchester University Press, Manchester)

Hall, T (1981), *King Coal: Miners, Coal and Britain's Industrial Future* (Penguin, Harmondsworth)

Hammond, T T (1974), *Lenin on Trade Unions and Revolution, 1893-1917* (Greenwood Press, Westport, Connecticut)

Handy, L J (1981), *Wages Policy in the Coalmining Industry* (Cambridge University Press, Cambridge)

Harman, C (1973), 'Communist Party in Decline: 2', *International Socialism* 1:63

Harman, C (1988), *The Fire Last Time: 1968 and After* (Bookmarks)

Harrison, R (ed) (1978), *Independent Collier: The Coal Miner as Archetypal Proletarian Reconsidered* (Harvester, Hassocks)

Heath, E (1998), *The Course of My Life: My Autobiography* (Hodder and Stoughton)

Hills, D H (1973), 'The National Industrial Relations Court—A Personal History', *British Journal of Industrial Relations* 11:2

Holmes, M (1982), *Political Pressure and Economic Policy: British Government, 1970-1974* (Butterworth)

Howe, G (1994), *Conflict of Loyalty* (Macmillan)

Hughes, J and R Moore (1972), *A Special Case? Social Justice and the Miners* (Penguin, Harmondsworth)

Hunter, B (1994), *They Knew Why They Fought: Unofficial Struggles and Leadership on the Docks 1945-1989* (Index Books)

Hurd, D (1979), *An End to Promises: Sketch of a Government, 1970-74* (Collins)

Hyman, R (1973), 'Industrial Conflict and the Political Economy', in R Miliband and J Saville (eds), *The Socialist Register* 1973 (Merlin Press)

International Socialists (1973a), *The 1973 Engineering Pay Claim*, International Socialists Industrial Pamphlet (IS)

International Socialists (1973b), *Pickets on Trial: Defend the North Wales 24*, International Socialists Industrial Pamphlet (IS)

Jackson, M P (1975), *Labour Relations on the Docks* (Saxon House, Farnborough)

James, L (1984) *Power in a Trade Union: The Role of the District Committee in the AUEW* (Cambridge University Press, Cambridge)

Jefferys, S (1975), 'The Challenge of the Rank and File', *International Socialism* 1:76

Jenkins, P (1970), *The Battle of Downing Street* (Charles Knight)

Jones, A (1973), *The New Inflation: The Politics of Prices and Incomes* (Penguin, Harmondsworth)

Jones, J (1986), *Union Man: The Autobiography of Jack Jones* (Collins)

Kelly, G (1991), *A History of LACSAB: Industrial Relations in Local Government* (Centurion Press)

Kerr, H (1973), 'Fair Rents—the Experience', *International Socialism* 1:56

King, C H (1975), *The Cecil King Diary, 1970-1974* (Jonathan Cape)

Knowles, K G J C (1954), *Strikes: A Study in Industrial Conflict—with Special Reference to British Experience between 1911 and 1947* (Blackwell, Oxford)

Lavalette, M and J Kennedy (1996), *Solidarity on the Waterfront: The Liverpool Lock-Out of 1995/6* (Liver Press, Birkenhead)

Lenin, V I (1974, first published 1917), 'The State and Revolution', in *Collected Works*, vol 25 (Lawrence & Wishart)

Lewis, G (1997), *Lord Hailsham: A Life* (Jonathan Cape)

Lewis, N (1973), 'Railroading the Workers—One Way or Another', in M Barratt Brown and K Coates (eds), *Trade Union Register 3* (Spokesman, Nottingham)

Lindop, F (1983), 'Unofficial Militancy in the Royal Group of Docks 1945-67', *Oral History* 11:2

Lindop, F (1998a), 'The Dockers and the Industrial Relations Act, Part 1: Shop Stewards and Containerization', *Historical Studies in Industrial Relations* 5

Lindop, F (1998b), 'The Dockers and the Industrial Relations Act, Part 2: The Arrest and Release of the "Pentonville Five" ', *Historical Studies in Industrial Relations* 6

Lindop, F (forthcoming), 'Racism and the Working Class: Strikes in Support of Enoch Powell in 1968', *Labour History Review*

Lyddon, D (1996), 'The Car Industry, 1945-79: Shop Stewards and Workplace Unionism', in C Wrigley (ed), *A History of British Industrial Relations, 1939-1979* (Edward Elgar, Cheltenham)

Lyddon, D (1998), 'Rediscovering the Past: Recent British Strike Tactics in Historical Perspective', *Historical Studies in Industrial Relations* 5

Lyddon, D (1999), ' "Glorious Summer", 1972: The High Tide of Rank and File Militancy', in McIlroy, Fishman and Campbell, 1999

McCarthy, W E J and S R Parker (1968), Royal Commission on Trade Unions and Employers' Associations, Research Paper 10: *Shop Stewards and Workshop Relations* (HMSO)

McCormick, B (1979), *Industrial Relations in the Coal Industry* (Macmillan)

McIlroy, J (1999a), 'Notes on the Communist Party and Industrial Politics', in McIlroy, Fishman and Campbell, 1999

McIlroy, J (1999b), ' "Always Outnumbered, Always Outgunned": The Trotskyists and the Trade Unions', in McIlroy, Fishman and Campbell, 1999

McIlroy, J and A Campbell (1999), 'Organizing the Militants: The Liaison Committee for the Defence of Trade Unions', *British Journal of Industrial Relations* 37:1

McIlroy, J, N Fishman and A Campbell (eds) (1999), *British Trade Unionism and Industrial Politics, vol 2: The High Tide of Trade Unionism, 1964-79* (Aldershot: Ashgate)

McLeod, C (1970), *All Change: Railway Industrial Relations in the Sixties* (Gower Press)

Mark, R (1978) *In the Office of Constable* (Collins)

Marks, M (1974), 'The Battle at Fisher Bendix', *International Socialism* 1:73

Marsh, A (1965), *Industrial Relations in Engineering* (Pergamon Press, Oxford)

Marsh, R (1978), *Off the Rails: An Autobiography* (Weidenfeld and Nicolson)

Martin, R M (1980), *TUC: Growth of a Pressure Group, 1868-1976* (Clarendon Press, Oxford)

Mathews, J (1972), *Ford Strike: The Workers' Story* (Panther)

Maudling, R (1978), *Memoirs* (Sidgwick and Jackson)

Mills, C Wright (1948), *The New Men of Power: America's Labor Leaders* (New York: Harcourt, Brace)

Minkin, L (1980), *The Labour Party Conference: A Study in the Politics of Intra-Party Democracy* (Manchester University Press, Manchester)

Monks, J (1992), 'Gains and Losses after Twenty Years of Legal Intervention', in W McCarthy (ed), *Legal Intervention in Industrial Relations: Gains and Losses* (Blackwell, Oxford)

Moran, M (1977), *The Politics of Industrial Relations: The Origins, Life and Death of the 1971 Industrial Relations Act* (Macmillan)

Mortimer, J E (1994), *History of the Boilermakers' Society, vol 3: 1940-1989* (Verso)

Oldham, J and others (1970), 'The Miners' Strike', in K Coates, T Topham and M Barratt Brown (eds), *Trade Union Register 1970* (Merlin Press)

Philips, J (1996), 'Inter-Union Conflict in the Docks, 1954-1955', *Historical Studies in Industrial Relations* 1

Pitt, M (1979), *The World on Our Backs: The Kent Miners and the 1972 Miners' Strike* (Lawrence & Wishart)

Ritson, J (1972), *Case Studies in Industrial Law and Relations* (Charles Knight)

Roberts, E (1994) *Strike Back* (Orpington: Ernie Roberts)

Roche, J (1970), 'The Leeds Clothing Strike', in K Coates, T Topham and M Barratt Brown (eds), *Trade Union Register 1970* (Merlin Press)

Routledge, P (1993), *Scargill: The Unauthorized Biography* (HarperCollins)

Scargill, A (1975), 'The New Unionism', *New Left Review* 92

Seifert, R V (1987), *Teacher Militancy: A History of Teacher Strikes, 1896-1987* (Falmer Press)

Sewill, B (1975), *A View from the Inside: In Place of Strikes* (Institute of Economic Affairs)

Shipley, P (1976), *Revolutionaries in Modern Britain* (The Bodley Head)

Smith, P (1969), 'The Engineering Settlement', in K Coates, T Topham and M Barratt Brown (eds) *Trade Union Register* (Merlin Press)

Spriano, P (1975), *The Occupation of the Factories: Italy 1920* (Pluto Press)

Taylor, A (1984), *The Politics of the Yorkshire Miners* (Croom Helm)

Taylor, R (1980), *The Fifth Estate: Britain's Unions in the Modern World* (Pan; 2nd edition)

Taylor, R (1993), *The Trade Union Question in British Politics* (Blackwell, Oxford)

Thatcher, M (1995), *The Path to Power* (Harper Collins)

Thompson, W and F Hart (1972), *The UCS Work-In* (Lawrence & Wishart)

Thomson, A W J and S R Engelman (1975), *The Industrial Relations Act: A Review and Analysis* (Martin Robertson)

Tomison, M (1972), *The English Sickness: The Rise of Trade Union Political Power* (Tom Stacey)

Topham, T (1973), 'The Attack on the Dockers', in M Barratt Brown and K Coates (eds), *Trade Union Register 3* (Nottingham: Spokesman)

Townsend, P (1979), *Poverty in the United Kingdom: A Survey of Household Resources and Standards of Living* (Penguin, Harmondsworth)

Trades Union Congress (1972a), *The Great March* (TUC)

Trades Union Congress (1972b), *TUC Handbook on the Industrial Relations Act* (TUC)

Turnbull, P (1993), 'Docks', in A Pendleton and J Winterton (eds), *Public Enterprise in Transition: Industrial Relations in State and Privatised Corporations* (Routledge)

Turnbull, P, C Woolfson and J Kelly (1993), *Dock Strike: Conflict and Restructuring in Britain's Ports* (Avebury, Aldershot)

Turner, H A, G Clack and G Roberts (1967), *Labour Relations in the Motor Industry* (Allen & Unwin)

Ulam, A B (1969), *Lenin and the Bolsheviks: The Intellectual and Political History of the Triumph of Communism in Russia* (Fontana)

Undy, R (1979), 'The Electoral Influence of the Opposition Party in the AUEW Engineering Section 1960-75', *British Journal of Industrial Relations* 17:1

Undy, R, V Ellis, W E J McCarthy and A M Halmos (1981), *Change in Trade Unions: The Development of UK Unions since the 1960s* (Hutchinson)

Wallace, M (1996), *Single or Return? The History of the Transport Salaried Staffs' Association* (TSSA)

Wallington, P (1972), 'The Case of the Longannet Miners and the Criminal Liability of Pickets', *Industrial Law Journal* 1:4

Wallington, P (1975), 'Criminal Conspiracy and Industrial Conflict', *Industrial Law Journal* 4:2

Wallington, P (1985), 'Policing the Miners' Strike', *Industrial Law Journal* 14:3

Walton, R E and R B McKersie (1965), *A Behavioral Theory of Labor Negotiations* (McGraw-Hill, New York)

Warren, D (1982), *The Key to My Cell* (New Park)

Watters, F (1992), *Being Frank: The Memoirs of Frank Watters* (Monkspring, Barnsley)

Webb, S and B Webb (1894), *The History of Trade Unionism* (Longmans, Green)

Webb, S and B Webb (1897), *Industrial Democracy* (Longmans, Green)

Weekes, B, M Mellish, L Dickens and J Lloyd (1975), *Industrial Relations and the Limits of Law: The Industrial Effects of the Industrial Relations Act, 1971* (Blackwell, Oxford)

Whitehead, P (1985), *The Writing on the Wall: Britain in the Seventies* (Michael Joseph)

Wigham, E (1973), *The Power to Manage: A History of the Engineering Employers' Federation* (Macmillan)

Wigham, E (1976), *Strikes and the Government, 1893-1974* (Macmillan)

Wilson, D F (1972), *Dockers: The Impact of Industrial Change* (Fontana)

Wood, L W (1979), *A Union to Build: The Story of UCATT* (Lawrence & Wishart)

Unpublished work

Armstrong, M (1978), 'The History and Organisation of the Broad Left in the AUEW (Engineering Section) until 1972, with Special Reference to Manchester', MA, University of Warwick

Austrin, T (1978), 'Industrial Relations in the Construction Industry: Some Sociological Considerations on Wage Contracts and Trade Unionism, 1919-1973', PhD, University of Bristol

McIlroy, J and A Campbell (1997), 'The Communist Party and Industrial Politics 1964-1975', paper presented to conference on 'British Trade Unionism, Workers' Struggles and Economic Performance, 1940-1979', University of Warwick, 19-20 September

Tuckman, A (1985), 'Industrial Action and Hegemony: Workplace Occupations in Britain 1971 to 1981', PhD, University of Hull

Index

Hawker Siddeley: 114, 132
Hays Wharf Transport: 146, 159
Heath, Edward: 36, 37, 65, 67-68, 80, 87, 92, 93, 149, 154, 156-157, 167, 171-172, 176, 190, 211, 223-224
Heaton Transport: 148, 149, 152, 155, 170
Heffer, Eric: 19
Henry, Jack: 193
Hicks, Mike: 167
Hildrew, Peter: 128
Hiles, Jim: 226
Holborn station: 89
Holmes, Joe: 46
Horner, Kevin: 127
Howe, Sir Geoffrey: 83, 86, 89, 91, 156-157
Howell, Denis: 62
Hunter, Laurence: 65
Hurd, Douglas: 13-14, 67, 72, 176, 224
Hyman, Richard: 10

I'm All Right Jack: 9
In Place of Strife: 17, 19, 20, 225, 226
Incomes Data Services: 106
Incomes Policy: 10-15
Industrial democracy: 26
Industrial Relations Act: 16, 19, 20, 71, 75, 77, 79, 82-83, 92, 102, 104, 106, 120, 121, 134, 141-177, 186, 222, 224, 226
  Industrial Relations Act Review of the Situation: 158
Inflation: 225, 276-277
Institute for Workers' Control (IWC): 210
International Marxist Group (IMG): 228
International Publishing Group: 79
International Socialism: 127
International Socialists (IS): 28, 53, 116, 125, 131, 160-161, 163, 165, 166, 184, 202, 227-228
Iron and Steel Trades Confederation: 21
Isle of Man: 70

Jackson, Tom: 14
James Mills steelworks: 111
Jarratt, Alex: 79, 81
Jenkins, Peter: 8
Johnson, Bob: 192
Jones, Aubrey: 11
Jones, Jack (NUM): 45
Jones, Jack (TGWU): 20, 27-28, 44, 81, 144, 148-150, 151, 152, 153, 154, 161, 167, 168, 172-173, 175, 176, 222-225
  Jones-Aldington Committee: 160, 175, 176, 212
Jones, McKinsie: 206

Kane, Jock: 67-68, 226, 238
Kavanagh, Peter: 186, 203, 220
Kent coalfield: 45-48, 51, 52, 54, 70
King Ludd pub: 162
King, Cecil: 56, 79, 120
Krushchev, Nikita: 29

Labour Party: 14, 17, 19, 75, 158, 162, 169, 184, 196, 224
  1945 government: 141-142
  1964 government: 7, 10, 16, 34, 143
  1974 government: 16, 224
  New Labour: 16
Labour Research: 49, 55
Lally, Jack: 57
Lancashire coalfield: 32, 41
Law Lords: 170-171
Law, Alan: 62
Lawrence, John: 164
Leicester: 187
Leicestershire coalfield: 39, 45, 57
Lenin: 26, 217-218
Lewis, Lou: 182, 184, 185, 191, 193, 194, 202, 203, 226, 258
Liaison Committee for the Defence of Trade Unions (LCDTU): 17, 18, 19, 147, 157, 165, 226
Light, Bob: 161, 164, 166-167, 229
Lindop, Fred: 170
Liverpool: 181, 182, 186, 187, 192, 195, 198, 201, 202
  dockers: 84, 140

National Society of Operative Printers
and Assistants (NATSOPA): 52,
163
National Union of General and
Municipal Workers (NUGMW): 1,
54-55, 59, 99, 111, 116, 166, 173,
187, 192, 197
National Union of Mineworkers
(NUM): 32, 35, 36, 37, 38, 40, 41,
42, 43, 44, 45, 46, 47, 50, 53, 56, 57,
62, 64, 67, 70-72, 164, 166, 211,
219-223, 227
National Union of Public Employees
(NUPE): 12
National Union of Railwaymen
(NUR): 43, 51, 75-6, 77, 80, 83-91,
215-216
National Union of School Students
(NUSS): 209
National Union of Vehicle Builders
(NUVB): 59, 61
Neap House Wharf: 175-176, 212,
272-273
New Statesman: 171, 190
NGA: 174
Norfolk: 190, 193, 196, 198
Northern Ireland: 2, 22, 264
Nottinghamshire coalfield: 33, 34, 39,
42, 48

Official Solicitor: 157, 171-173, 219,
255-256
Oldham, Jim: 33
Order 1305: 141
Owen, Bill: 119

Pain, Peter: 157
Paisley, Ian: 57
Panalpina: 153
Pannell, Charles: 212
Panorama: 12, 38
Panter, Bernard: 109, 111, 113, 122,
125, 134
Parry, Terence: 205
Paterson, Peter: 172
Paynter, Will: 32
Peel, Jack: 20

Pentonville Five: 21, 137-138, 160-
162, 164-166, 172, 174, 175, 177,
217, 219-223, 229
Pickets: 17, 210, 211-213
flying: 139, 197, 207
secondary: 42-5
victimised: 203-7
Pitt, Malcolm: 46, 69
Plessey: 23
Police: 46, 48-49, 58, 197, 206, 218
Ports: 143-167
Hull: 143, 145, 147, 152-153
London: 143, 145-147, 154, 167
Liverpool: 143-149, 152, 165, 167
Postal workers: 14-15, 49
Powell, Enoch: 144
Power stations:
Bankside: 52
Battersea: 50
Cliff Quay: 48
Cockenzie: 43
Ferrybridge: 43
Fiddlers Ferry: 52
Greenwich: 216
Keadby: 57
Kincardine-on-Forth: 43
Kirkstall: 51
Leicester: 45
Longannet: 64, 70, 212, 218, 219
Thorpe Marsh: 49
West Ham: 54
West Thurrock: 54
Woolwich: 54
Power workers: 12-13, 25, 47, 48, 53-
55, 62-64, 80, 91, 211-212, 219
Prentice, Reginald: 169
Preston: 147, 152, 187, 196
Prevost, Eddie: 160-161, 164
Price, John: 204
Printworker: 162, 174
Prior, Alan: 186, 220
Pritchard, Ross: 164, 174
Private detectives: 254

Racism: 144
Railways: 1, 3, 5, 15, 16, 25, 75-93
Railway Staff National Tribunal: 79